*Agrarian Capitalism in Theory and Practice*

Susan Archer Mann

# Agrarian Capitalism in Theory and Practice

The University of North Carolina Press

Chapel Hill and London

Manufactured in the United States of America

The paper in this book meets the guidelines for permanence and durability of the Committee on Production Guidelines for Book Longevity of the Council on Library Resources.

94 93 92 91 90 5 4 3 2 1

Library of Congress Cataloging-in-Publication Data

Mann, Susan, 1950–
Agrarian capitalism in theory and practice / by Susan Archer Mann.
p. cm.
Based on the author's thesis.
Includes bibliographical references.
ISBN 0-8078-1885-2 (alk. paper)
1. Agriculture—Economic aspects—United States—History.
2. Capitalism—United States—History. I. Title.
HD1761.M35 1990 89–22656
338.1'0973—dc20 CIP

Portions of Chapter 2 appeared in Susan A. Mann and James M. Dickinson, "Obstacles to the Development of a Capitalist Agriculture," *The Journal of Peasant Studies* 5, no. 4 (July 1978): 466–81. Copyright 1978 by Frank Cass & Co. Ltd. Reprinted with permission of Frank Cass & Co. Ltd.

Portions of Chapter 4 are a revised version of an article first published as "Sharecropping in the Cotton South: A Case of Uneven Development in Agriculture," *Rural Sociology* 49, no. 3 (1984): 412–29. Copyright 1984 by the Rural Sociological Society. Reprinted with permission of the journal and the Rural Sociological Society.

Portions of Chapter 5 appeared in Susan A. Mann, "The Rise of Wage Labour in the Cotton South: A Global Analysis," *The Journal of Peasant Studies* 14, no. 2 (January 1987): 226–42. Copyright 1987 by Frank Cass & Co. Ltd. Reprinted with permission of Frank Cass & Co. Ltd.

Portions of Chapter 6 appeared in Emily Blumenfeld and Susan Mann, "Domestic Labour and the Reproduction of Labour Power: Towards an Analysis of Women, the Family and Class," in *Hidden in the Household: Women's Domestic Labour under Capitalism*, ed. Bonnie Fox (Toronto: The Women's Press, 1980), pp. 267–307. Reprinted with permission of The Women's Press.

*In loving memory of*
*Hunter Reece Mann, Jr.*

# *Contents*

# Tables

# *Figures*

# Acknowledgments

My father once remarked that he was sure the Bible was written faster than I wrote my dissertation. Since my dissertation only provided the first draft of this book, I easily have over a decade's worth of people and institutions to thank. First, I owe much to the support provided by my alma mater, the University of Toronto, and to my dissertation committee, especially Harriet Friedmann, Jack Wayne, Miguel Murmis, and my external adviser, Fred Buttel. I also am indebted to the University of New Orleans for its institutional support and to the National Endowment for the Humanities for a summer research stipend.

From the beginning of this undertaking, James Dickinson fortified me with his confidence in our thesis and his like-minded approach to theory and history. Our collaboration over the years has been invaluable to this book. Although I often stubbornly resisted his painful, but witty, criticisms of my early drafts, his good sense usually prevailed in the final copy. This, of course, does not mean that he or any other person mentioned here is responsible for the final outcome. My debts are many and varied, but the errors are mine alone.

My friends and mentors, Gordon Welty and Emily Blumenfeld, deserve special thanks. In addition, the detailed and thorough reviews of my manuscript by Fred Buttel, Philip McMichael, and an anonymous reviewer suggested many useful revisions and saved me from making foolish mistakes. The patience of my editor, Paul Betz, helped me maintain my sanity, while his close scrutiny of the manuscript greatly enhanced the final product. From all of these friends I have benefited as much from the kind word as from the kind criticism.

I am also grateful to Loretta Burchett for designing the graphs and to Hennessey Hayes, Lonnie Hauptmann, and Karen Bishop for typing, retyping, and in many other ways preparing countless pages of the final manuscript. A special thanks to Paul Stekler for permitting me to use the title of his fine film, *Hands That Picked Cotton*, in my chapters on the American South.

The writing of this book spanned the death and birth of two Mann men. The book is dedicated to the memory of my father, a strong-minded man who had a healthy skepticism in regard to sociology. The book also took sustenance from my new son, Joshua, whose daily care made me realize that many of the feminist concerns raised in the text should be given a higher profile.

My deep thanks to Michael Sartisky, whose support was so fundamental and varied that only an author and a wife can appreciate it. I am also especially grateful to my women friends for keeping me in their hearts while I was often so far away. A final thanks to all of my family and friends who helped me survive this past year's two major gestations.

Susan Archer Mann
New Orleans, Louisiana
March 1989

# *Agrarian Capitalism in Theory and Practice*

# *Introduction*

> All theories of progress and modernization, left, right and centre, subscribed to the belief that . . . the free wage labourer represents the "vision of the future" for all those who are not yet wage labourers and for most of mankind. But . . . the proletarian wage labourer is a minority phenomenon . . . and is limited to a few areas of the earth.—Claudia von Werlhof, *Women: The Last Colony* (1988)

The so-called "Agrarian Question," as posed by late-nineteenth-century Populist and Marxist theorists, was essentially a question of the nature of capitalist development in agriculture. Much of the contemporary interest in this question stems from the reality of a world still marked by uneven capitalist development almost a century later. This book is about such uneven development. It is about the survival and revival of traditional forms of production as an integral part of the modern world. Indeed, the very forms of production that many nineteenth-century social theorists predicted would be swept away by modernization and industrialization have not become remnants of the past; some simply never passed away, while others have been resurrected unexpectedly in the modern global economy.

The term "traditional" has often been used by social scientists to refer to forms of production that failed to adopt certain key features of modern industrial production, such as the separation of industry from household; the development of a highly specialized division of labor; and the replacement of personal, patrimonial, or familial labor relations by impersonal wage contracts. Such diverse social theorists as Emile Durkheim, Max Weber, and Karl Marx all viewed these features as central to modern industrial capitalist development. Durkheim's treatise on the division of labor in society, Weber's notion of the rationalization of the modern world, and Marx's predictions regarding the concentration and centralization of capital share the general view that traditional forms of production would wither away in the face of the greater efficiency and competitive superiority of the modern industrial enterprise.[1] As Marx put it, the cheap commodities produced by capitalist enterprise "compel all nations, on pain of extinction, to adopt the bourgeois mode of production." Hence, modern capitalism "creates a world after its own image" (Marx 1970, 39).

Yet, in fact, modern capitalism has created a world that appears grotesquely uneven, unequal, and distorted. The past continues to impress itself on the present, as seemingly archaic forms of production persist in the modern era. This uneven development is most evident in Third World societies, where peasants, who ostensibly could have stepped out of another century, still constitute the majority of the population. Moreover, these peasants are no longer isolated in rural village communities, but are shaping and being shaped by highly developed world markets as their commodities become ever more incorporated into a modern global network of exchange. Some of these peasants have even won protracted wars and socialist revolutions against the technological and military might of highly industrialized opponents—developments that shook the foundations of modern global politics and undermined any simplistic equations of political hegemony with technological superiority.

Although most visible in the Third World, uneven development also characterizes the advanced industrial societies—particularly in the sphere of agriculture—where traditional forms of production continue to exhibit a remarkable vitality. No doubt many people think of American agriculture as modern, given its use of advanced technology and its high levels of productivity. However, the social organization of most American farms remains quite traditional. The majority of American farms are not "factories in the fields" employing hundreds of wage laborers, but rather are family farms, many of which employ no wage labor at all. Moreover, these rural enterprises do not exhibit other key features of modern industrial production, since there is no separation of industry from the household and no highly specialized division of labor.

In addition, American agriculture has experienced what in earlier decades would have seemed to be a reversal of normal patterns of development. For example, despite the decline of American farms over the last century, today the number of small family labor farms is increasing in the United States and in many other Western industrialized societies (Bonnano 1987, 1–2). In some agrarian sectors, development even appears to have moved backwards as factory farms employing wage labor have been replaced by more traditional forms of production, such as family sharecropping (Wells 1984).

In contrast, readers will be hard put to think of many or any major industrial commodities that are still produced by family labor in highly developed societies. While much has been written recently about the rise of small businesses in the industrial sector of countries like the United States, these nonfarm businesses are seldom so small as to be predicated on family labor.[2] Rather, the vast majority of the people who work in the urban or industrial centers of these societies are wage or salary workers employed by highly specialized private or public organizations.

These differences between wage and nonwage labor, as well as the differences between industry and agriculture, are the central features of uneven development addressed in this book. Specifically, I focus on the survival and revival of nonwage forms of production in agricultural sectors of one of the most highly industrialized societies to date—the United States. American agriculture presents an especially intriguing case, because a major peculiarity of its history, as compared to the histories of many other industrialized societies, has been the absence of feudal landlord and peasant classes. The pattern of American economic development through settler colonialism and the virtual liquidation of the indigenous Indian populations created forms of production that were comparatively more highly commoditized and, hence, more integrally linked to markets in land, labor, and capital as prime competitors for the agrarian domain. Even agrarian slavery in the United States was predicated on highly developed markets, given the important role of American cotton in the world economy. In the view of Max Weber (1972, 365), such a high level of commoditization meant that industrial capitalism in the United States would have fewer obstacles to contend with than was the case for its European or Asian counterparts, but this is yet another prediction that has not been fully realized.

In order to address the theoretical anomalies presented by the persistence of nonwage forms of production, I will proceed as follows. Chapter 1 examines the strengths and weaknesses of major classical and contemporary theories of agrarian capitalism. This review of the literature illuminates how other writers have ignored important differences between the production processes in agriculture and those of industry—differences that may account for the greater resistance of certain types of agricultural production to the use of wage labor.

Chapter 2 elaborates on these differences between agriculture and industry by presenting a theory of natural obstacles to the use of wage labor. I argue that because agricultural production is by definition centered in nature, it is crucial that we understand how various natural features of certain branches of agriculture can serve as impediments to the efficient use of advanced technology and wage labor. Natural obstacles include such problems as the lengthy production time of certain crops or the uneven nature of seasonal labor requirements, which can make certain types of farming risky and unprofitable avenues for capital investment.

A decade ago, James Dickinson and I published a shorter version of this theory, and it has since come to be known in the literature on the political economy of agriculture as the Mann-Dickinson thesis (Mann and Dickinson 1978). Prior to this publication, many writers had noted how the unpredictability and biological rhythms of nature were difficult to synchronize to the requirements of industrial production. However, few had attributed any major significance to these natural obstacles to capitalist development. After the publication of our thesis, it was lauded by some as a "pioneering" and "seminal work" and criticized by others for being theoretically or empirically impotent.[3] Chapter 2 further develops the Mann-Dickinson thesis and addresses its critics. In subsequent chapters a variety of methodological approaches are used to examine its validity empirically.

A quantitative analysis of United States census data is used in Chapter 3 to examine the employment of wage labor in American agriculture over the period from 1900 to 1930. This empirical study documents changes in the forms of production that characterized American agriculture over this interval. Unlike more traditional studies of rural stratification, it uses a commodity-specific analysis to examine whether a given type of farming has any relationship to the use of wage and family labor. Through the approach taken here, the Mann-Dickinson thesis is empirically tested, the aim being to determine whether variations in the natural features of rural production processes are related to differences in the social organization of production.

In Chapters 4 and 5 I present a history of Southern cotton farming from the abolition of slavery to the rise of family sharecropping in the years between the Civil War and the Great Depression, and then onward to the establishment of fully developed capitalist cotton farms employing wage labor in the following decades. Because of its history of wage and nonwage forms of production, Southern cotton production provides a particularly interesting case with which to examine in more detail the natural, social, and technical factors that fostered or impeded the use of wage labor. Moreover, by focusing special attention on the natural features of cotton production and how different social classes adapt to, clash with, and modify natural impediments, this study presents a new framework for understanding the social history of the American South.

The final chapter relates what has been learned from the empirical and historical analyses to a more general theory of modern capitalist development. Hence, by examining agrarian capitalism in theory and in practice, this study answers the "Agrarian Question" by showing how the nature of capitalist development is integrally related to the development of capitalists' ability to control and subordinate—to civilize—nature.

# One

# The New Sociology of Agrarian Capitalism

It is necessary to fight narodism everywhere—be it German, French, English, or Russian.
—Friedrich Engels, Letter to Vera Zasulich (1890)

We are presented with an unforeseen fusion of the Marxist and Populist traditions . . . and the peasant becomes proletarian.—Goodman, Sorj, and Wilkinson, *From Farming to Biotechnology* (1987)

The major theoretical approaches to rural development that emerged in the late 1960s and early 1970s differed markedly from the theories that had characterized American rural sociology in earlier decades.[1] Not only did these approaches draw heavily on the conflict theories of Karl Marx and Max Weber, but they also represented a more interdisciplinary approach to agrarian analysis because they integrated the work of historians, political economists, anthropologists, and sociologists. As Buttel, Larson, and Gillespie point out in their impressive new overview of the field of American rural studies, *The Sociology of Agriculture* (1989), these more conflict-oriented and critical approaches were themselves a product of major conflicts experienced by American society, both at home and abroad.

Domestically, the civil rights movement, the anti–Vietnam War movement, and the women's movement gave rise to a new generation of American scholars interested in understanding the structural conflicts dividing their society. In turn, the heightened role of the United States in international conflicts extended such interests to a global scale, particularly when these conflicts abroad directly entered American homes through the mass media and mass conscription. Although the response of many academics was to focus more critical attention on the distorted development of Third World countries, some scholars began to examine uneven development in highly industrialized countries—particularly in the sphere of agricultural production. Though drawn from a variety of disciplines, the evolving critical approach to uneven development has come to be known as "the new sociology of agriculture" (Buttel, Larson, and Gillespie 1989, chap. 4).

In this new sociology of agriculture, two distinct interpretations of uneven capitalist development have been advanced. Macro-oriented scholars tend to view capitalism as the hegemonic mode of production shaping modern rural class structures. Such writers contend that nonwage forms of production are destined to disappear as capitalism extends and deepens its control over the countryside, or else they focus on factors that delay or avert this process. In contrast, more micro-oriented theorists focus attention on factors internal to nonwage forms of production that presumably provide the means of resisting capitalist penetration. From the latter perspective, nonwage enterprises are viewed as having some internal logic or set of characteristics that enable them to successfully compete with capitalist enterprises and to remain relatively permanent oases in a hostile capitalist world.

These antithetical approaches reflect fundamental differences between Marxist and neoclassical economics—between a political economy that focuses on social classes and structural relations of production and one that focuses on individuals, and subjective market considerations.[2] While often framed in terms of a Marx-Weber debate in sociology, these antithetical perspectives in many ways mirror a debate that took place almost a century ago, when Lenin engaged in his famous exchanges with the Narodniks over the nature of capitalist development in Russian agriculture. Although the major issues in the classical and contemporary debates are similar, the terms of debate have been significantly extended in recent years. In reviewing this literature below, I examine various ways in which contemporary theorists have transformed or refined the works of their predecessors.

### *Macro-Oriented Classical Marxist Theories*

Karl Marx is generally thought to be a theorist of *industrial* capitalism rather than a theorist of agrarian structures. Yet, even disregarding his writings on precapitalist societies, Marx wrote hundreds of pages on agriculture under modern capitalism; in *Capital* alone there are over 400 pages where agricultural production is discussed.

One of Marx's major contributions to a sociology of agriculture is his conceptual framework for understanding different forms of production. Indeed, his analytical and deductive concepts stand in sharp contrast to the more descriptive and inductive concepts used in traditional rural sociology. For example, in the old sociology of American agriculture, a family farm was defined quantitatively by the number of man-hours of family labor and wage labor it used.[3] Studies of rural stratification tended to counterpose "family farms" to "corporate farms." However, this counterposition was deceptive, because "corporate farm" refers to a legal arrangement and specifies nothing about the social relations of production involved. As a result, often these concepts could be used interchangeably to refer to the same unit of production. For example, a study of corporate farming in the United States in the 1970s found that 66 percent of corporate farms were actually family-owned and family-run enterprises (Wilcox, Cochrane, and Herdt 1974, 12).

In contrast, Marx's categories of social class reveal an analytical preference for qualitative, as opposed to quantitative—and therefore arbitrary—distinctions. Moreover, because his conceptual categories represent social relations of production rather than occupational categories, they are relevant to both urban and rural settings. Specifically, Marx used the terms capitalist production and simple (or petty) commodity production to differentiate wage labor from family labor enterprises. The major feature these forms of production have in common is that they are both dependent on markets for the sale of their commodities and for their personal and productive consumption.

For Marx, the distinguishing feature of the capitalist labor process is that all factors of production—including labor power—are commoditized. Hence, capitalist production presupposes the existence of two classes: a class of wage laborers divorced from their means of production and thereby forced to sell their labor power, and a class of private entrepreneurs who own the means of production and thus are able to employ wage labor. According to Marx, the accumulation of profit under capitalist production is predicated on this separation of wage labor from the means of production and occurs through the appropriation of surplus value. This surplus or additional value arises from the difference between the value added by labor at the point of production and value of labor on the labor market. It therefore arises from the difference between the use value and the exchange value of labor power. As such, surplus value is a term Marx specifically reserves for profits derived from wage labor; indeed, it is a value that can only be calculated in relation to commoditized labor.

In contrast, neither commoditized labor nor the separation of property and labor is an essential feature of simple commodity production. Simple commodity producers maintain ownership of the commodities they produce, and family labor constitutes the majority, if not all, of the labor on the farm. Consequently, unlike capitalist production, simple commodity production is not predicated on class exploitation as one of its intrinsic internal features. Rather, patriarchy is the form of domination that tends to prevail, since family labor is generally differentiated by gender and age.

Marx noted several different types of simple commodity production that reflected different degrees of producers' alienation from private property. These types ranged from independent simple commodity production, where producers own all of their means of production, to tenant farming and sharecropping, where the unity of land and labor has been severed because land and sometimes other capital assets are not owned but rented. While sharecroppers and tenant farmers still maintain ownership of the commodities they produce, they exist in a subordinate relation to another class—a class of landowners. In this instance, class exploitation or the appropriation of surplus labor takes the particular form of ground rent. Ground rent and rentier classes will be discussed at more length in subsequent chapters; suffice it to say at this point that sharecropping usually entails more landlord control and supervision than tenant farming. In addition, with sharecropping, rent is variable because it is tied to the production of a finished commodity (rent in kind), rather than to a fixed monetary agreement. For these reasons, sharecropping is generally considered to be a more exploitative and less developed form of production than tenant farming (Wright 1978, 162–63).

There are a number of other variations on simple commodity production inhabiting the modern agricultural landscape that are analyzed at some length in Appendix 1. These include indebted farms, contract farms, and new forms of production somewhat akin to sharecropping. Because these forms of production appear to hold more ambiguous class positions that do not fit easily into Marx's conceptual scheme, they have been the subject of numerous attempts at reconceptualizing agrarian class structures in the new sociology of agriculture.[4] Despite such limitations, there are several important advantages to using Marx's analyses of different forms of production.

First, compared to the atheoretical concepts used in the old sociology of agriculture, Marx's conceptual framework allows for the specification within a deductive theory of the conditions necessary for the social reproduction of these units of production. That is, patterns or tendencies as regards the alternatives facing rural producers, such as questions concerning the expansion or curtailment of production, can be deductively determined because they are a function of objective market determinations (Friedmann 1980b).[5]

Second, by analytically basing his conceptual scheme on the presence or absence of both income-producing property and exploitation, Marx has chosen criteria that have implications for the way different forms of production act politically. The political import of Marx's theoretical categories is evident, for example, in his analysis of how the structural position of simple commodity producers—as both property owners and direct producers—is reflected in the political vacillation of this social class. On the one hand, the frequent anticapitalist stance of petty producers reflects their vulnerability to competition from large-scale capital, which threatens to undermine their social order. On the other hand, their permanent fear of proletarianization is expressed in their resistance to the radical restructuring of society, preferring reformist solutions to the abolition of private property. Modern writers, such as Barrington Moore and Eric Wolf, have confirmed Marx's political analysis by documenting how this class has served not only as the foundation for the democratic republican order and fascist regimes, but also as the mass base that provided at least initial support for a number of socialist revolutions in the twentieth century (Moore 1966; Wolf 1973).[6]

In a similar way, Marx discussed how the scattered property and relatively atomized existence of petty producers often provided little basis for the development of either class consciousness or political organization. Because of this structural situation, Marx characterized peasants as being "incapable of representing themselves" and, hence, at the beck and call of those external forces capable of mobilizing their support (1972a, 515–16). Through this analysis Marx again foretold the antithetical role of this class in both fascist and communist revolutions, as well as the fact that the leadership of peasant movements tends to come from the more educated and well-to-do classes.[7] While these views reflect his general assessment of the political behavior of petty commodity producers, Marx recognized that under certain historical conditions the structural atomization constricting class consciousness was reduced, such as under communal forms of land distribution.[8]

In *The Peasant Question in France and Germany*, Friedrich Engels (1970) took Marx's rudimentary analysis a step forward by suggesting that the industrial proletariat could provide the leadership for those rural producers incapable of representing themselves. Later, in a number of his writings, Lenin expanded this discussion into his famous theory of the peasant-proletarian alliance. Like Engels, Lenin highlighted how the proletariat would provide the leadership for this class alliance, expressing views very similar to those of Marx about the peasantry's inability to organize themselves.[9] These writings on the peasant-proletarian alliance have transformed the theory and praxis of social revolution, particularly in Third World societies. As Barrington Moore writes: "For those who savor historical irony it is indeed curious that the peasant in the modern era has been as much the agent of revolution as the machine, that he has come into his own as an effective historical actor along with the conquests of the machine" (1966, 453).

However, Moore is careful to point out that while petty producers are major agents in the making of the modern world, they are also modernization's major victims (1966, 11). Marx and Lenin would certainly agree with this statement, given their view of petty commodity production as a transitional form of production. Because this issue is at the crux of many criticisms leveled against orthodox Marxist analyses of agriculture, I will examine at some length Marx's and Lenin's views on this subject.

To put it simply, Marx argued that market competition would result in differential rates of accumulation, whereby producers either survived by adopting the capitalist mode of producing or were gradually ruined through the erosion of their market viability—an erosion that eventually would lead to their proletarianization. The superiority of capitalist enterprise included many factors, such as the more efficient use of labor and advanced technology through a highly specialized division of labor, accumulated capital from the appropriation of surplus value to invest in the continued expansion of production, larger volume sales, and more privileged access to credit. Together these factors would ostensibly undermine the long-term viability of more traditional forms of production as capitalism spread across the globe.

As part of his general theory of capitalist development, then, the demise of traditional forms of production was an essential component of Marx's major predictions regarding the global universality of capitalism, the concentration and centralization of capital, and the polarization of modern social classes into the bourgeoisie and the proletariat. These predictions seem to be based on a fundamental belief in the superiority of large-scale production, a belief that is carried through Marx's writings from his earlier to his later works. For example, in *The Communist Manifesto* Marx foresees how petty producers will "sink gradually into the proletariat, partly because their diminutive capital does not suffice for the scale on which Modern Industry is carried on, and is swamped in the competition with the large capitalists" (1970, 42). Later, in *Capital,* he describes even more vividly the fate of petty commodity production: "It must be annihilated. It is annihilated. Its annihilation, the transformation of the individualised and scattered means of production into socially concentrated ones, of the pygmy property of the many into the huge property of the few . . . comprises the prelude to the history of capital" (1967a, 714).

In some of his writings Marx actually appears to welcome the demise of traditional forms of production as a progressive development.

Consider his comment about British petty commodity production: "It is compatible only with a system of production and a society moving within narrow and more or less primitive bounds. To perpetuate it would be, as Pecquer rightly says, to 'decree universal mediocrity' " (1967a, 713–14). Similarly, in his brief, but much-quoted analysis of the French peasantry in *The Eighteenth Brumaire*, he unsympathetically likens petty producers to a dull and homogenous "sack of potatoes" when he writes: "Their field of production, the small holding, admits of no division of labour in its cultivation, no application of science, and therefore, no multiplicity of development, no diversity of talents, no wealth of social relations" (1972a, 515). His later writings on British rule in India, while vehement in their attack on British colonialism, also reveal a contempt for the "stagnatory" aspects of peasant life and the "barbarian egotism" he saw as myopically "concentrating on some miserable patch of land." He writes: "We must not forget that these idyllic village communities, inoffensive as they may appear, had always been the solid foundation of Oriental despotism, that they restrained the mind within the smallest possible compass, making it the unresisting tool of superstition, enslaving it beneath traditional rules, depriving it of all grandeur and historical energies" (1972b, 582).

In many ways these writings constitute a rudimentary phenomenology of work, in which the relatively isolated and atomized structure of the scattered farms that make up rural life is contrasted with the cooperative nature of work found in the modern factory, where industrial laborers are organized under one roof, working together under a highly specialized division of labor (Marx 1967a, 713). The lack of social interaction or "mutual intercourse," as Marx calls it, associated with more isolated work settings is the structural basis for a social psychology of political consciousness and organization. In turn, Marx argues that such limited social settings lead not only to a lack of class consciousness, but also to dull minds susceptible to superstition and prejudice—in his words, "the idiocy of rural life" (1970, 39). This view of petty commodity production as a potential breeding ground for false consciousness and reactionary politics was shared by Lenin as well.[10]

However, it is not clear whether these descriptions applied only to peasant agriculture or to all forms of rural petty commodity production. Unfortunately, neither Marx nor Lenin adequately distinguishes between peasants and family farmers. Sometimes these writers counterpose "commercial agriculture" to "natural economy," using the latter to refer to peasant production and to suggest that it is not as commoditized as more developed forms of simple commodity production. In other words, while peasants may produce commodities, their means of subsistence and/or their means of production often are not purchased, but are produced by their own hands (Marx 1972a, 515; Lenin 1967, 164–69; Lenin 1974, 30–31). Because of this ability to revert to production for use, peasants are generally less dependent on markets than are contemporary family farmers. The implications of such differences for modernization, as well as the development of a more sophisticated sociology of peasants, have been important concerns of the new sociology of agriculture.[11]

Yet, interestingly, whether or not Marx was referring to all types of petty commodity production, the critics of Marx in American rural sociology seem not to have noticed his harsh remarks about the mind-sets of petty producers. Rather, they were considerably more disturbed by the specter of capitalist development resulting in the dissolution of family farms.[12] Indeed, the fact that Marx's writings ran counter to the hegemonic ideology of traditional American rural sociology concerning the viability of American family farms may account, in part, for the fact that Marxist writings on agriculture were largely ignored in the United States until the 1970s.[13] This neglect stands in sharp contrast to the significant impact these writings had on debates in a country where capitalism was far less developed—Russia.

Here the expansion of Marxist writings on agriculture occurred primarily in response to the Russian Narodniks. The term "Narodnik" referred to the adherents of a rather broad current of populist social thought that idealized the peasant community in the late nineteenth and early twentieth centuries. Politically, the romanticization of rural life was part of a more general belief in the unique historical destiny of Russia to find a path of development different from the West. This belief combined an unremitting hostility to capitalism with a glorification of both petty commodity production and the peasant commune (*mir*) as the foundations for Russian noncapitalist development.

Specifically, the Narodniks held that the relatively backward position of Russia in the world economy precluded Russian commodities from competing successfully on external markets. This, coupled with their idea that impoverished peasants, who made up the bulk of Russia's population, could not provide the purchasing power to foster internal markets, led them to argue that capitalist development was in fact impossible in Russia.[14] V. I. Lenin's most famous work on the agrarian question—*The Development of Capitalism in Russia* (1899)—was written primarily as a refutation of the Narodniks' claims. Using an impressive array of agricultural data, Lenin documented how capitalism was developing in Russia, using such indicators as the decline in traditional labor service, the expansion of the home market through the increasing commoditization of rural life, the transformation of landlords into capitalist farmers, and the accompanying transformation of peasants into a rural proletariat. Thus Lenin's detailed empirical study also documented Marx's predictions regarding the demise of petty commodity production in the late-nineteenth-century Russian countryside.

By discussing at length the process he called the "differentiation of the peasantry," Lenin expanded on Marx's notion that rural capitalism led to increasing class stratification in the countryside. Like Marx, he argued that petty producers would either rise into the ranks of the capitalist farmer by competing successfully and expanding their production to the point of requiring wage labor, or conversely they would fail in competition and fall into the ranks of the proletariat. This differentiation left the countryside tiered into three analytically distinct social strata—the rich, the middle, and the poor peasant—with the middle peasants or family labor enterprises being the strata destined eventually to disappear. Lenin also noted how these strata were not always empirically distinct in late-nineteenth-century Russia; thus, he did discuss peasants in more ambiguous class positions, such as the "rural proletarian who has been allotted a patch of land." However, he mentioned these anomalous cases only briefly, suggesting that they were neither typical nor likely to endure as capitalism developed (1967, 316).

The impending doom of the petty producer was an essential component of Lenin's writings throughout his life because of the importance of the peasant-proletarian alliance to the success both of the Bolshevik revolution in 1917 and of the New Economic Policy in the 1920s, when rural instability threatened the young Soviet Republic. In a country composed of millions of middle peasants, Lenin wanted to show unequivocally that the capitalist road of development only offered them increasing misery and impoverishment. Consequently, while the demise of petty production was a recurring subject in his writings on Russia, he also used empirical data from half a dozen other countries to show that the same process was happening elsewhere (Rochester 1942, 34 and 42).

It is for this reason that Lenin became one of the first writers to examine the development of capitalism in American agriculture. Using U.S. census data, he carefully documented how large farms were increasing their use of wage labor and gaining a greater proportion of farm sales relative to small and medium-sized farms (Lenin 1974). Indeed, in the more highly commoditized setting of American agriculture, as compared to the Russian countryside, Lenin could show how the rise of capitalism and the dissolution of petty commodity production was even more pronounced. From his analysis, he concluded "a comparison of corresponding data on industry and agriculture for the same period shows that although the latter is incomparably more backward, there is a remarkable similarity in the laws of evolution, and that small-scale production is being ousted from both" (1974, 102). This idea, that there were no significant differences between the capitalist development of agriculture and industry, and his prediction of the eventual disappearance of small-scale production were to become two of the most criticized subjects of his writings on agriculture.

One early attack on Lenin's conclusions was led by the revisionist wing of the German Social Democratic Party, which argued that the existing structure of European agriculture, where capitalist and noncapitalist farms seemed to coexist quite peacefully, did not support the Leninist view. In response, Karl Kautsky wrote another of the more famous Marxist analyses of agriculture, *Die Agrarfrage* (1899). Here Kautsky reasserted Lenin's position with some important qualifications. Most notably, he discussed countervailing factors that might limit or slow down the pace of capitalist development in agriculture. He even went so far as to admit the possibility that noncapitalist forms of agriculture might become permanent features of the agricultural landscape (Kautsky 1976; Hussain and Tribe 1981a).

Kautsky's countervailing factors included various ways in which the maintenance of family labor farms might be protected when this benefited capitalist production, such as when such farms provided surplus labor for capitalist enterprises, or where particular conditions, such as the inability to acquire contiguous land, precluded the expansion of production and thereby reduced capitalists' interests in investing in agricultural production (Kautsky 1976; Bonnano 1987, 12–14). Because Kautsky's analysis specifically acknowledged tendencies that would lead to the coexistence of capitalist and family farms in the modern era, it has received a good deal of attention in recent years from both Marxist and non-Marxist scholars (de Janvry 1980; Friedland, Barton, and Thomas 1981; Newby 1978 and 1983).

Some of the early studies of U.S. agriculture by contemporary American Marxist scholars followed the macro-oriented, empirical models established by Lenin and Kautsky by documenting the increasing hegemony of capitalist production in rural America and the increasing marginalization, if not elimination, of family labor farms. Anna Rochester (1940) found empirical evidence for such developments in American agriculture during the decades preceding World War II, and similar findings for the post–World War II decades have been documented by Goss, Buttel, and Rodefeld (1980), among others. The impressive empirical data published by these scholars showed how large-scale capitalist farms were cornering a larger proportion of farm sales, how medium-sized family farms were declining, and how poor family farmers were becoming indebted or dependent on off-farm work.

These studies played an important role by introducing Marxism into American rural sociology. Nevertheless, they were not without problems. First, they were primarily empirically oriented and did little to extend or develop Marxist theory.[15] Second, while these studies clearly documented the hegemony of the capitalist mode of production in terms of its increasing domination of the countryside, they often did not address adequately its incomplete and uneven development. Consequently, because their opponents could point to the persistent empirical reality of remaining family farms and even to the increase of small family farms in recent years, debates over the capitalist development of American agriculture too often degenerated into statistical battles over how many capitalist versus noncapitalist farms were currently in operation in the United States.

As a result, more recent debates in the new sociology of agriculture have shifted slightly from the major arguments in the Lenin-Narodnik exchange. In contrast to Lenin's more orthodox position regarding the transitional nature of family labor farms, many contemporary Marxist theorists agree with their non-Marxist colleagues that rural noncapitalist forms of production may be a long-term feature of the modern agricultural landscape.[16] Where Marxist and non-Marxist writers continue to disagree is over whether or not capitalist production is the dominant force shaping modern agriculture. Non-Marxist writers tend to locate the reason for the persistence of noncapitalist farms in certain advantages internal to family labor enterprises, their argument being that these nonwage forms have an economic logic sufficient to withstand capitalist competition. In contrast, the assumption of capitalism's superiority and its capacity to destroy, shape, or selectively leave intact noncapitalist forms is shared in the macro-perspectives of the theories presented by the orthodox Marxists just discussed, as well as by various writers who try to synthesize the writings of Marx and Weber.

### *Macro-Structural Syntheses of Marx and Weber*

Over the last three decades, a number of contemporary sociologists developed alternative theories of uneven development that, intentionally or not, use a combination of the macro-structural theories of Marx and Weber. Specifically, these are the dependency and world-systems theories initially created to explain the uneven development of entire societies, but which have also been used to explain regional imbalances and the survival of traditional forms of production. While more prevalent in analyses of the Third World, these relatively new theoretical perspectives also have been used to study agriculture in advanced industrial societies.

Dependency and world-systems theories initially arose as a critique of the modernization theories that dominated mainstream sociology in the post–World War II era. Building on nineteenth-century conceptions of evolution, modernization theories argue that all societies follow certain unilinear and evolutionary stages of development but that some societies proceed through these stages more quickly than others (Hoselitz 1960; Parsons 1966; Rostow 1960). The major explanations given for the faster or slower pace of a particular society rest primarily on factors internal to that society. Among these factors, the social-psychological orientations of people are considered central, whereby people in less-developed societies often are portrayed as victims of their own traditional and parochial orientations. The solution, according to modernization theorists, is increased contact between developed and less-developed nations, because more contact would advance cultural diffusion and the "benefits" of economic aid, trade, and technology. In short, modern men and women could be produced in tradition-bound societies by contact with modern institutions (Chirot and Hall 1982, 83).

In direct opposition, dependency theorists argue that existing contacts between developed and less-developed societies are in fact the cause of, rather than the solution to, uneven development. They claim that the economic and political relations between the developed and less-developed nations put a brake on development in the Third World and create neocolonial forms of dependency. For example, historical case studies are used to show how terms of trade, investment, and foreign "aid" often result in "unequal exchanges" between developed and less-developed countries and thus foster economic stagnation and the distorted "underdevelopment" of these societies. Conversely, they argue that the developed nations may have been at one time "undeveloped," but they were never "underdeveloped" (Frank 1970). Rather, the development of the highly industrialized societies is seen as both the cause and the effect of the underdevelopment of the Third World, since the developed societies modernized at the expense of the less developed. The later world-systems theories of such scholars as Immanuel Wallerstein (1973, 1974a and 1974b, and 1983), Samir Amin (1978), and Arghiri Emmanuel (1972) merely extended this focus from bilateral relations between countries to a global perspective that situated each nation as part of an international market, a global division of labor, and, hence, a world system of stratification and exploitation (Chirot and Hall 1982; Margavio and Mann 1989).

Dependency and world-systems theories have made important contributions to the new sociology of agriculture. Of general importance has been their role in forcing modern researchers to take seriously the effect global developments have on local, regional, and national events. As a result, studies utilizing these new approaches have called into question the underlying assumptions and conclusions of major writings in the fields of history, sociology, and political economy.[17] In addition, as compared to the notoriously ahistorical and positivistic character of traditional mainstream sociology, these new global approaches promoted comparative-historical analyses that helped to reunify theory and history (McMichael 1987c).

However, one of the more problematic aspects of many dependency and world-systems theories is their analysis of class stratification. Indeed, despite their claim to Marxist roots, such writers as Wallerstein, Amin, and Emmanuel argue that virtually all forms of production in the modern world (wage, nonwage, and even socialist) are capitalist by virtue of their participation in markets dominated by a world capitalist system.[18] As critics were quick to point out, such market-oriented class analyses owed more to the legacy of Max Weber than they did to Karl Marx (LaClau 1971; Bettleheim in Emmanuel 1972; Kay 1976; Brenner 1977; Goodman and Redclift 1982).

Weber is often credited with rounding out and improving upon Marx's analysis of social class by adding to Marx's focus on property ownership such other dimensions of stratification as status, power, and market relations.[19] Of particular relevance here, Weber noted the importance of examining a given individual's life chances on the credit, commodity, and labor markets. These market relations play a salient role in Weber's work because of his neoclassical approach to economics and the centrality he gives to rationality and calculability in his writings on modern capitalism.[20] Certainly, market forces epitomize the objective and calculable, as opposed to the subjective and incalculable, assessment of economic values.

The different foci of Weber's and Marx's analyses of stratification, of course, also stem from their different research agendas. Weber's goal was academic: to develop a sociology of stratification. Marx's goal was political: to expose the material basis of exploitation. Consequently, Marx paid less attention to market exchanges because he viewed them as essentially equal exchanges, in which commodities were generally exchanged at their value.[21] Indeed, Marx went to great lengths to show that industrial capitalist profits did not result from manipulations of the market. His most explicit writings on this subject are those that differentiate between merchant and industrial capital. Merchant capital was described as being predicated on market relations and as spanning both precapitalist and capitalist eras. Industrial capital, in contrast, was described as a specifically modern phenomenon whereby exploitation took place at the point of production. These distinctions have been central to the debates in the development literature over the last two decades (LaClau 1971, 24–28; Bettleheim in Emmanuel 1972, 301; Kay 1976, 86–95; Goodman and Redclift 1982, 24–67; Goodman, Sorj, and Wilkinson 1987, 150–51).

By ignoring these distinctions and coupling Marx's notion of the dominance of capitalism with Weber's emphasis on market relations, many dependency and world-systems theorists continue to define capitalist development by market participation. John Emmeus Davis's analysis of American agriculture provides a good example of this approach. He writes: "Forms of social and economic organization . . . , while not always resembling typical capitalist structures, are not survivals of a precapitalist past; they are not evidence of a lack of capitalist development. They are, instead, an integral part of the world capitalist system, within which they have been shaped and maintained through decades of dependency and exploitation" (1980, 134).

In particular, Davis argues that the survival of the family farm in the United States is not indicative of a dearth of capitalist development, but rather represents a new form of rural proletariat, despite family farmers' formal ownership of property. Here Davis argues that finance and industrial capitalist enterprises which intersect with the farm sector (such as banks, food processing companies, marketing firms, and/or industries that provide agricultural inputs like farm machinery or fertilizers) "exploit" family farmers by extracting value through the manipulation of credit and commodity markets (1980, 146).

While Davis wants to maintain a Marxist conceptual scheme, he argues that the more orthodox analysis of class based on wage labor and property ownership is too narrowly conceived, given the loss of control over production experienced by many family farmers. For example, Davis suggests that a more accurate Marxist class analysis must determine whether formal property ownership effectively provides farmers with "independence" and "autonomy" over their production processes (1980, 138–39). For Davis, this problem is most evident in contract farming, where farmers make marketing agreements with capitalist entrepreneurs who specify and require extremely detailed production procedures, so that the planning of farm production is removed from its actual execution (1980, 142–44).[22]

Along with contract farmers, Davis includes different types of indebted farmers in his notion of a rural proletariat. He includes not only farmers who are so deeply in debt that they may be on the verge of bankruptcy, but also farmers who purchase farm machinery or equipment on credit and those who have mortgages on their farms. Here Davis argues that capitalist exploitation occurs through "transfers of value" resulting from interest payments and from "monopoly overcharges" on the prices farmers pay for goods produced by monopolistic or oligopolistic agribusinesses. Loss of entrepreneurial control may also result from indebtedness when financial institutions insist upon sharing farm management decisions as a condition of credit (Davis 1980, 145).

By illuminating how market and credit relations place external constraints on the operation of family farms, writers like Davis have increased our understanding of the specific conditions that foster or hinder agricultural production at different times in history. For example, a nineteenth-century family farm was not enmeshed in the same sophisticated credit and marketing relations facing a contemporary family farm, so to ignore these different structural parameters governing production makes for inadequate comparisons. However, for Davis to call such farms "capitalist" results in a class analysis that is seriously flawed. Following his logic, almost every farmer and, indeed, almost every person in the United States would be a proletarian. That is, if paying interest is a form of capitalist exploitation, we would have to conclude that all indebted consumers—rural or urban—belong to the proletariat regardless of the labor processes in which they are engaged.[23] Similarly, because almost all Americans purchase commodities produced by oligopolistic corporations, these consumers could be paying "monopoly overcharges" and, hence, could fall into the ranks of Davis's new proletariat.

By confusing capitalist exploitation with market relations, writers like Davis ignore the analytical differences between merchant capital and industrial capital, between consumption and production, and between surplus value and other forms of surplus labor. To many readers such analytical distinctions may appear to be simply academic or semantic squabbles. However, they have serious implications for the sociopolitical resolutions of these problems (Bettleheim in Emmanuel 1972; Brenner 1977). For example, since surplus value is intrinsic to the capitalist production and reproduction process, capitalism would have to be abolished to negate this form of class exploitation. In contrast, unequal market exchanges could simply be renegotiated through political-economic reforms, such as price controls, rather than requiring a restructuring of the economic system. Such a difference between revolution and reform is far from being simply academic.

To summarize, the world according to dependency and world-systems theories is no longer characterized by the survival and revival of traditional forms of production. By equating the universality of capitalism with the mere existence of a world market,[24] theorists have transformed peasants and family farmers into proletarians by the stroke of a pen. However, changing the labels does not change the empirical realities that have puzzled social theorists to this day. Regardless of the labels used, there remains the problem of explaining why the forms of production that characterize the agricultural landscape look so different from those that characterize the industrial sector. Indeed, simply redefining family farmers as "proletarians who work at home" cannot erase the distinct labor processes that distinguish both agriculture from industry and family farms from capitalist enterprises (Mouzelis 1977, 484).

### *Micro-Oriented Weberian Theories*

In contrast to the perspectives outlined above, which all view capitalism as the dominant, determinant force behind uneven development, non-Marxist writers often locate the reason for the persistence of traditional forms of production in certain advantages internal to family labor enterprises.[25] For lack of a better term, I refer to these micro-oriented approaches as Weberian. On the one hand, this is appropriate because Weber's most celebrated writing on agrarian capitalist development, "Capitalism and Rural Life in Germany" (1972), uses a micro-level, idealist analysis. Here Weber locates the major reason for the persistence of family farms in farmers' desire for freedom and autonomy in the workplace.

On the other hand, labeling micro-oriented approaches to rural analysis as Weberian is somewhat misleading, because Weber's work contains many different and, at times, conflicting theoretical positions. For example, while Weber presents his micro-oriented social action approach as the fundamental building block of his sociology (Weber 1949), most of his analyses do not utilize this approach at all, but rather remain at a macro-structural level of analysis.[26] In turn, some of Weber's writings use a materialist analysis, such as his *General Economic History* (1950), while others rely on an idealist analysis, such as *The Protestant Ethic and the Spirit of Capitalism* (1958). Because he never fully succeeded in synthesizing all of the disparate elements in his sociology, his work is difficult to categorize as representing a particular approach or a single coherent theory.[27]

Weber's failure to integrate his different approaches and levels of analysis is evident in his explanation for the persistence of family farms in Prussian agriculture. Here Weber takes an idealist approach by identifying the farmer's quest for freedom or what he calls the "psychological magic of freedom" as the major factor responsible for the tenacious endurance of petty commodity production in Prussian agriculture (Riesebrodt 1986, 487). Though Weber admits that there is a tendency for petty producers to be replaced by wage labor, he argues that it is subverted by family farmers who will endure the most extreme privations and the heaviest possible indebtedness in order to preserve their independence (Giddens 1971, 122–23). Thus, along with subjective value orientations toward freedom and independence, Weber uses the notion of self-exploitation to explain the survival of simple commodity production in the face of capitalist competition.

This discussion of Prussian agriculture is Weber's most explicit statement on the subject of the survival of family farms. Though written early in his career, this idealist analysis of family farms is quite in keeping with two central components of Weber's more mature sociology, found in the posthumously published *Economy and Society* (1968). Indeed, the focus on the meanings and motives behind farmers' behaviors is in keeping with both his social action approach and his advocacy of *verstehen* or a hermeneutical methodology as essential for understanding the meaning of social acts from the perspective of the actor, rather than the researcher (Weber 1968, 8; Weber 1949; Bakker 1987; Ritzer 1983, 133–35 and 125–27).

In the new sociology of agriculture, some modern writers have followed Weber's lead here by using farmers' values to explain uneven development (Mooney 1983; Bonnano 1987) or by highlighting the general benefits of bringing Weber's notion of *verstehen* "back into rural sociology" (Bakker 1987). These subjectivist approaches contrast sharply with the structural approaches used by the macro-oriented theorists discussed above. While none of the macro-theorists are likely to deny the value of *verstehen* for understanding the meaning behind social action, they probably would distinguish between its value for understanding social behavior at the level of meaning, rather than at the level of causality. In addition, neither Weber nor these modern Weberians ever deal adequately with the problem of false consciousness and how it can be reconciled with a hermeneutical approach. For example, if one took seriously Marx's concern that petty commodity production provides a structural context that fosters prejudice, superstition, and other forms of false consciousness, it would be unwise to accept causal (as opposed to interpretive) explanations of uneven development based on a *verstehen* analysis of the values and beliefs of rural petty producers.

A more rigorous articulation of the internal logic of family farms that avoids this problem—because it does not rely simply on the values and beliefs of farmers—can be found in the writings of the Russian agricultural economist A. V. Chayanov (1966a and b).[28] For many academics and political activists, Chayanov's theory stood as an idealist and populist alternative to Lenin's historical materialism in the Lenin-Narodnik debates.[29] Although Lenin's theoretical attacks were directed primarily at an earlier generation of Narodnik theorists, such as Nicholas Danielson and V. P. Vorontsov, Chayanov actually provides the most developed idealist theory of the viability of petty commodity production.

A fundamental thesis of Chayanov's work rests on the claim that the absence of the category of wages in units of production based on family labor makes the calculation of profit in the capitalist sense of the term an impossibility. Hence, if an objective assessment of an average rate of profit cannot serve as the criterion for decisions concerning the expansion or curtailment of production, one must look elsewhere for the key to the economic behavior of family labor farms. According to Chayanov, the key lies in the farmer's subjective assessment of the amount of drudgery required in production weighed against the consumption demands of the household unit, which he called the "labor/consumption balance" (Chayanov 1966a, 4–6).

Since consumption demands vary over the demographic lifespan of the household as families add members through procreation or adoption and lose members through death and the marriage of children, every family farm, depending on its stage in the life cycle, represents a particular ratio of producers to consumers. While Chayanov recognized that such demographic factors are not the only variables affecting economic differentiation, they were in his view decisive (1966a, 5; 1966b, 69, 254). Consider the following statement: "Farms may increase or decline with unchanged family compositions due to purely economic causes. . . . There is, nevertheless, no doubt at all that demographic causes play the leading part in these movements" (1966b, 249).

Demographic factors and the subjectively driven economic behavior of family farms are the major variables Chayanov uses to explain the maintenance and persistence of family labor farms. For example, Chayanov argues that unlike capitalist farmers, family farmers will consider it worthwhile to acquire any plot of land that enables the household to achieve an internal balance between drudgery and consumption. Consequently, if family farmers are willing to pay high and (in capitalist terms) unprofitable prices for land, over time this family farm valuation may become dominant and in effect drive capitalists out of agriculture (Chayanov 1966b, 234 and 237). Chayanov makes an analogous argument when he explains why family farmers would hazard what would appear to capitalists as economically nonrational rent payments, farm investments, and labor intensification (Chayanov 1966a, 10; 1966b, 39, 88–89, 113, 115, 237–39). Such nonrational forms of economic behavior are predicated on subjective assessments and the ability of family farmers to engage in self-exploitation, major positions that Chayanov shares with Weber.

Contemporary empirical studies of the subjective orientations of farmers, which Weber and Chayanov presume make family farms resilient to objective market conditions, have not provided sufficient evidence to convince critics. Some studies have found that value orientations of family farmers do reflect Weber's notion of subjective interests in autonomy and work gratification (Mooney 1983; Bonnano 1987). Other studies have found that family farmers in the weakest structural positions and, therefore, in the most need of holding their own against adverse market conditions are in fact the most alienated from farming in terms of their subjective orientations (Schroeder, Fliegel, and van Es 1985, 317; Rosenfeld 1985, 175–78). In addition, conflicting data from more macro-oriented comparative historical studies have led some scholars to argue that theorists must move "away from social-psychological modes of explanation" if they are to make progress toward adequate explanations of social change (Skocpol 1982, 576).

Similarly, empirical studies of economic differentiation and family life cycles have resulted in contradictory findings (Friedmann 1978a; Shanin 1972; Schulman, Garrett, and Newman 1988; Sivakumar 1976; Welty 1987).[30] However, a common thread running through these empirical studies is that Chayanov's life-cycle analysis has greater validity if confined to forms of production that are not fully integrated into a market economy (Friedmann 1980b; Meillassoux 1983; Seccombe 1986).[31] Although Chayanov did not limit his theory to such forms of production (Chayanov 1966b, 125 and 224), this finding should be a warning to rural scholars who want to use life-cycle analyses to understand family labor enterprises in highly developed market economies.

In addition, the notion of self-exploitation used by both Weber and Chayanov has come under critical scrutiny in recent years. One of the most detailed critiques of this concept can be found in the work of Gordon Welty (1987). Along with other problems presented by this concept, Welty points out how the notion of self-exploitation conceals the patriarchal domination entailed in family labor enterprises, in which the male head of the household in fact controls both farm income and property, as well as the labor of women and children. Hence, self-exploitation is in fact a euphemism for patriarchal domination, covering up sexual and intergenerational structural inequalities. Because historical analyses are replete with evidence of the patriarchal nature of petty commodity production, Welty's analysis should also be sobering to scholars who continue to romanticize rural family relations and who uncritically view self-exploitation simply as a virtue.[32]

Yet, ironically, while Weber and Chayanov are criticized for overgeneralizing their concept of self-exploitation, their theories as a whole can be criticized for their lack of generalizability to other spheres of production. That is, on logical grounds their theories should hold true for nonrural, as well as rural, enterprises based on family labor. Yet, in most spheres of industrial production, neither ultimate values nor the peculiar economic behavior of family labor enterprises has been sufficient to forestall the penetration of capitalism. Rather, it is only in agricultural production that we find a significant coexistence of capitalist and noncapitalist units of production.

### *Macro-Micro Theoretical Syntheses*

The understandable frustration over the fact that neither rural sociology nor sociology in general has developed a theory that adequately links the macro and the micro dimensions of social life has led some rural sociologists to attempt more comprehensive theoretical syntheses. To date, most of these attempts have been largely unsuccessful. What has occurred, instead, is that some theorists have eclectically mixed the macro-structural components of Marx's theory with the micro-subjectivist components of Weber's theory (Bonnano 1987; Mooney 1983). These rather forced marriages between Marx and Weber have produced works devoid of any serious reconciliation of the major contradictions between the two approaches—contradictions that have been noted by Marxist and Weberian scholars alike (Bendix 1960; Gerth and Mills's introduction to Weber 1972, 49–50; Mommsen 1965; Welty 1983).[33]

Far more interesting for the new sociology of agriculture is the analysis of the reproduction[34] and transformation of simple commodity production developed by Harriet Friedmann. Because of the truly synthetic nature of her work, it is difficult to categorize as Marxist or non-Marxist. On the one hand, she employs a world-systems approach that combines some of the macro features of both Marx's and Weber's writings. On the other, she avoids the major pitfalls of her predecessors by viewing agrarian social classes as having an internal logic not entirely subsumed or defined by market relations. Indeed, Friedmann's conceptual distinctions between forms and modes of production have clarified and advanced many of the ongoing debates over agrarian forms of production (Friedmann 1981).[35]

Her focus on specifying the conditions necessary for the reproduction of different forms of production has also served to move the debates from abstract theories to more historically specific studies. Here the internal logic of specific wage and nonwage forms of production is viewed as operating within the context of objective market conditions, which set certain parameters or possibilities for their reproduction or transformation. Concrete historical conditions determine which of these possibilities is realized (Friedmann 1980a, 652). Because the former can be theoretically deduced, while the latter must be empirically induced, theory and history enrich each other, but neither loses its specific role in the development of knowledge.

Friedmann also incorporates Marx's macro-structural analysis with some of the micro-elements of Chayanov's theory. This integration of macro- and micro-theory is partially achieved by using Marx's distinction between simple and expanded reproduction to explain Chayanov's earlier point that family farmers and capitalists do not have the same criteria for making economic decisions (Friedmann 1980b and 1981). Simple reproduction refers to the ability of farms to continue producing so long as their costs of production (including farm inputs and consumption costs) do not exceed the realized value of their commodities on the market. This means that simple commodity producers can "dispense entirely with the category of profits as a precondition for their reproduction and replace the inflexibility of the wage with the flexible costs of personal consumption" (Friedmann 1981, 17). In contrast, capitalist enterprises must operate at the level of expanded reproduction, not only because their wage costs are less flexible, but also because their profits must tend toward the average rate of profit to ensure their competitive reproduction. Hence, rather than following Weber and Chayanov by using subjective assessments as her explanatory variables, Friedmann focuses on the structural ability of family farmers to operate at the level of simple reproduction to explain their greater market flexibility as compared to capitalist enterprises.[36]

Friedmann's melding of Marx and Chayanov to explain social reproduction is only partly successful because she is unable to integrate Chayanov's life-cycle analysis into her theory. Indeed, her writings on this point are quite contradictory. In her historical analysis of the reproduction of simple commodity-producing wheat farms in the late 1800s, life-cycle analysis is used to explain why family farms were able to outcompete capitalist producers (Friedmann 1978a). In her theoretical analysis of the transformation (or the failure of reproduction) of simple commodity production, demographic or life-cycle factors are relegated to a subordinate role in relation to objective market conditions (Friedmann 1980b and 1981).

In sum, Friedmann's conceptual rigor has done much to clarify many key issues in the modern debates. Her contributions to understanding the social reproduction and transformation of simple commodity production, while incomplete, stand alone in terms of bridging the gap between the competing Marxist and non-Marxist traditions. Yet despite these advances, her work fails to explain why the internal logic of simple commodity production did not serve to protect nonrural producers from their rather evident demise. That is, like many of her predecessors, she fails to explain why the social reproduction of simple commodity production has been more successful in agriculture than in industry.

## *Conclusion*

From this review of the literature on agrarian capitalism, it appears that no theoretical perspective adequately explains why the labor processes that characterize agriculture continue to be significantly different from those in modern industry. In most of the writings by the orthodox Marxists, agriculture has no unique features that would preclude capitalist class relations typical of the industrial factory from being reproduced in the countryside. Rather, industry and agriculture are portrayed as having "a remarkable similarity" in their "laws of evolution," which would eventually eradicate the differences between town and country.[37] Even Kautsky, who recognized that "agriculture does not develop according to the same process as industry" (Kautsky 1976, 39), did not see any significant opposition or incompatibility between capitalism and agriculture. Rather, in all of the macro-level theories examined above, capitalism is viewed as the dominant mode of production that selectively destroys or leaves intact traditional units of production—rural or urban—depending on whether they are functional or dysfunctional to capitalist accumulation.

The micro-subjectivist theories of Chayanov and Weber present the exact opposite problem. Proponents of these theories go to great lengths to detail how the internal features of family labor farms provide an adequate defense against the onslaught from capitalist enterprises. However, these theorists never explain why self-exploitation, demographic life cycles, or farmers' subjective value orientations fail to protect nonrural family labor enterprises from being undermined by capitalist competition, even though the logic of their theories would imply that family labor enterprises should continue to exist in both agriculture and industry. In short, the micro-subjectivist theorists are unable to explain why family labor enterprises are not reproduced in industry, while the macro-structural theorists cannot explain why wage labor/capital class relations are not reproduced in the countryside.

This theoretical impasse results from the fact that the specific context in which all of these ostensible economic activities take place—agricultural production—is ignored. In other words, these theorists fail to ask whether agriculture itself has any unique or peculiar features that distinguish it from industrial production and that inhibit capitalist development. As such, the following characterization of the classical Marxist-Narodnik debates by Goodman, Sorj, and Wilkinson is equally relevant to many modern writings in the new sociology of agriculture:[38] "The problematic of agriculture as a natural production system, as such, remains hidden behind debates on the respective merits of capitalist versus peasant modes of production, and an overriding—almost exclusive—preoccupation with the social relations of production. . . . The terms of the classical debate thus were soon frozen. . . . As a result, the specificity of agriculture either was denied by transposing capitalist social relations from the industrial town to the countryside or was defended on the basis of the alleged superiority of a peasant mode of production" (1987, 145 and 149).

To address this serious omission in the classical and the contemporary literature on the agrarian question, the following chapter examines the attempts made by contemporary rural sociologists to understand certain natural obstacles to rural capitalist development. I argue that many of the peculiar natural features of agricultural production which serve to protect family farms from capitalist penetration were discussed by Karl Marx almost a century ago. His important analyses in this regard went largely unnoticed because they are found only in some of his less well known or less well read writings. Certainly the anti-Marxist bias that until recently characterized American rural sociology did not foster a close examination of his writings. Thus it is one of the ironies of the history of American rural sociology that its own ideological biases are, in part, responsible for the underdevelopment of an adequate theory of the very phenomenon it has traditionally held as sacred and immutable: the persistence of the family farm.

# *Two*

# *Natural Obstacles to Agrarian Capitalism*

Beyond earth, water, weather and wind.
—John W. Gartrell and C. David Gartrell,
*Rural Sociology* (1980)

Agriculture and industry both entail the transformation of nature by socially organized labor. However, unlike industry, the social organization of agricultural production is *centered in nature* as its name implies: *agri* (meaning "field") and culture. Although this understanding seems elementary, few scholars have given this notion any serious attention. I am not suggesting here that scholars who specialize in rural studies are unaware of the seasonal nature of crop production, the natural gestation period entailed in animal husbandry, or agriculture's particular vulnerability to the vagaries of weather and climate. Such a claim would be ludicrous. However, until recently, few writers had mentioned these natural features of agricultural production in more than a descriptive fashion, and even fewer had assigned them any theoretical significance. Yet, as I argued at the end of the last chapter, an analysis of the natural obstacles to capitalist development is prerequisite to surmounting the theoretical obstacles to an adequate understanding of modern agriculture.

In the "new sociology of agriculture," some of the first theoretical analyses of the natural impediments to rural capitalism centered on the issues of land and ground rent. Consequently, it is these analyses that will be examined in the first section of this chapter. This will be followed by an elaboration of a more general theory of natural obstacles to the use of wage labor that James Dickinson and I originally formulated a decade ago. In light of the rather lengthy interval since the Mann-Dickinson thesis first appeared, I will also take this opportunity to examine critically some of the responses to our thesis.

## *Natural Obstacles to Agrarian Capitalism*

### *Land and Ground Rent*

Most of the contemporary writings that focus on the peculiar features of land as impediments to capitalist development derive their theoretical analyses from Karl Marx's writings on ground rent in Volume 3 of *Capital* or from Karl Kautsky's discussion of land in *Die Agrarfrage* (Mandel 1970; Murray 1977 and 1978; Vergopoulos 1978; Goss, Buttel, and Rodefeld 1980; Mann 1982). Consequently, in my review of this literature, some of these classical Marxist statements on land and ground rent will be interwoven with writings by contemporary authors.

In discussing various problems associated with land as a major factor of production, both Marx and Kautsky highlighted the simple fact that land is a fixed resource—fixed because it is both of limited quantity and a relatively immovable form of capital. Hence, it can neither be socially created and multiplied at will nor easily transported to more suitable locations in order to expand production and profits (Marx 1967c, 118, and 1967b, 165; Kautsky 1976, 30). Additional constraints on the expansion of production can result from the quality and/or the spatial characteristics of land, such as rolling terrain or irregular-sized fields that do not lend themselves to certain types of mechanization.[1] Similarly, natural and social conditions that obstruct capitalists from acquiring contiguous territories can prevent the expansion of production, as well as the use of appropriate economies of scale. These problems can also result in significant differences between agriculture and industry in terms of the concentration and centralization of production. As Kautsky writes: "In industry, accumulation proceeds independently of centralization: A big capital can form without suppressing the autonomy of smaller capitals. When this suppression occurs it is the *effect* of the formation of big industrial capital. Accumulation is here the starting point. On the contrary, where the land is fragmented into different properties and where small ownership prevails, large holdings can only acquire land by centralizing smaller ones" (1976, 30 [his emphasis]). Consequently, the importance of acquiring contiguous territories in agricultural production could mean that centralization—the union of scattered capitals into one capital—would have to precede significant accumulation of wealth by any single capitalist farm. This reversal of the normal process of expanded reproduction could entail large expenses at early stages of production and, thereby, thwart rural capitalist development.

Another reason certain types of land-based agriculture might entail large expenses in their early stages is related to Marx's concept of the organic composition of capital, that is, the ratio of the value of capital inputs to the value of labor inputs (Marx 1967a, 574 and 583–84). Extensive types of agriculture generally have a high organic composition of capital even at the earliest stages of the production process because of the large amounts of land and/or livestock required for successful production.[2] However, capital assets, like land or livestock, do not function to increase labor productivity in the same way as do capital investments in labor-saving technology. To a capitalist, the implications of these different types of capital for generating surplus value are significant.

By contrast, in industrial production a high organic composition of capital usually signifies major investments in labor-saving technology and, hence, major advances in labor productivity.[3] Moreover, such a high organic composition of capital in nonfarm production is also generally the result of capital accumulation—not its beginning—since technology is added as capitalism advances. Concern for the expenses entailed in a high organic composition of capital at early stages of the production process could present a problem to capitalists' initial entry into land-based agriculture, especially when the bulk of such capital assets do not enhance labor productivity (Mann and Dickinson 1978, 475).[4]

While it might appear that any impediments that land presents to farm production and expansion would obstruct both capitalist and noncapitalist forms of production, these impediments, in fact, have different effects on different social classes. For example, as I noted in the previous chapter, although both family farms and capitalist farms can operate at the level of expanded reproduction, only capitalist enterprises require such expanded reproduction or capital accumulation for their long-term viability. Hence, obstacles to farm expansion have more serious and detrimental consequences to capitalist enterprises. For this reason, such obstacles can actually protect family farmers faced with market competition from capitalist farms.

Another protection for landowning family farmers can arise from the surplus income Marx termed differential rent. This type of rent flows simply from the differential natural qualities of land. Hence, even if the labor of farmers is equally intense or productive and even if farmers invest the same amount of capital in land improvement, differential incomes can arise as a result of natural factors, like the variability of different soils or more advantageous geographical locations. As Murray points out, this differential rent can serve as a cushion that partially insulates landowning family farmers from the effects of market determinations, thus forestalling their demise (Murray 1978, 19).[5]

By contrast, the appropriation of ground rent by another noncapitalist class of landlords presents obstacles to farm expansion for any tenant farmer—capitalist and noncapitalist alike. Here the peculiar nature of land as a factor of production can actually serve as a disincentive for capital investments in land improvement. This occurs because many improvements made to land become inseparable from the land itself, such as drainage canals, irrigation works, leveling, or fertilization. Hence, the benefits from such improvements would revert to the landlord when the lease expired. In turn, if such improvements were made, landlords would have less interest in renewing leases so as to reap a greater proportion of income by renegotiating new leases in their favor (Marx 1967c, 618–19; Mandel 1970, 281–82; Goss, Buttel, and Rodefeld 1980, 92).

As many writers have noted, the existence of a landlord class also presents a barrier to the free mobility of capital in agriculture and, thus, serves as an impediment to capital accumulation as a whole (Murray 1977 and 1978; Vergopoulos 1978). Breaking the hold of such a landlord class can be achieved through a variety of different mechanisms, such as breaking their political hegemony through state intervention or outright revolution; circumventing their control by opening new frontiers or reclaiming unused lands, such as marshland; or eliminating the need for land altogether by developing new types of landless production, such as hydroponics or fast-fattening feedlots (Goodman, Sorj, and Wilkinson 1987, 154–56).

Such solutions to the immobility of land as capital, however, also have different consequences for different social classes. For example, in the United States, the settlement of the frontier fostered the development of simple commodity production, particularly in prairie wheat production. In contrast, the development of landless types of production would be more likely to undermine simple commodity production, by making certain types of agriculture more amenable to factory farming. The integral relationship between nature, class, and history is even more visible in the more general discussion of natural obstacles to rural capitalist development below.

## *The "Mann-Dickinson Thesis"*

Over a decade ago, James Dickinson and I published an article, "Obstacles to the Development of a Capitalist Agriculture" (1978), in which we discussed a number of natural barriers to the use of rural wage labor. Unlike the preceding analyses of land and ground rent, which were rooted in relatively well known writings by Marx and Kautsky, our thesis was derived from some of Marx's less well known writings in the *Grundrisse* (1973) and in Volume 2 of *Capital* (1967b).

With the notable exception of an article in Spanish by Ariel Contreras (1977),[6] these observations by Marx had been largely overlooked by Marxist and non-Marxist scholars alike. Because our thesis placed Marx's analysis of natural obstacles to agrarian capitalism more clearly within the context of the ongoing theoretical debates in rural sociology or, perhaps, simply because of the ethnocentrism of First World rural sociology, our thesis received far greater attention from both supporters and critics.[7]

This attention was in many ways a mixed blessing. Indeed, in subsequent interpretations and critiques of the Mann-Dickinson thesis, several important analytical points we had originally used to qualify our thesis were often overlooked. To avoid such misinterpretations in the future I will highlight these points before presenting our more general analysis of natural obstacles to rural capitalist development. Readers should recognize that these points not only suggest important qualifications to our thesis, but they also provide valuable insights for any study of rural stratification or development.

First, we did not treat agriculture as a monolithic whole, but rather drew attention to the peculiar nature of the production processes in certain spheres of agriculture. Indeed, numerous writers had documented how capitalism had successfully conquered the production of certain rural commodities (Lenin 1974; Rochester 1940; Goss, Buttel, and Rodefeld 1980). Therefore, the issue was no longer the problem of explaining obstacles to the capitalist development of agriculture, but rather why *some* branches of agriculture become capitalist more rapidly than others.

Second, the Mann-Dickinson thesis is not a biological or natural determinist theory, but rather an analysis of the contradictions faced by a specific form of production—capitalist production. As we wrote in our original piece: "An appeal to nature alone is an ahistorical argument." Rather, we presented our arguments in terms of the historically specific conditions required by capitalist production, recognizing that these same conditions are not necessarily required for farms that produce only use values or even farms engaged in simple commodity production. Consequently, we go "beyond earth, water, weather and wind" by examining the interrelationship between natural and social conditions as an essential component of our thesis.[8] Indeed, "what appears then, as a natural barrier, is only a barrier to capitalist forms of production" (Mann and Dickinson 1978, 478–79).

Finally, unlike some neo-Marxist theorists, we do not view the maintenance and survival of nonwage forms of production as providing alternative forms of dependency and exploitation that are, from a capitalist's viewpoint, either equivalent to or preferable to the extraction of surplus value through wage labor.[9] Rather, we argue that non-wage forms of production continue to exist, not because they are preferred avenues of capital accumulation, but because they are unavoidable features of the modern landscape. That is, they cannot be conquered by capitalist production *at this point in time*. Hence, while capitalism is viewed as the dominant mode of production in our thesis, it is neither so invincible nor so powerful as to successfully contend with the erratic and capricious character of nature—as I shall document below.

## *The Nonidentity of Production Time and Labor Time*

According to Marx's labor theory of value, the production of any commodity is based on the socially necessary labor time needed for its production. Socially necessary labor time refers to the prevailing conditions of production existing in a given time and place. Consequently, in a local market, competition would be far more limited than would be the case for commodities that must compete on a world market. Yet the actual labor time expended in any concrete production process is distinct from socially necessary labor time (Singer, Green, and Gilles 1983).[10] Whether or not a farmer's actual labor time approaches this social average determines his or her viability in a given market.

Actual labor time can further be distinguished from production time. As Marx writes: "Working time is always production time; that is to say, time during which capital is held fast in the sphere of production. But vice versa, not all time during which capital is engaged in the process of production is necessarily labor time" (1967b, 242). Marx explained this passage by saying that production time consists of two parts: one period when labor is engaged in production and a second period when the unfinished commodity is "abandoned to the sway of natural processes" (1967b, 243, and 1973, 668–69). Instances of the latter include the natural, chemical, and physiological changes that occur in such processes as the gestation period of livestock, the drying stage of pottery production, bleaching, or fermenting. Although labor generally initiates these processes, after the initial labor input the process proceeds on its own.

According to Marx, the intervals when labor is not being used create neither value nor surplus value. In Volume 2 of *Capital* he writes: "There is no expansion of the value of productive capital as long as it stays in that part of its production time which exceeds labor time, no matter how inseparable from these pauses the carrying on of the process of self-expansion may be" (1967b, 127). Thus, it follows that the more production time and labor time coincide, the greater the productivity and self-expansion of capital in a given time period (Contreras 1977, 887; Mann and Dickinson 1978, 472–73).

In some industries, such as automobile production and mining, these two periods—production time and labor time—almost completely overlap. For example, in car production, special ovens coupled with special paints circumvent the natural drying process of paint on metal. However, in other spheres of production, the gap between production time and labor time proves extremely problematic. This divergence is of particular importance in certain types of agricultural commodity production (Marx 1967b, 244).

For example, cereal grain production entails a relatively lengthy total production time because the produce takes months to mature and can be produced only annually. It is also characterized by a long interval between production time and labor time, since labor time is almost completely suspended in various stages of production, as when the seed is germinating in the earth (Marx 1967b, 244, and 1973, 668). In this case, the reduction of production time is severely restricted by natural factors and cannot easily be socially modified or manipulated.

One of the central tenets of the Mann-Dickinson thesis was that capitalist development progresses most rapidly in those spheres where production time can be successfully reduced and where the gap between production time and labor time can be minimized. Conversely, we argued that spheres of production characterized by a more rigid nonidentity of production time and labor time were likely to prove unattractive to capitalist investment and thus were more likely to be left in the hands of petty producers. That the nonidentity of production time and labor time also establishes an entire series of obstacles to rural capitalist development will become apparent as its effect on turnover time, profits, marketing, and the utilization of machinery and wage labor is examined below.

### *Turnover Time and Profits*

In our original thesis, we discussed how the production time of many agricultural commodities would also reduce the turnover of capital, due to the long interval it takes to renew the productive cycle again. Since capitalist firms extract profits during each turnover of capital, they can also use these profits to replenish and expand their production. Using this logic, we argued that the more turnovers of capital in a given period of time, the more this enhanced profits and reduced capitalists' need to borrow from others for their productive activity (Marx 1967b, 317; Contreras 1977, 888; Mann and Dickinson 1978, 473–74).

This point is more obvious when one compares two capitalist enterprises that are identical in every respect except that one enterprise has a number of turnovers annually, while the other has only a single annual turnover (such as capitalist wheat farming). The former not only extracts surplus value more times during the year, but also can replenish and even expand production out of the surplus value appropriated. In contrast, the latter enterprise must await the annual sale of its commodities and is not in a position to expand production as often. Thus, the gains that accrue to the former are similar to the advantages of compound over simple interest.

Consequently, we maintained that it was in the interests of capital to reduce production time as much as possible, so that the turnover of capital would be speeded up and profits enhanced. However, since the seasonal nature of agricultural production often operates effectively to prevent any meaningful reduction of production time, we concluded that "capital would shy away from such areas of production precisely because turnover time, like production time, is relatively fixed" (Mann and Dickinson 1978, 474).[11]

One of the earliest, as well as some of the most recent, critics of our thesis argued that our rate-of-profit argument was not sufficient to explain the inability of capitalism to penetrate agriculture (Perelman 1979; Goodman, Sorj, and Wilkinson 1987).[12] For example, Goodman, Sorj, and Wilkinson argued that the rate of profit alone cannot explain uneven rural development, since capitalist farmers are competing against family labor enterprises for whom the rate of profit is not a criterion (1987, 154).

We agree that successful capitalists—whether in agriculture or in nonfarm industries—must be able to outcompete family enterprises that can operate at the level of simple reproduction (Mann and Dickinson 1980, 300). However, this does not significantly change our argument. It simply means that a more fundamental point should have been highlighted in our original thesis. That is, the natural features of agricultural production can impede capitalist enterprises from sufficiently reducing the socially necessary labor time needed to produce commodities. In contrast, in industrial production where inflexible natural obstacles do not present as severe a problem, capitalist enterprises have clearly succeeded in reducing the socially necessary labor time even *below* that of petty producers operating at the level of simple reproduction. Indeed, it is only by producing below this level that the cheap prices of capitalist commodities can serve as the "heavy artillery" that batters down more traditional forms of production (Marx

1970, 39). Otherwise petty producers would be playing a much more dominant role in the industrial sphere. Capital's inability to replicate these accomplishments in certain branches of agriculture stems from the greater difficulty entailed in socially modifying or manipulating the natural foundations of rural production. How these difficulties also plague the marketing of agricultural commodities will be addressed below.

### *Peculiar Features of Agricultural Marketing*

While all producers—industrial and agricultural alike—incur unavoidable costs in marketing their products, the form in which the commodity exists is not the same for all spheres of production. For example, some commodities are perishable by nature and, consequently, if they are not consumed quickly (either as raw materials in another production process or in household consumption), they spoil and lose—along with their use value—their exchange value. The spoiling of commodities sets, then, the absolute limit for the circuit of commodity capital. As Marx writes: "The more perishable the commodity is and the greater the absolute restriction of its time in circulation as a commodity on account of its physical properties, the less it is suited to be an object of capitalist production" (Marx 1967b, 131). Because a number of agricultural commodities are perishable by nature, Marx predicted that this would make capitalist penetration in the countryside a higher-risk venture than in industry (Contreras 1977, 887; Mann and Dickinson 1978, 475–76).

Moreover, Marx noted that the peculiar features of agricultural marketing extended beyond perishability to include more durable agricultural commodities, such as wheat or soybeans. As he argued, these commodities have their own particular problems associated with circulation. Their relatively lengthy production times require that a certain amount of the finished commodity be stored because their consumption takes place over the entire year, whereas their production occurs in many areas only annually. While marketing firms often provide the bulk of this storage, these firms do so only by charging high rates for storage and/or by buying the commodities at a cheaper rate than the farmer could receive at different points in the year.

In addition, the storage of agricultural commodities can also involve the problem of shrinkage. Different types of commodities vary in their degree of shrinkage. At the turn of the century, farmers usually expected a loss of about 10 percent when potatoes were stored for six months after harvest. Tests done on corncobs in the early 1900s indicated a shrinkage estimated at 12 to 20 percent in the first year (Warren 1917, 417–19). In contrast, industrial commodities seldom entail the same degree of deterioration.

Another marketing problem that is much more acute in agricultural production than in industry is the problem of price fluctuations (U.S. Bureau of Labor Statistics 1959, 25 and 27). The perishability of many farm products, as well as agriculture's greater vulnerability to natural factors such as harmful climatic conditions or pest infestations, can result in sharp variations in the volume of marketable produce. In turn, the relatively lengthy production time of certain agricultural commodities impedes the farmer's ability to respond to changes in price.

Such delayed reactions occur because it is more difficult to quickly augment production in agriculture than in industry (Contreras 1977, 886; Mann and Dickinson 1980, 287). In the middle of a production cycle, the farmer may be able to increase output slightly by the greater use of fertilizer or more intensive feeding. For example, milk production shows an immediate, but small, increase if cows are given more food (Cohen 1940, 97). Between production cycles, the lengthy production time of certain commodities also presents a problem. For instance, one of the most prolific of farm animals—the pig—has a gestation period of four months. In addition, pigs have to be four to six months old for slaughter as pork and eight months old for slaughter as bacon (Cohen 1940, 98). Conversely, curtailing production can frequently entail overhead costs, since livestock that are not slaughtered for market still have to be fed, while fields lying fallow may quickly become overgrown with weeds and bushes.

Moreover, in industry, the entrepreneur responding to the dictates of the market can generally increase or decrease production by almost the exact amount intended. In contrast, farmers have considerable difficulty achieving such precision. The range of error for crops is compounded by the fact that the total output for many crops varies more with yield per acre, which the farmer cannot easily control, than with acreage, which can be controlled. For example, in areas with temperate climates, potato acreage varied on the average during the decade preceding World War II by no more than 6 percent from year to year, while yield per acre varied by 9 percent. In areas subject to less temperate climates, variations in crop yields per acre were even greater (Cohen 1940, 100).

All of these natural factors accentuate the frequency and degree of price fluctuations in agriculture. In subsequent chapters, a number of social developments that have reduced the risk of adverse price fluctuations, such as the growth of food processing and preservation industries, trading on crop and livestock futures markets, and government price supports, will be discussed. Nevertheless, despite advances, none of these developments has provided foolproof security to farmers (Goss, Buttel, and Rodefeld 1980).

### *Farm Machinery, Labor, and Nature*

Marx also pointed out how the lack of synchronization between production time and labor time resulted in the inefficient use of farm machinery (Marx 1967b, 176 and 246). Since machinery depreciates as a result of both physical deterioration and social obsolescence, the value of machinery after it is purchased is calculated according to the time in which it depreciates, rather than according to the time in which it functions (Marx, 1967b, 176 and 246). Thus, it is not surprising that capitalists strive to keep their machines running as a means of utilizing as much value as they possibly can.

Yet such continuous production is often precluded by the biological rhythms of agricultural production. For instance, farm machinery often lies idle with its value being whittled away by social obsolescence during off-seasons and other periods characterized by an excess of production time over labor time. Here, again, the high organic composition of capital in certain branches of agriculture can exacerbate this problem (Wilcox, Cochrane, and Herdt 1974, 13–15). Idle machinery is therefore a burden to the farmer and something to be avoided by the capitalist.

Goodman, Sorj, and Wilkinson point out that the spatial and temporal features of agricultural production present another serious natural obstacle to the efficient use of certain types of machinery in the countryside: "In manufacturing, 'nature' is broken down by processing and introduced into the machine as a raw material input, which thus can be adapted to the speed of machine production. By contrast, nature in agricultural production cannot be reduced to an input; indeed it is the 'factory' itself. . . . Rather than the Copernican revolution of manufacturing whereby nature must circulate around the machine, nature in agriculture maintains its predominance and it is the machine which must circulate" (Goodman, Sorj, and Wilkinson 1987, 21). This wonderful imagery of machines circulating around nature, rather than nature being subservient to machines, captures a significant difference between agriculture and industry in terms of their respective technological histories. For example, Goodman, Sorj, and Wilkinson use their spatial analysis to explain why the steam engine provided the motive power for nineteenth-century industry, while agricultural technology continued to be drawn primarily by horse and mule. The notable exception here was threshing, where the machine no longer had to maneuver around nature, but rather could act on the more compact finished product, much as it did in the industrial factory. The development of the internal combustion engine, which led to widespread adoption of machinery powered by gasoline engines in the twentieth century, was a major breakthrough in this regard, because it produced more maneuverable farm machinery and thereby reduced the spatial constraints of land-based agriculture (Goodman, Sorj, and Wilkinson 1987, 20–21).[13]

Along with such spatial constraints, another problem that Marx did not discuss is the relationship between the continuous production often used in the processing of agricultural commodities and the consequent need for continuous or near-continuous harvests in agriculture. For example, some crops undergo a substantial reduction of bulk during processing. Tanganyikan sisal undergoes a reduction to about 4 percent of its bulk during the mechanical extraction of fibers (Paige 1975, 15; A. M. O'Connor 1966, 90). Similarly, Peruvian sugar undergoes a reduction to less than 5 percent of its former bulk during the extraction of refined sugar from sugarcane (Paige 1975, 15). An adequate return for processing these crops requires that machinery be kept in almost constant operation. Only a relatively small number of crops grown in certain locales—sisal, sugar, tea, and palm oil—both involve bulk reduction and satisfy the condition of near-continuous harvesting. Given the closer identity of labor time and production time entailed in continuous harvesting, it is not surprising that these crops can be produced on plantations using wage labor and centralized factory forms of organization (Paige 1975, 15; Courtenay 1965, 50–67).

In industry, labor (at least shift labor), like machinery, can fulfill the requirements of continuous production. Labor can even circulate around nature if necessary. However, if labor is forced to be idle during the excess of production time over labor time, due to the seasonal nature of labor requirements or the underemployment of labor on a daily basis, this can give rise to serious labor supply and recruitment problems. Such problems have given the wage labor force in agricultural production a much different complexion than that found in industry proper.

My choice of the term "complexion" here is not accidental. Indeed, it appears that where capitalist agriculture has developed most fully in an industrialized fashion, it has relied on a marginalized wage labor force that is vulnerable to inequalities arising from ethnicity, citizenship status, and gender, and thus is subject to greater control (Friedland and Barton 1975; Friedland 1980; Friedland, Barton, and Thomas 1981; Majka and Majka 1982; Thomas 1985; Thomas-Lycklama a Nieholt 1980). Today, most of the research on wage labor in agriculture has focused on this migrant and marginalized labor—labor that is not at all typical of the primary labor force in the industrial sphere (Buttel, Larson, and Gillespie 1989, chap. 4). Yet, while these nonpermanent, marginalized farm workers constitute the majority of the American rural wage labor force, the *majority of hours of hired labor* are provided by wage workers employed on a more permanent basis.

The vast majority of these permanent wage laborers in agricultural production are not members of a minority group (Rodefeld 1978; Buttel, Larson, and Gillespie 1989). However, here a crucial difference between industry and agriculture is that in the rural sphere, permanent, white, male workers are not employed on the most fully developed capitalist operations, but rather on what have come to be called "larger-than-family farms." While these farms hire labor, they do not exhibit many of the features of full-scale capitalist factory farming because they are family-owned, family-managed, and they employ only a few (an average of eight) wage workers (Buttel 1983).[14]

Another peculiar way in which wage labor relationships have been established in agriculture arises from the seasonal nature of agricultural production. Here capitalist farmers are often forced to hire family farmers as a necessary supplement to their wage labor force during peak harvest seasons (Bonnano 1987, 14; McMichael 1984, 221). This was one of the reasons why Kautsky argued that the coexistence of family farms alongside capitalist production was functional to capitalism. In contrast, although industrial capitalists may make use of such petty bourgeois overtime workers, they do not rely on such labor for their ongoing production, as Kautsky implied was the case for many rural capitalists (1976).

These significant differences between the characteristics of the wage labor force in agriculture as compared to industry again draw our attention to the peculiar natural rhythms of rural production, which result in the much sharper peaks and gluts in the cycle of labor demand. Indeed, that rural wage labor presents a caricature or mirror image of the industrial wage labor force exemplifies the difficulty of duplicating the requirements of capitalist enterprise in a sector of production that is centered in nature.

## The Historical Specificity of Natural Impediments

The Mann-Dickinson thesis also discussed how private and public agricultural research is given over to efforts to reduce the natural impediments to capitalist development through such advances as artificial insemination, fast-fattening processes, the development of hybrid seeds, and hydroponics (Mann and Dickinson 1978, 474).[15] In addition, we explicitly noted in the original thesis that: "When the conditions of production are sufficiently altered . . . so as to overcome these barriers, then there is no reason to believe that capitalism will not move in and conquer them as it has done in industry proper" (Mann and Dickinson 1978, 478). From these discussions we thought it was clear that any natural impediments to capitalist development should be viewed in a historically specific and relative manner.

Some modern writers recognized this and used our thesis constructively to show how various natural obstacles were modified or reduced in particular historical settings (Singer, Green, and Gilles 1983; Pfeffer 1983; Koc 1987).[16] In contrast, other writers criticized our thesis for ostensibly arguing that the natural obstacles we identified were immutable barriers to the use of wage labor in agriculture.[17] Because of these contradictory interpretations of the Mann-Dickinson thesis, it is necessary to reemphasize the historical specificity of any and all natural impediments to agrarian capitalism.

For example, when we discussed how the reduction in agricultural production times is severely limited by natural barriers, we quoted Marx's observations on livestock production, where "neither the period of gestation nor the growth to economic maturity could be easily shortened" (Marx 1967b, 241 and 248). Yet certainly in the modern era there have been remarkable advances in capitalists' control over livestock production. The post–World War II developments in reproductive technologies, such as artificial insemination, superovulation, embryo transplants, and estrus detection and synchronization, surmounted many biological obstacles present in Marx's lifetime. Prior to these developments, a cow normally only produced one embryo a year. Today, following artificial insemination, the fertilized superovulated ova are recovered and transferred to surrogate mothers whose estrus cycles have been synchronized to those of the donor. With these methods it is estimated that superior donors can produce fifty to sixty calves a year (Goodman, Sorj, and Wilkinson 1987, 53; U.S. Congress 1986, 36).[18] Such incredible new methods of controlling nature could not have been foreseen by nineteenth-century writers like Karl Marx.

Some of the most interesting work in the new sociology of agriculture is focusing precisely on this issue of how capitalism comes to increase its control over nature in order to conquer the seemingly recalcitrant sphere of agriculture. The recent work by Goodman, Sorj, and Wilkinson *From Farming to Biotechnology* (1987) provides one of the best analyses to date of the historical attempts by capital to reduce or eliminate the natural resistance of agriculture to the use of wage labor. Even though almost a decade had elapsed since the publication of the Mann-Dickinson thesis, this also was the first major publication to share our view that the inability to subordinate nature to capitalist production requirements was the *fundamental key* to understanding uneven rural development.[19] Indeed, while many other writers had used our thesis in their work, none had given nature such a central role in explaining the so-called agrarian question. Below I examine Goodman, Sorj, and Wilkinson's contributions to an analysis of natural obstacles to agrarian capitalism.

### *Recent Work on Capitals' Conquest of Nature*

Contrary to the subtitle of their book, *A Theory of Agro-Industrial Development*—Goodman, Sorj, and Wilkinson do not actually present a *theory* as to why certain natural features of agriculture conflict with the logic of capitalist development. Rather, they simply state this to be the case. That is, they say that agricultural development took a "decisively different path" from industrial capitalist development because of the structural constraints presented by nature, and then they use the rest of the book to describe how capital has "responded" by adapting to, modifying, or eliminating natural obstacles to its development (1–5). These descriptions are so fascinating that they reveal a great deal about the conflicts and contradictions between capitalism and nature even in the absence of a developed theory.

Moreover, in an earlier work by Goodman and Redclift (1982), as well as in the later book, a number of new concepts are introduced that provide important analytical distinctions for studies of agrarian capitalism. In particular, the distinction between different ways that forms of production are subordinated or subsumed by capital—formal subsumption versus real subsumption—provides a simple, but intriguing, way out of the seemingly endless debate over whether to characterize modern nonwage forms of production as capitalist or noncapitalist. Real subsumption refers to capitals' control over the actual labor process and its economic logic or laws of production and reproduction. By contrast, formal subsumption refers to capitals' control over the parameters within which nonwage forms of production operate, such as control over credit or commodity markets, without actually transforming the labor process. In this way the different means and degrees of capitalist penetration of the countryside can be better articulated. In turn, while these distinctions do not resolve all of the issues in the debate,[20] they provide a useful, nonpartisan vocabulary that enables theoretical opponents to clarify their essential points of agreement and controversy.

Interestingly, however, even this conceptual breakthrough is downplayed in the 1987 book, where nature takes on a much more fundamental role in the authors' analysis. As they write: "For capital, the central constraint is not the (limited) autonomy of the farmer or owner-operator but the inability to eliminate the risks, uncertainties, and discontinuities intrinsic to a natural or biological production process" (156). Hence, "we must look not to rural production for the secret of capitalist subordination," but rather to "the growth of the agro-industrial work force, with the dynamic of rural social structures being determined by the degree and form of the industrialization of nature" (152–53). In this way, these writers have come to share the view of the Mann-Dickinson thesis that the real subsumption of rural forms of production is dependent on capital's ability to civilize nature.

With nature now in the center of their analysis, Goodman, Sorj, and Wilkinson introduce two more useful concepts—appropriationism and substitutionism—which analytically guide their historical descriptions of capitals' struggles to subordinate nature. Appropriationism refers to attempts by industrial capital to reduce or weaken the importance of nature in rural production, so as to increase the social manipulation and control of this sphere of production. Substitutionism entails the actual elimination of the natural base of production, either by using nonagricultural raw materials or by creating industrial substitutes for food or fibers (2–3 and 57–58). For example, the advances in livestock reproduction cited above reflect the process of appropriationism because they only modify the natural base of agriculture. By contrast, the creation of synthetic dyes and fibers and the development of socially fabricated foods, like margarine, exemplify the process of substitutionism.[21]

Goodman, Sorj, and Wilkinson also provide insights into the future structure of the American agricultural landscape when they discuss how a qualitative leap in both appropriationism and substitutionism is under way, given the developments in biotechnology over the last few decades.[22] For example, in the realm of appropriationism, recombinant genetic engineering or "gene-splicing" and the removal of species barriers to reproduction will give plant breeders access to genetic characteristics not found in the natural gene pool. While serious obstacles still remain before this becomes a practical method of plant breeding, illustrative examples of the application of genetic plant engineering include the introduction of nitrogen-fixing and pest-resistant crops, the development of more nutritional varieties of cereal grains, and the better adaptation of crops to the requirements of food-processing industries (105–17). Improved plants from such gene transfer methods are expected to be commercially available within a decade (U.S. Congress 1986, 47).

A more immediate impact is expected on livestock production, where growth hormones are currently being used to substantially increase milk production and livestock body weight. In turn, the insertion of genes into animal reproductive cells to increase growth or disease resistance has revolutionary implications for the future, since such gene manipulations can permanently affect future generations of livestock. Already, rabbit genes inserted into mice embryos have produced mice that are more than twice as large as normal mice. It is not surprising that these developments, which already border on transcending our current sensibilities about the world, could eliminate the most serious remaining obstacles to greater efficiency in livestock production (U.S. Congress 1986, 35–36).

Recent biotechnological developments in the realm of substitutionism may sound less foreboding but have even more revolutionary implications, since they can eliminate the need for agriculture. For example, the low-calorie, artificial sweeteners already widely used in the food industry represent the modern application of enzyme technology. Another recent innovation is the production of mycoprotein, a microscopic fungus that can be used to simulate animal protein textures. Meat, poultry, and fish have all been imitated in both texture and flavor. Many of these new simulated foods are being marketed on the basis of their nutritional qualities, particularly because they do not contain animal fats and cholesterol (Goodman, Sorj, and Wilkinson 1987, 127–36).

As Goodman, Sorj, and Wilkinson point out, the appropriational and substitutional uses of biotechnology are currently on two different and opposing trajectories. On the one hand, the appropriational methods, such as the development of new plant breeds through genetic engineering or the production of essential amino acids to cheapen and enhance animal feed, help to buttress and maintain the grain-meat complex as the fulcrum of the modern food system. On the other hand, the substitutional methods, such as the development of simulated foods, undermine the grain-meat complex through competition (144).

In terms of the future of family farms, Goodman, Sorj, and Wilkinson predict two different outcomes which, again, depend on the natural features of different branches of agricultural production. In branches of agriculture like livestock or horticultural crops, where the need for land can be virtually eliminated by confined settings, environmentally controlled conditions, and hydroponics, they foresee increased vertical integration and capitalist factory farming. In contrast, where the possibilities for the elimination of land are far more limited, as in the case of field crops, they foresee a reduction of the farmer's role in crop management practices, an increase in part-time farming, and the transformation of many petty producers into virtual or actual "rentiers." In both scenarios, the role of the farm operator is "qualitatively redefined," giving way to the "bio-manager" and the peripheralization of family labor farms (Goodman, Sorj, and Wilkinson 1987, 177–84). Somewhat similar predictions are described by a report by the U.S. Office of Technology that portends the likelihood of increased contract farming and the enhanced role of large farms in the American rural economy (U.S. Congress 1986, 9 and 12).

I introduced the work of Goodman, Sorj, and Wilkinson as a fine example of an analysis that has taken seriously both the role of natural impediments to rural capitalist development and the historical specificity of these natural obstacles. However, as they are aware, their analysis is vulnerable to the charge of technological determinism, because advances in technology are seen as the major means by which the natural foundations of agricultural production are modified or transcended. More emphasis on how social events and forces can foster or obstruct technological innovations would have significantly enhanced this study. Perhaps because these authors are so critical of earlier analyses of agrarian capitalism that, in their view, were so "preoccupied with the social relations of production" that they were blind to the natural features of agricultural production, Goodman, Sorj, and Wilkinson err in the opposite direction by ignoring in their own analysis the role of social classes and class conflict in the history of industrial capitals' attempts to conquer nature.[23] In other words, along with technological advances, the "social struggles" and the "socio-historical circumstances" that make obstacles of the specific conditions of agricultural production should have been pursued at more length.[24]

By contrast, in my own historical analyses in subsequent chapters, the social and the natural are integrally intertwined in the making of modern agriculture. Indeed, while I argue that the natural features of any commodity are the key to understanding uneven capitalist development, such natural features "are as much a reflection of the social relations which structure its production as they are given in nature" (Wilson 1986, 52). However, before I examine how different social classes encounter and counter the natural foundations of agricultural production, I will address, perhaps, the most serious criticism to date of the Mann-Dickinson thesis—the claim that this thesis is empirically invalid (Mooney 1982).[25] In the remainder of the book several different research methodologies are used to empirically test this claim and, thus, our thesis. In particular, the next chapter uses U.S. census data to examine whether the specific natural obstacles I have identified had any impact on the capitalist development of different branches of American agriculture during the period from 1900 to 1930.[26] In this way, I shall begin to determine whether my theory of agrarian capitalism accurately reflects agrarian capitalism in practice.

# *Three*

# *Capitalism in American Agriculture*

A leading country of modern capitalism is of special interest to the study of the socio-economic structure and evolution of present-day agriculture. The U.S.A. is . . . in many respects the model for our bourgeois civilisation and is its ideal.—V. I. Lenin, *New Data on the Laws Governing the Development of Capitalism in Agriculture* (1915)

A central tenet of this book is that the marked differences between the class structures that characterize agriculture and industry are in large part attributable to the natural foundations of agricultural production. To examine this thesis, the present chapter uses U.S. census data to document trends in the capitalist development of American agriculture by type of rural commodity. This commodity-specific analysis is necessary to determine whether uneven rural development is related to the peculiar production processes in certain branches of agriculture. If such a relationship exists, one would expect to find that agricultural commodities vary in their degree of capitalist development. In addition, since I have argued that natural factors play an important role in obstructing capitalist development, various natural obstacles I have identified will be examined in terms of their effect on the use of wage labor.

I had intended that this empirical chapter, like the subsequent chapters on the history of Southern cotton production, would cover the time period from the Civil War to the Great Depression. This period is often referred to as the "Golden Age" of family farming in the United States because it was marked by an unprecedented expansion in the number of farms and a spectacular increase in farm production (Rasmussen 1960, 104; Carstensen 1974, 2).[1] This so-called "heyday" of family farming seemed an appropriate era in which to examine obstacles to rural capitalist development. However, my plans were thwarted by the fact that few censuses from 1870 to 1930 provided commodity-specific data; only the 1900 and the 1930 censuses categorized farms by the commodities they produced. As a result the empirical analysis below is more narrowly circumscribed to the periods of 1900 and 1930.

### *Type of Farm and Capitalist Development*

In the censuses of 1900 and 1930, farms were grouped according to their principal source of income and categorized in commodity groups if the value of a particular commodity produced exceeded the value of all other commodities produced and constituted at least 40 percent of the farm's total income (U.S. Bureau of Census 1930b, 3–4; U.S. Bureau of Census 1900, xlii). This scheme of categories places some limitations on the degree of precision that can be achieved, since many of these farms still represent varying degrees of mixed farming, and commodities are not categorized separately but are placed into commodity groupings.[2] Fortunately, the similarities in the nature of the production processes that characterize specific commodities within larger commodity groupings do provide a reasonable basis upon which to examine the Mann-Dickinson thesis.

This commodity-specific analysis has certain advantages over earlier studies of stratification in American agriculture. For many decades it was typical for researchers studying rural capitalist development to focus their attention primarily on the relationship between size of farm and expenditures on wage labor. By doing so, they were able to show that large farms had the largest expenditures on wage labor and how, over time, these large capitalist farms increased their proportion of total farm sales at the expense of small and medium-sized farms. Conversely, they showed how smaller farms appeared to be on the road to proletarianization by documenting the increase in farm tenancy, indebtedness, and/or farmers engaged in off-farm employment.[3]

While these studies often did an excellent job of shattering the myth of the "Golden Age" of family farming by documenting how capitalism was increasing its control over the American countryside, their methodology still left something to be desired. Indeed, by focusing too narrowly on the relationship between size of farm and employment of wage labor, they frequently lumped all farms together, regardless of the type of commodity being produced, and simply compared them in terms of their degrees of capitalist development.[4] Not only did this methodology implicitly assume that all agricultural commodities are equally amenable to production along capitalist lines, but also it gave little consideration to variations in the nature of the production processes of different commodities.

This neglect of a commodity-specific analysis is particularly sur-

Table 3-1. Percentage of Farms and Average per Acre and per Farm Expenditures on Labor, by Type of Farm in Terms of Principal Source of Income, 1900

| | | Expenditures on Labor | |
|---|---|---|---|
| Farms by Principal Source of Income | Percentage of Total Number of Farms | Average per Acre in 1900 Dollars | Average per Farm in 1900 Dollars |
| All Farms | 100.0 | .43 | 64 |
| Hay and Grain | 23.0 | .47 | 76 |
| Livestock | 27.3 | .29 | 63 |
| Cotton | 18.7 | .30 | 25 |
| Vegetables | 2.7 | 1.62 | 106 |
| Fruits | 1.4 | 2.46 | 184 |

Source: U.S. Bureau of Census 1900, cxxviii.

prising because as early as 1900 compilers of the agricultural census pointed out that alongside size of farm the most important factor associated with the employment of wage labor was the *type of agricultural commodity being produced* (U.S. Bureau of Census 1900, cxxviii). Yet it was not until the rise of the new and more critical rural sociology of the last two decades that writers began to recognize more fully the virtues of commodity-specific analyses for understanding rural stratification (Friedland, Barton, and Thomas 1981; Friedland 1984a; Buttel 1980; Friedmann 1980b; Gilbert and Akor 1988). I shall demonstrate some of the benefits of such analyses in the following examination of the capitalist development of American agriculture.

Table 3-1 provides data on a number of different commodity groups in terms of expenditures on wage labor per farm and per acre in 1900 dollars. As this table indicates, in 1900, livestock and cash-grain farms could be classified as average in terms of their degree of capitalist development, since their expenditures for hired labor per farm were nearest to the average for all farms in the United States. Vegetables and fruits had the highest degree of capitalist development of all the commodity groups represented here. Per farm expenditures on labor for vegetable and fruit production were significantly higher than for the other groupings, while per acre expenditures were approximately four and six times the national average, respectively. In contrast, cotton farms exhibited the least capitalist development: their expendi-

Table 3-2. Average per Acre Expenditures on Wage Labor, by Type of Farm in Terms of Principal Source of Income, 1900 and 1930

| | Average per Acre Expenditures on Wage Labor in 1930 Dollars | |
|---|---|---|
| Farms by Principal Source of Income | 1900 | 1930 |
| All Farms | .98 | .97 |
| Cash Grains | 1.07 | .70 |
| Cotton | .69 | .84 |
| Vegetables | 3.71 | 10.55 |
| Fruits | 5.63 | 11.21 |

Source: U.S. Bureau of Census 1900, cxxviii; U.S. Bureau of Census 1930a, 12 and 16.

tures for wage labor per farm were considerably below the national average and the ratings of the other commodity groupings.

Unfortunately, existing data only allow us to make comparisons over time for some of the commodity groupings discussed here.[5] Tables 3-2 and 3-3 provide comparisons in terms of expenditures on wage labor per acre and per farm for four major commodity groupings in 1900 and in 1930. Here figures are presented in comparable 1930 dollars. According to these tables, fruit and vegetable production involved the largest expenditures on wage labor per acre and per farm in both 1900 and 1930, ranking high above the average for all farms. These commodity groupings also show the largest increases in expenditures on labor over these three decades. In contrast, in cotton production, expenditures on wage labor per acre and per farm remained far below the average for all farms in 1930, even though these expenditures had increased slightly over the preceding thirty years. While in 1930 cotton production showed a higher expenditure on labor per acre than commercial grain production, the average expenditure per farm was much lower.[6]

These data confirm my general prediction that agricultural commodities would vary in their degree of capitalist development. I will now move on to examine specific natural features of these different commodity groupings so as to determine their effect on the employment of wage labor.

Table 3-3. Average per Farm Expenditures on Wage Labor, by Type of Farm in Terms of Principal Source of Income, 1900 and 1930

| Farms by Principal Source of Income | Average per Farm Expenditures on Wage Labor in 1930 Dollars | |
|---|---|---|
| | 1900 | 1930 |
| All Farms | 147 | 159 |
| Cash Grains | 174 | 245 |
| Cotton | 57 | 61 |
| Vegetables | 243 | 635 |
| Fruits | 421 | 796 |

Source: U.S. Bureau of Census 1900, cxxviii; U.S. Bureau of Census 1930c, 891.

## *The Peculiar Nature of Land as a Factor of Production*

In 1900 and 1930, all of the commodity groups examined in this chapter were land-based types of production. To examine the role played by the peculiar nature of land as a factor of production, extensive and intensive types of production will be compared in terms of their use of wage labor. Table 3-4 compares different commodity groupings in terms of average acreage per farm in 1900 in order to get an indication of the extensive versus intensive nature of these various types of agricultural production. Here, the most extensive types of farms include livestock and cash-grain farms. The most intensive forms of production are represented by the fruits, vegetables, and cotton commodity groupings. A comparison of the data in tables 3-1 and 3-4 suggests that, with the notable exception of cotton production, extensive types of production may be less amenable to capitalist development than intensive types of production.

Data from the 1930 census, which classified farms employing wage labor in terms of their economic size as well as by type of agricultural commodity, corroborate this general finding even for the seemingly anomalous case of cotton. Here, the dividing line, where the number of farms employing wage labor exceeded those that did not, varied according to the extensive or intensive nature of production. In specialized fruit farming, many farms with less than $1,000 gross income were employing wage labor. On vegetable and cotton farms, the dividing line was roughly estimated at a gross income above $1,000. On the more extensive livestock and grain farms, the dividing line came

Table 3-4. Average Acreage per Farm, by Type of Farm in Terms of Principal Source of Income, 1900

| Farms by Principal Source of Income | Average Acreage per Farm in 1900 |
|---|---|
| All Types | 147 |
| Fruit | 75 |
| Vegetables | 65 |
| Cotton[a] | 90 |
| Livestock | 227 |
| Hay and Grain | 159 |

Source: U.S. Bureau of Census 1900, lvi.

[a] Here sharecropping units are each counted separately even though some landowners had their sharecroppers work all of their land as one unit, as in the through and through method (Paige 1975, 64). Consequently the data above on average acreage per farm may understate the extensive nature of cotton production (Rochester 1940, 90). Nevertheless, other data on man-hours per acre indicate that cotton is a far more intensive type of production than most livestock or cash grains (Hopkins 1973, 118, 123, 126, and 131).

in the next higher income group, over $1,500 (Rochester 1940, 87–89). These data suggest that the more extensive forms of cultivation generally require larger scales of operation in order to develop successfully along capitalist lines—an outcome that would be expected if land served as an obstacle to capitalist development.

Another problem we identified as stemming from agriculture's reliance on land as a major factor of production was a high organic composition of capital or a high ratio of the value of capital inputs to the value of labor inputs. We posited that concern for the expenses entailed in a high organic composition of capital would be greater in agriculture than in industry because forms of capital that did not significantly enhance labor productivity—like land and livestock—would make up a large percentage of capital costs even at the initial stages of the production process. Of course, this problem was expected to be most serious in extensive types of agrarian production.[7]

During the period from 1900 to 1930, beef production was especially likely to have a high organic composition of capital because cattle ranches were generally extensive forms of production where grazing land was an important factor of production. Moreover, since cattle not only required relatively small labor inputs but also were themselves components of farm capital as well as being the finished commodity, such ranches had a relatively high organic composition of capital

Table 3-5. Index of Capital Composition by Type of Farm for 1,116 Large Capitalist Farms, 1930

| Type of Farm | Acreage | Persons Employed per 1,000 Acres | Capital, Including Land | |
|---|---|---|---|---|
| | | | Per Worker | Per 1,000 Acres |
| Truck | 1,710 | 51.6 | $ 2,758 | $ 142,250 |
| Fruit | 2,240 | 36.1 | 3,631 | 131,150 |
| Crop-specialty | 5,728 | 17.1 | 4,017 | 68,660 |
| Cotton | 4,170 | 15.6 | 4,676 | 72,994 |
| General | 9,645 | 6.2 | 6,713 | 41,341 |
| Poultry | 1,020 | 20.4 | 11,387 | 232,201 |
| Dairy | 2,127 | 9.7 | 12,026 | 116,470 |
| Animal-specialty | 4,748 | 5.4 | 16,390 | 88,372 |
| Cash-grain | 6,646 | 2.5 | 20,151 | 49,727 |
| Stock Ranches | 57,851 | 0.4 | 24,653 | 9,631 |

Source: Rochester 1940, 282. Reprinted with permission of International Publishers Co., Inc., New York, © 1940, 1968.

(Warren 1917, 119). Consequently, during this time period one might expect cattle ranches to have the highest organic composition of capital, followed by other extensive types of production.

Measuring the organic composition of capital entails a number of difficulties.[8] For example, this concept, as used by Marx, is stated in terms of his labor theory of value, while the census presents data in terms of actual prices. Without maintaining that the actual price is synonymous with value, it has been convincingly argued that trends in relative price magnitudes can describe trends similar in logic to those of relative value magnitudes (J. Wayne 1981, 81–83). Accordingly, table 3-5 uses an approximate index of capital composition to compare extensive and intensive capitalist farms in 1930. As the data demonstrate, stock ranches and farms devoted to cash grains, animal specialty, dairy, and poultry all had a much higher index of capital composition than did the more intensive types of farming. Along with other factors to be discussed below, the index of capital composition may help to explain why extensive types of production were less capitalistically developed during the early 1900s.

In the modern era the problem of a high organic composition of

Table 3-6. Average per Acre Value of Farm Implements and Machinery, by Type of Farm in Terms of Principal Source of Income, 1900 and 1930

| Farms by Principal Source of Income | Average per Acre Value of Farm Implements and Machinery in 1930 Dollars | |
|---|---|---|
| | 1900 | 1930 |
| All Farms | 2.00 | 3.35 |
| Cash Grains | 2.38 | 3.91 |
| Cotton | 1.21 | 2.35 |
| Vegetables | 4.85 | 11.11 |
| Fruits | 5.36 | 11.68 |

Source: U.S. Bureau of Census 1900, lix; U.S. Bureau of Census 1930a, 12 and 904.

capital largely has been reduced in certain types of livestock production by removing the production requirement for grazing land through fast-feeding lots and livestock confinement production.[9] The separation of livestock from the land was not as feasible in the historical periods examined in this study because of the fear of disease. It took until the mid-twentieth century for advances in antibiotics, vaccines, and other methods of disease control to ensure that the total confinement of livestock was safe enough for profitable investments (Goodman, Sorj, and Wilkinson 1987, 48–54).[10]

While separating grazing animals from the land fostered the capitalist development of certain types of livestock production, eliminating the need for land is much more difficult in the other commodity groupings examined here. Because the relationship of livestock to land is mediated by crop consumption, social intervention can take place at this point of mediation. However, crops live *in* the land, rather than *off* the land, which presents significantly greater problems. Currently, controlled plant environments and the use of hydroponics are largely restricted to horticultural crops that have higher planting densities, smaller spatial requirements, and more rapid turnovers than field crops (Goodman, Sorj, and Wilkinson 1987, 120–22).[11]

Along with the necessity of living in the land, the spatial features of field crop production can present other problems to capitalists, since, as discussed in chapter 2, farm machinery often must maneuver around the crop, rather than the crop being maneuvered around the machine. With this in mind I present the data in tables 3-6 and 3-7 to

Table 3-7. Average per Farm Value of Farm Implements and Machinery, by Type of Farm in Terms of Principal Source of Income, 1900 and 1930

| Farms by Principal Source of Income | Average per Farm Value of Farm Implements and Machinery in 1930 Dollars | |
|---|---|---|
| | 1900 | 1930 |
| All Farms | 305 | 550 |
| Cash Grains | 380 | 1,374 |
| Cotton | 103 | 170 |
| Vegetables | 316 | 669 |
| Fruits | 401 | 829 |

Source: U.S. Bureau of Census 1900, lix; U.S. Bureau of Census 1930c, 891 and 904.

examine the relationship between expenditures on farm machinery and type of crop. Here cash-grain, cotton, vegetable, and fruit farms in 1900 and in 1930 are compared in terms of the value of their farm implements and machinery. As one can see, the two most intensive types of production—fruits and vegetables—have the largest increase in the value per acre of these components of farm capital. Only in the cases of fruit and vegetable production did that value increase by a factor greater than two. Moreover, for both of these commodity groupings the value per farm was above the national average. In contrast, cotton production had the smallest value of farm machinery per acre and per farm in both census years. Since cotton's low ratings on farm machinery match its low ratings on capitalist development, in all of the cases cited above there appears to be a direct relationship between capitalist development (the employment of wage labor) and investments in farm implements and machinery. These are important findings because they call into question the claim that labor-saving technology has inhibited the use of wage labor in American agriculture (Nikolitch, 1969).

The data on cash-grain farms, however, present quite a different picture. This category showed relatively low values of machinery per acre in both censuses, which is not surprising, given the fact that per acre ratings are likely to be lower on more extensive forms of cultivation. Much more significant are the per farm ratings, in which cash grains outstripped all other commodity groupings (including the more capitalistically developed commodity groupings) in terms of an increase in the value of farm machinery per farm over the period between 1900 and 1930.

This tremendous increase might be attributed to the major breakthrough in mechanization that followed the development and diffusion of farm machinery using internal combustion engines—an outcome analyzed by Goodman, Sorj, and Wilkinson (1987). As they point out, unlike the steam engine, such internal combustion engines could more easily maneuver around fields and could thereby reduce some of the natural constraints posed by the spatial features of land. The sales of maneuverable tractors increased rapidly following the introduction of Henry Ford's "Fordson" in 1917 and were further fostered by the development of International Harvester's "Farmall" in 1925—a tractor more suitable to all types of field work, as its name implies (Goodman, Sorj, and Wilkinson 1987, 21–23).

Given the direct relationship between capitalist development and expenditures on farm machinery associated with all of the other commodities examined above, one would expect such advances in the mechanization of grain production to have fostered the capitalist development of this extensive type of agriculture. However, while the mechanization of grain farming reduced one barrier to capitalist development, it seems to have exacerbated another natural impediment. That is, by reducing labor time, mechanization increased the "discontinuities" between "labour time and biologically determined production time" (Goodman, Sorj, and Wilkinson 1987, 25). Whether such discontinuities can help explain why cash-grain farms were not very developed along capitalist lines in 1900 and in 1930 will be addressed below.

### *Production Time and Labor Time in Different Types of Farming*

Two major propositions of the Mann-Dickinson thesis were that the length of production time and the nonidentity of production time and labor time could present serious natural obstacles to the use of wage labor. Below, I shall use as an index of the natural constraints on production time estimates of the approximate weeks to economic maturity required by various crops as compiled by personnel at State Agricultural Experiment Stations in 1901.[12] These estimates were based on the opinions of a large number of state agricultural researchers throughout the country (U.S. Department of Agriculture 1901, 692). Because the amount of moisture, daylight, and temperature all interact in the process of the growth and development of crops from germination to maturity, there will be regional differences in the maturation

Table 3-8. Weeks to Economic Maturity, by Type of Crop and by Region, 1901

| | Type of Crop | Weeks to Economic Maturity by Region | | | |
|---|---|---|---|---|---|
| | | New England States | Middle Atlantic States | Central and Western States | Southern States |
| | *Cash Grains*: | | | | |
| | Wheat[a] | 20 | 41–43 | 40–42 | 43 |
| | Corn | 14–17 | 16–18 | 16–20 | 18–20 |
| (Least Capitalist Developed) | Oats | 11–15 | 16–17 | 12–14 | 17 |
| | Barley | 10–15 | 13–16 | 11–13 | 17 |
| | Rye | 40 | 40–43 | 35–40 | 43 |
| | *Cotton* | —[b] | — | — | 20 |
| | *Vegetables*: | | | | |
| | Tomatoes | — | — | — | 14–20 |
| (Most Capitalist Developed) | Cabbage | — | 8–15 | — | — |
| | Onions | — | — | — | 16–24 |
| | Beans | — | 13–14 | 12 | 7–8 |
| | Peas | — | — | — | 6–8 |

Source: U.S. Department of Agriculture 1901, 692–94.

[a] Spring wheat requires approximately 20 weeks to economic maturity. All other figures represent winter wheat.

[b] — indicates no data available or crop not produced in that region.

time for any specific crop. Where possible, these regional differences will be taken into account.

Table 3-8 shows variations in the weeks to economic maturity of a number of different crops. These crops can be categorized into three of the commodity groupings discussed above. Moreover, since these commodity groupings represent different degrees of capitalist development from the least developed—cotton and cash grains—to the most developed—vegetables—we can make valid comparisons as to whether the length of maturation time is associated with variations in the use of wage labor.

According to table 3-8, natural constraints on production time, as measured by weeks to economic maturity, bear a relationship to the use of wage labor. Vegetables, which were the more capitalistically developed rural commodities, have on average a somewhat shorter maturation time than either cotton or cash grains. Winter wheat and rye have particularly long periods of maturation. Nevertheless, this relationship on the whole is weak, since the maturation time of many vegetables is close to that of cotton, corn, oats, and barley.[13]

What may be a more important obstacle to the use of wage labor is the *coincidence of a lengthy production time with the absence of a continuous use of labor throughout the productive cycle.* According to the Mann-Dickinson thesis, it is the *gap* between production time and labor time that led to the inefficient use of machinery and to labor recruitment and management problems. Consequently, it could be predicted that capitalist relations of production would be most developed in those spheres where labor time is more evenly distributed throughout the production cycle.

In order to examine this argument empirically, different types of farming are compared in terms of their distribution of labor requirements over the production cycle. Figure 3-1 provides a number of graphs representing the labor requirements for different crops in 1913.[14] From these graphs it is evident that all of the agricultural commodities represented have an uneven distribution of labor requirements. However, the largest gaps between production time and labor time occur in the commercial grain category (wheat), the least capitalistically developed of the commodity groupings represented. Poultry production, represented in graph F, had the most even distribution of labor requirements, providing work throughout the productive cycle.[15] However the amount of labor time required on a daily basis (represented by the vertical axis) was very low. In the case of this particular farm, which is taken as an average, the flock would require only two hours of labor per day, except during the incubation period, when it would require six hours (Warren 1917, 121–22). Next to poultry, the commodities that had the most even distribution of labor requirements and also provided a full day's work during much of the labor period were the most capitalistically developed commodities: the vegetables.

Since I could not obtain a graph of the labor requirements for cotton production in 1913, figure 3-2 presents graphs of the monthly distribution of labor requirements for cotton and corn production in a later time period, 1939. Unlike the graphs in figure 3-1, these new graphs do not show how much labor was required per day (there are no vertical axes on these graphs). Rather they only show that cotton production had a more even seasonal distribution of labor requirements than corn production. So long as the labor required on a daily basis is unknown, a lower variance in seasonal labor requirements does not in

Figure 3-1. Distribution of Labor Requirements in the Production of Different Agricultural Commodities, 1913

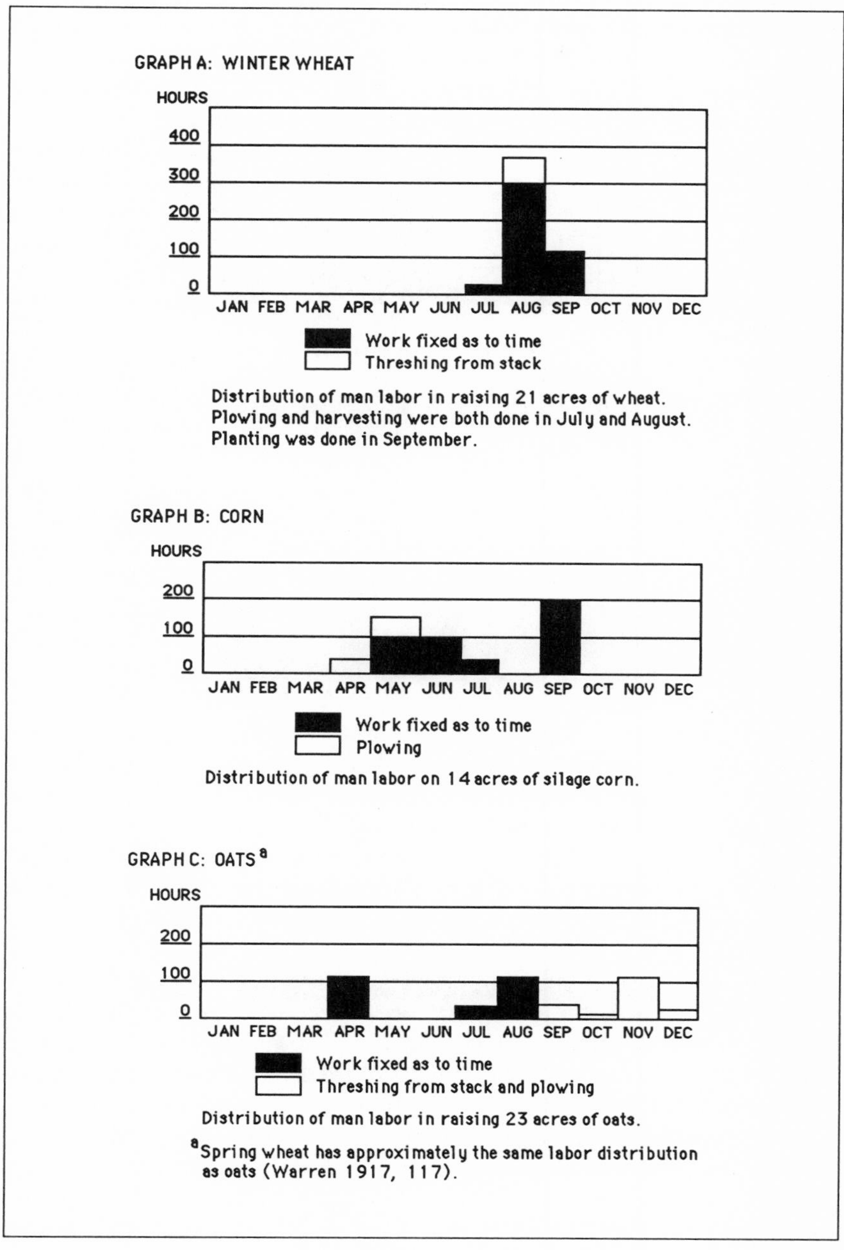

Figure 3-1. Continued

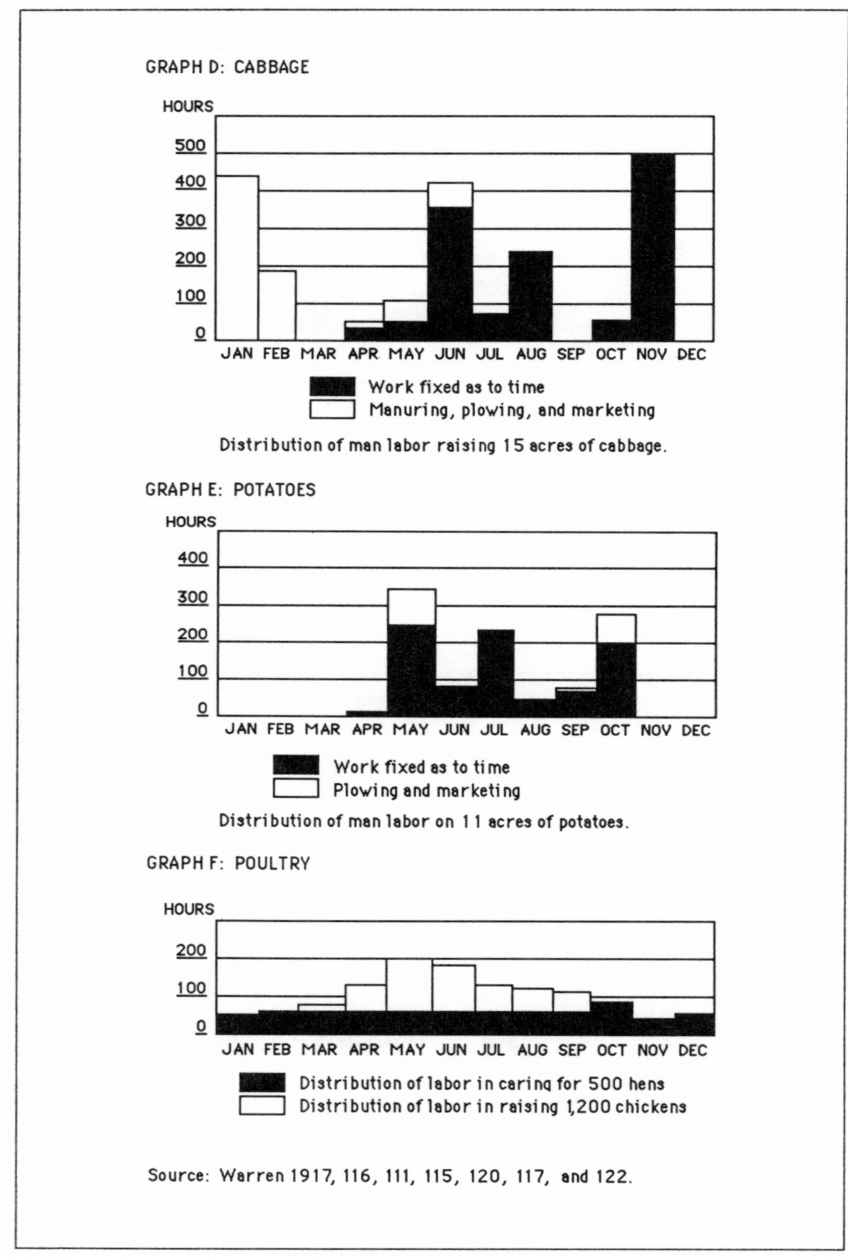


Source: Warren 1917, 116, 111, 115, 120, 117, and 122.

Figure 3-2. Distribution of Labor Requirements in the Production of Corn and Cotton in the Mississippi Delta Region, 1939

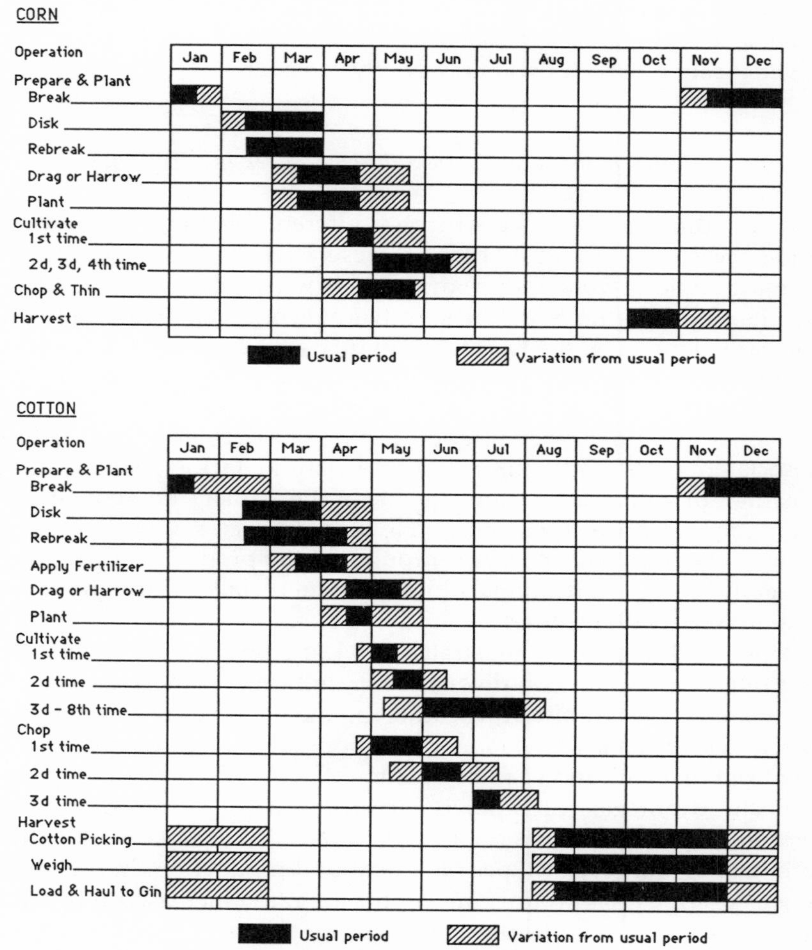

CORN

Operation

Jan Feb Mar Apr May Jun Jul Aug Sep Oct Nov Dec

Prepare & Plant
Break
Disk
Rebreak
Drag or Harrow
Plant
Cultivate
1st time
2d, 3d, 4th time
Chop & Thin
Harvest

Usual period
Variation from usual period

COTTON

Operation

Jan Feb Mar Apr May Jun Jul Aug Sep Oct Nov Dec

Prepare & Plant
Break
Disk
Rebreak
Apply Fertilizer
Drag or Harrow
Plant
Cultivate
1st time
2d time
3d - 8th time
Chop
1st time
2d time
3d time
Harvest
Cotton Picking
Weigh
Load & Haul to Gin

Usual period
Variation from usual period

Source: Langsford and Thibodeaux 1939, 61 and 59.

itself represent a closer identity of production time and labor time.[16] However, it is still interesting to note that by 1939—the time period represented by these graphs—capitalist social relations were more highly developed in cotton production than in corn production, a transformation that is discussed at some length in Chapter 5.

In summary, the data presented above suggest that capitalist development may be obstructed when labor is distributed unevenly on a daily basis and throughout the production cycle. These findings also imply that any mechanisms that increased the continuous use of labor would serve to enhance the amenability of that type of production to the use of wage labor. One such mechanism is mixed farming or crop diversification, which I will now briefly consider.

### *Reducing Natural Barriers through Diversified Farming*

By providing a crop mix whereby different planting, cultivation, and harvesting times could be more closely synchronized, diversified farming could serve to reduce the periods when labor and machinery lie idle. Indeed, one of the major advocates of diversified farming in the early decades of the twentieth century—G. F. Warren—presented arguments in favor of diversified farming that closely parallel my discussion of natural obstacles to the use of wage labor. For example, Warren argues that diversification can reduce the risk of crop failure associated either with uncontrollable natural factors, such as the weather, or with social factors outside of the farmer's immediate control, such as price fluctuations. He also discusses how diversification can better distribute labor throughout the productive cycle, thus "keeping men, draft animals and machinery busy throughout the year" (Warren 1917, 108–9).

Figure 3-3 graphically illustrates this last point by depicting the labor requirements on two diversified grain farms. If these graphs are compared to the graphs of wheat, corn, and oats production in figure 3-1, a clearer image of the more continuous labor requirements resulting from diversification can be obtained.[17]

Such advantages for capitalist enterprise arising from diversified farming would also suggest further differences between industrial production and certain types of agricultural production. In the initial stages of industrial production, profits are often increased through a specialization of production that allows for a greater specialization of skill and a more efficient division of labor. Here the labor process can be broken down into its simplest component parts and assigned to different laborers working cooperatively. This not only increases the efficiency with which each particular task is performed, but it also reduces the costs of labor power, since labor can be divided by payments as well as by tasks. Cheaper, unskilled labor, therefore, can be assigned to tasks requiring little skill, while higher paid, skilled labor can be reserved for specialized, skilled tasks (Braverman 1974, 75–83).

However, as Cohen points out, the situation in agriculture is differ-

Figure 3-3. Distribution of Labor Requirements on Two Diversified Grain Farms, 1913

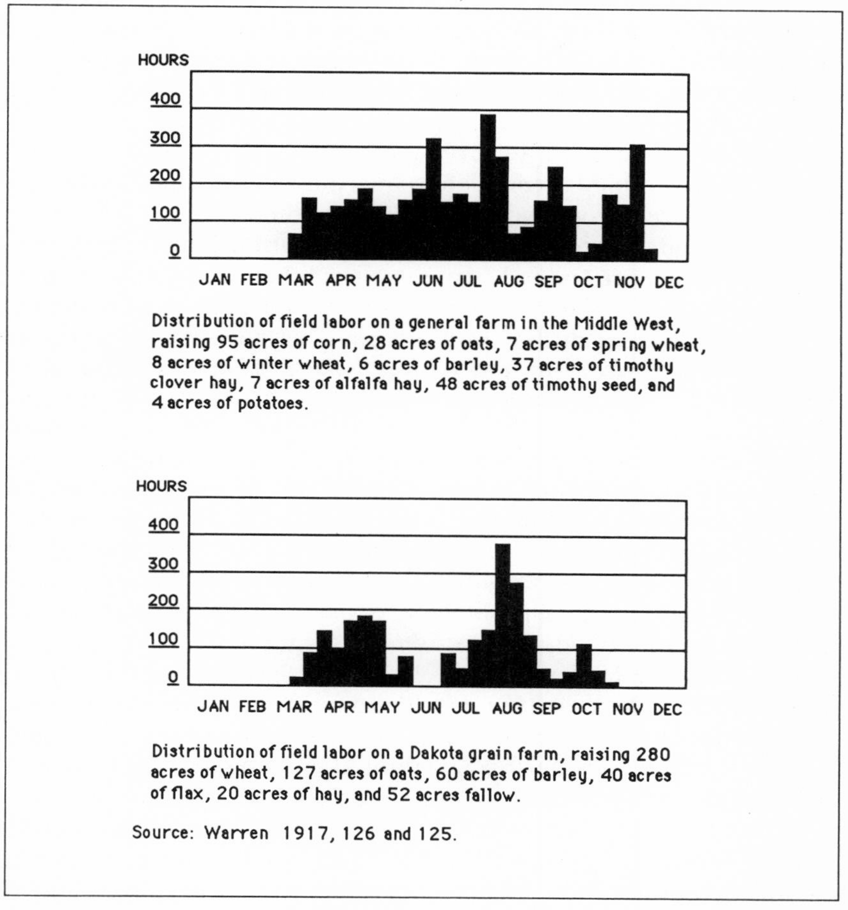


Distribution of field labor on a general farm in the Middle West, raising 95 acres of corn, 28 acres of oats, 7 acres of spring wheat, 8 acres of winter wheat, 6 acres of barley, 37 acres of timothy clover hay, 7 acres of alfalfa hay, 48 acres of timothy seed, and 4 acres of potatoes.

Distribution of field labor on a Dakota grain farm, raising 280 acres of wheat, 127 acres of oats, 60 acres of barley, 40 acres of flax, 20 acres of hay, and 52 acres fallow.

Source: Warren 1917, 126 and 125.

ent: "The scope for economies through acquiring skill is, once again, generally smaller in agriculture than in industry. There are few operations in agriculture which must be repeated for all the day, so that a man has no opportunity of concentrating on one small motion. A farm worker can only plough, harrow, and harvest the crops at the right season of the year and must be able to perform all of these operations. Cows must be milked twice a day and pigs fed; but the stockman cannot spend all of this time on these tasks" (Cohen 1940, 53).

Moreover, in industry, a diversification of production generally occurs only after substantial accumulation through a prior specialization of production. Hence, the pattern of industrial capitalist development often proceeds in the following manner: concentration or accumulation of capital through specialization; centralization or the horizontal integration of like capitals; vertical integration that incorporates various stages of the production process directed to the finished production of a particular commodity; and finally, full diversification through the establishment of conglomerates (Baran and Sweezy 1966, 14–51). By contrast, in agriculture, diversification may be necessary in the early stages of capital accumulation in order to overcome the discontinuities between production time and labor time.

Goodman and Redclift point out yet another qualitative difference between agriculture and industry in terms of the specialization of production. That is, in the industrial sphere, specialization does not normally bring about a decline in the productive potential of factors of production. However, in agriculture, "too great a specialization in terms of the crops produced, and the methods employed to produce them, commonly leads to a lack of nutrients in the soil, erosion, and the destruction of natural habitats on which the human population depends" (Goodman and Redclift 1982, 12–13). For this reason, crop rotation has been a guiding principle of agricultural production for centuries. There are few comparable situations in the industrial sphere of production that so seriously militate against specialization.

Studies comparing the profitability of diversified versus specialized types of farm production have resulted in contradictory findings (Warren 1917, 133–42; Holley and Arnold 1938, 110; Langsford and Thibodeaux 1939, 73; DeCanio 1974, 13). However, it appears that specialization is more profitable under situations where: a particular commodity provides or approximates full year-round employment for labor and equipment; highly specialized farm machinery is required for each crop in a given crop mix; there is an abundant source of labor for peak harvest seasons; and the labor requirements for a particular crop with high market value seriously conflict with other crop mixes (Cohen 1940, 53–54; DeCanio 1974, 13; Holley and Arnold 1938, 110; Langsford and Thibodeaux 1939, 73; Paige 1975, 14–15; Warren 1917, 114 and 131–32). Hence, the advantages of specialization in agricultural production tend to vary not only by type of farming, but also by the specific natural and social conditions under which production is carried out.

It is not possible to establish whether the number of mixed and specialized farms in American agriculture increased or decreased over the period from 1900 to 1930 because of the absence of comparable data.[18] However, the fact that the dividing line according to which the census classified a farm as specialized was relatively low (i.e., that the agricultural commodity accounted for at least 40 percent of total farm income) suggests that many of these farms were not highly specialized, monocrop enterprises.[19] Possibly one of the ways in which farmers balance the particular advantages and disadvantages of specialization in agricultural production is to maintain some mixed farming as a supplement to their major crop.

## *Price Fluctuations in Agricultural Production*

In the preceding chapter I discussed how certain branches of agricultural production are marked by volatile price fluctuations that can present a risk for capitalist investment. To provide empirical support for this argument, I shall examine data on the frequency and amplitude of wholesale price changes of various agricultural and industrial commodities compiled by the United States Bureau of Labor Statistics. Because of restrictions on confidentiality, specific commodities are not published separately, but rather are included in larger commodity groupings, such as Farm Products or Metal and Metal Products (U.S. Bureau of Labor Statistics 1959, 3). Figure 3-4 presents in graphic form the frequency of price changes in a number of these different commodity groupings.[20]

In chart A of figure 3-4, the volatile nature of price movements in the farm products commodity grouping is apparent. Processed foods, represented by chart B, also show a high concentration at the upper end of the frequency scale. However, a sizable number of items in this grouping have relatively few price changes. As the report by the U.S. Bureau of Labor Statistics points out, the items with relatively low frequencies of price change are mostly cereal products, such as bread, cookies, and spaghetti; condensed and dried milk; and some canned foods—all of which represent more durable commodity forms resulting from the processing and/or preserving techniques used for raw agricultural products (U.S. Bureau of Labor Statistics 1959, 5).[21]

Chart C in figure 3-4, which presents price changes in textile and apparel products, provides an additional contrast between the price movements of raw agricultural products and the price movements of manufactured goods that rely on these raw materials for their base. The vast majority of textile and apparel products showed relatively infrequent price changes. However, the Bureau of Labor Statistics reported that over the same time period cotton, silk, and most of the foreign and domestic wools (all of which were included under the farm products commodity grouping) ranked in the high frequency ranges (U.S. Bureau of Labor Statistics 1959, 5).

Figure 3-4. Distribution of Commodities by Frequency of Wholesale Price Changes, January 1954–December 1956, by Commodity Groups

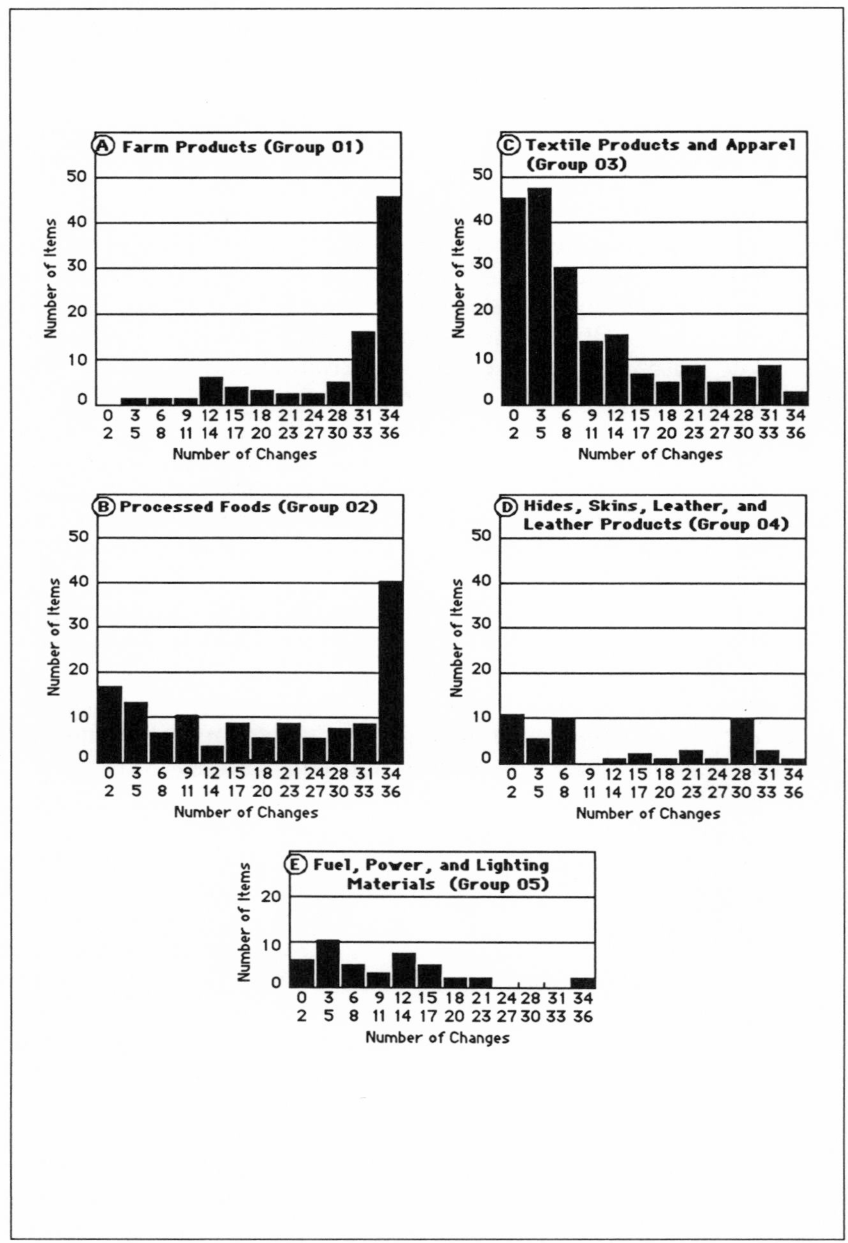

Figure 3-4. Continued

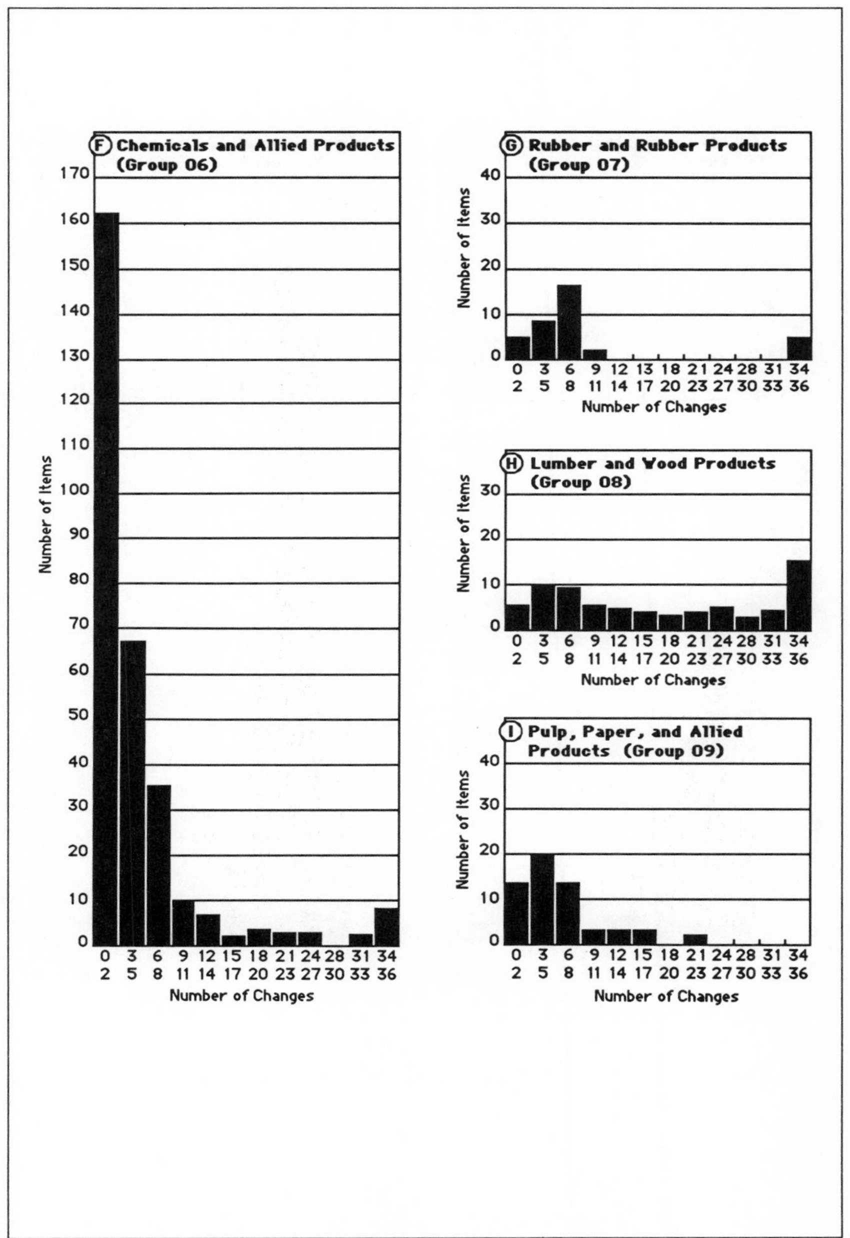

Figure 3-4. Continued

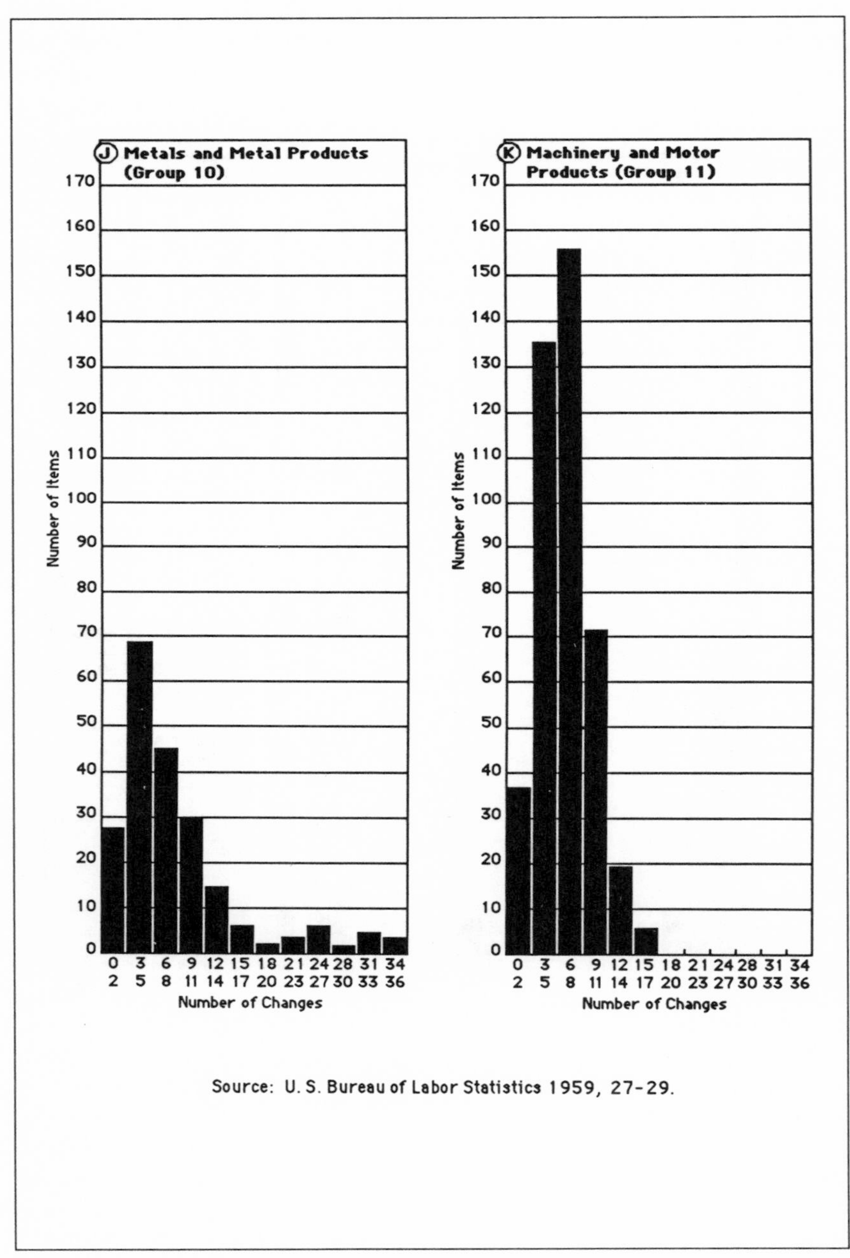


Source: U. S. Bureau of Labor Statistics 1959, 27-29.

A similar contrast between the price movements of manufactured goods and those of their raw material base can also be seen in charts H and I, where the frequency of price changes for pulp, paper, and allied products is shown to be much lower than is the case for lumber and wood products. These examples further illustrate a general tendency found by the bureau that frequency of price changes was inversely related to the degree of fabrication involved in the production of the commodities that were examined (U.S. Bureau of Labor Statistics 1959, 7).

Of all of the commodity groupings represented in these charts, the groupings that represented the very basis of industrial production, in terms of their role in the production of industrial means of production, exhibited a marked concentration at the lower end of the frequency scale. These included the chemicals, metals, and machinery groupings (charts F, J, and K, respectively, in figure 3-4), all of which tend to be highly developed along capitalist lines.

These comparisons help to substantiate the argument that agricultural production is more susceptible to price fluctuations than industrial production. Data from the U.S. Bureau of Labor Statistics also show that the amplitude of price changes was the greatest for farm products during this same time period (1959, 2–4 and 25). Moreover, the association of agricultural commodities with a higher frequency of price change existed even when price movements of farm products were compared with price movements of industrial or manufactured commodities that relied on raw agricultural products as part of their material base. Now, I shall limit my analysis of price fluctuations only to differences between agricultural commodities.

In the preceding chapter, I explained the greater fluctuation of agricultural prices by discussing the role of such factors as the length of production time, the seasonal nature of labor requirements, the costs of storage, and the perishability of certain agricultural commodities. However, I did not discuss which of those factors had the greatest impact on price fluctuations. According to literature on farm prices during the period I am examining, it appears that the most severe fluctuations in agricultural prices tend to be associated with the most perishable crops (Warren 1917, 78 and 88–89; Shepherd 1941, 70–77).

The importance of the durability of agricultural produce to greater price stability can be illustrated by comparing the price movements of a perishable crop, potatoes, with the price movements of more durable crops, such as cotton, corn, and oats. These comparisons can also illuminate the relative impact of durability as compared to the length of production time or seasonal labor requirements on price fluctuations, since potatoes, while more perishable, have a shorter production time and a more even distribution of labor requirements than any of the other crops.

Table 3-9 provides data on annual average farm prices of cotton, corn, oats, and potatoes over the ten-year period from 1902 to 1911. From these price data I have calculated the mean deviation of annual farm prices from a ten-year average price as a measure of the amplitude of price fluctuations. As table 3-9 shows, of the four crops whose price movements are represented, potatoes had the most extreme variations in price, with prices deviating annually by an average of plus or minus 8.1 cents from the ten-year average price. Similar findings resulted when price fluctuations for these same commodities were compared on a monthly, rather than an annual, basis.[22]

Shepherd provides other data that concur with my findings. From a comparison of average seasonal price fluctuations among eleven different farm products during the period from 1921 to 1939,[23] he also found that, on the average, the prices of perishable crops fluctuated more than the prices of durable crops (1941, 70–73). Egg prices showed the greatest average seasonal fluctuation of any of the farm products examined (75). In turn, by more closely examining the relative impact of various aspects of egg production and marketing, such as the relatively high costs of egg storage[24] and the seasonal nature of egg production, he concluded that the most important factor in determining egg price fluctuations was the perishability or deterioration of eggs that takes place during storage (77).

These findings confirm the general consensus in the farm-price literature that more perishable crops tend to have more severe price fluctuations than nonperishable crops. However, since the most capitalistically developed of the commodity groupings examined here—fruits and vegetables—are also some of the most perishable agricultural commodities, this calls into question my thesis regarding the role of both perishability and price fluctuations as obstacles to rural capitalist development.

It is possible that this anomaly can be explained by certain historical developments. For example, when Marx identified perishability as an impediment to agrarian capitalism, a scientific understanding of food preservation was only in its infancy. This was to change quickly in the decades that followed. Advances in the dehydration of milk, as well as the application of mechanical refrigeration to railway cars and wholesale distribution facilities, were just getting under way when Marx died in 1883. By the 1890s American bacteriologists had used the work of Pasteur to greatly enhance their understanding of the role of microorganisms in the deterioration of food, and in the early 1900s canning had become fully automated (Goodman, Sorj, and Wilkinson 1987, 63–

Table 3-9. Average Annual Farm Prices and Mean Deviation from Average Farm Price of Cotton, Corn, Oats, and Potatoes in the United States, 1902–1911[a]

| Year[b] | Cotton (cents per pound) | Corn (cents per bushel) | Oats (cents per bushel) | Potatoes (cents per bushel) |
|---|---|---|---|---|
| 1902 | 8.3 | 40.3 | 30.7 | 47.1 |
| 1903 | 12.2 | 42.5 | 34.1 | 61.4 |
| 1904 | 8.7 | 44.1 | 31.3 | 45.3 |
| 1905 | 11.0 | 41.2 | 29.1 | 61.7 |
| 1906 | 10.1 | 39.9 | 31.7 | 51.1 |
| 1907 | 10.4 | 51.6 | 44.3 | 61.8 |
| 1908 | 8.7 | 60.6 | 47.2 | 70.6 |
| 1909 | 13.9 | 59.6 | 40.5 | 54.9 |
| 1910 | 14.2 | 48.0 | 34.4 | 55.7 |
| 1911 | 8.8 | 61.8 | 45.0 | 79.9 |
| Mean over 10 year period | 10.6 | 48.9 | 36.8 | 58.9 |
| Mean Deviation | 1.8 | 7.5 | 5.9 | 8.1 |

Source: Calculated from data in Warren 1917, 570.

[a]Data for cotton prices in 1901 were not available.

[b]Average farm price on December 1 of each year.

69). These developments in food processing and preservation could go some way to explaining why perishability was not a serious obstacle to rural capitalism in 1900 and in 1930.[25]

In turn, since the farm-price data show that the greater the degree of fabrication of a commodity, the less its price fluctuates, it would logically follow that an increase in the proportion of perishable crops sold to food-processing industries, rather than as fresh produce, could help explain the negligible role the price fluctuations associated with perishable crops had as an impediment to agrarian capitalism.[26] While it would be beyond the scope of this book, an analysis of the impact of the expansion of food-processing industries on perishability, price fluctuations, and other natural obstacles to capitalist development would greatly enhance our understanding of these issues. Moreover, such an analysis also would provide a new angle for examining the relationship between industrial agribusinesses and farm production, as compared to the more typical focus on market relations between these two sectors of the economy.[27]

### *Conclusion*

The empirical analyses in this chapter have illuminated some expected and unexpected trends in the nature of rural capitalist development. The analysis of the relationship between type of farm and capitalist development confirmed the thesis that agricultural commodities vary in their degree of capitalist development and that the type of commodity being produced is an important factor in determining the use of wage labor. By examining an entire series of natural obstacles, it also became apparent that some types of farming were characterized by more than one natural impediment to employing wage labor and that, in some cases, the modification or reduction of one obstacle could serve to exacerbate another. The latter problem was illustrated by advances in mechanization, which could reduce the spatial constraints of land, but also could increase the gaps between production time and labor time. This suggests the need for a more holistic approach, where various natural obstacles are seen as interrelated, rather than a mechanistic approach, where each obstacle is viewed as separate and autonomous in terms of its possible impact on capitalist development.

Cotton was the only commodity grouping I examined that presented serious anomalies to my empirical analyses. Given cotton's intensive nature and its greater synchronization of production time and labor time, I would have expected cotton production to be more capitalistically developed than extensive types of farming. However, my empirical analyses indicated that by 1930 cotton was the least capitalistically developed and the least mechanized of any of the rural commodity groupings discussed in this chapter.

Thus, with the notable exception of cotton production, I found that capitalist class relations tended to be less developed in extensive types of farming. These extensive types of farming also generally required a larger economic size of farm before the employment of wage labor was feasible. Along with the higher organic composition of capital on extensive farms, all of these findings suggest that when land is a major factor of production it presents particular problems to capitalist development.

This study also found that other natural obstacles, such as a lengthy production time and the nonidentity of production time and labor time, tended to be associated with agricultural commodities that were less developed along capitalist lines. Whether a diversification of production that provides a crop mix allowing for a greater synchronization of production time and labor time fostered capitalist development was also examined. Although studies comparing the profitability of specialized versus diversified farming provided no conclusive findings, the conditions under which specialization was more profitable closely reflected various natural features of agricultural production.

In contrast, neither price fluctuations nor the perishability of certain agricultural commodities appears to have significantly impeded capitalist development during the time periods examined in this study. This highlighted the historical specificity of certain obstacles to capitalist development, since the impact of perishability and the volatile price fluctuations associated with it could have been reduced by the advances in food processing and preservation that had taken place by the turn of the twentieth century.

The analysis of farm-price data also indicated that price fluctuations were much more severe in agriculture than in industry. Other differences between agriculture and industry illuminated in this chapter included the distinct ways in which these two spheres often develop in terms of capital accumulation, the specialization of production, and the stage at which they encounter problems resulting from a high organic composition of capital.

All of these findings help to refine the Mann-Dickinson thesis. Nevertheless, like any methodology, using census data to analyze rural capitalist development has its weaknesses, as well as its strengths. While censuses are generally noted as being superior to other sets of data because of their more representative nature, they are only representative of the population of a given nation state. Indeed, by definition they exclude data on events and processes outside of a nation's geographical boundaries. This is a serious omission when studying American agriculture, since many rural commodities are produced for world markets and are affected by developments in the international economy. Moreover, while census data are also noted for being relatively detailed and reliable, they still only provide a snapshot of existing conditions in a given census year. They do not show how these conditions came into being or how they were shaped or modified over time.[28] Hence, they cannot reveal the *process* of capitalist development.

In the next two chapters I will address some of the shortcomings of the census analyses presented above by examining the capitalist development of cotton production in the American South from the end of the Civil War through the Great Depression. This historical study not only provides the opportunity to consider in detail why the specific instance of cotton production should present serious anomalies to the Mann-Dickinson thesis, but also it uses a global analysis to understand how international production and exchange relations affected the capitalist development of this major export crop. In turn, by focusing special attention on the natural features of cotton production and how different social classes adapted to, clashed with, or modified natural impediments to the use of wage labor, the following chapters should present a new framework for understanding the uneven growth of agrarian capitalism in the American South.

# Four

# Hands That Picked Cotton: From Slavery to Sharecropping

Yes, all God's dangers aint a white man.—Ned Cobb, quoted in *All God's Dangers: The Life of Nate Shaw* (1974)

On the eve of the American Civil War, cotton was king of far more than just Southern agriculture. Cotton was the most important agricultural commodity used in American industry and the most valuable American commodity sold on world markets (Hobhouse 1986, 149–50). While it is one of the ironies of uneven development that agrarian slavery fed the textile mills that provided the basis for the Industrial Revolution in England and the most important capitalist industry in the United States, the agrarian slave system was replaced by yet another noncapitalist form of production—the family sharecropping system. The continued production of cotton in a noncapitalist fashion was to have a long-term effect on the uneven regional development of the American South and the class and racial conflicts that these forms of production generated.

However, while the nonwage, family-based, sharecropping system replaced slavery in the older cotton-producing areas of the South, it did not come to dominate all areas of the American South.[1] Indeed, a peculiarity of Southern cotton production was the marked regional differences in the rural class structures that prevailed during the postbellum era. In the younger Southwestern cotton-producing regions, wage labor came to dominate cotton production on a permanent and significant scale. By 1930, Texas, Oklahoma, and the newly irrigated lands in New Mexico, Arizona, and southern California all had a relatively high proportion of capitalist cotton farms, while the noncapitalist sharecropping system dominated the older cotton-producing areas of Georgia, Alabama, Louisiana, Mississippi, and the Carolinas (Fulmer 1950, 74–75; Rochester 1940, 61).

This pattern prevailed despite the fact that the emancipation of almost four million slaves provided a ready-made class of propertyless laborers, the majority of whom were initially concentrated in the cotton belt of the Old South.[2] Such an abundance of poor, propertyless laborers should have made it easy for landowners to replace slavery with wage labor and to continue producing cotton on large estates in a highly centralized fashion. This, however, clearly did not occur. Rather, in the older cotton-producing areas, plantation lands were broken up into tenant family plots and farming was organized on the basis of family labor.

Coupled with the marked regional disparities in the capitalist development of American cotton production, the failure of wage labor to serve as a substitute for slavery in these older areas presents an intriguing historical case by which to examine obstacles to the use of wage labor. To address these issues, I will first provide an overview of some of the major social and economic conditions that characterized Southern agriculture in the aftermath of the Civil War. I will then examine how natural and social factors intertwined to give rise to the family sharecropping system in the older cotton-producing areas of the Southeast. Last, I will highlight various obstacles to the use of wage labor in cotton production through a comparative analysis of two regions of the American South during the period from 1870 to 1930.

### *Labor Instability in the Postbellum Rural South*

Much has been written about the defeat of the Confederacy and the domestic and international economic disruptions that plagued the postbellum South. While agriculture remained the primary occupation of the majority of the population after the Civil War, Southern farmers faced acute economic problems. Landowners—large and small—were without adequate capital, credit, transportation, and marketing facilities. The destruction of farm capital, the virtual collapse of the Southern financial and banking system, and the precipitous decline in agricultural output during the war all precluded the possibility of sufficient capital being generated internally to aid in the reconstruction of the postwar economy (Coulter 1947; Knox 1900; Ransom and Sutch 1972 and 1977; Saloutos 1960; Shannon 1945). Together with the failure of Northern capital to be attracted in sufficient quantities to restore the shattered Southern economy and the more general decline in world cotton demand, all of these factors contributed to the stagnation and slow recovery of the cotton economy (Saloutos 1960, 11; Wright 1978, 94–98 and 631–35).

Because the largest part of most slave owners' capital had been invested in slaves (Coulter 1947), the emancipation represented a significant transformation in the redistribution of wealth.[3] However, a redistribution of landed property was not forthcoming. While the prewar slave had hopes for the division of the large estates after the war, such a measure, which would have expropriated private property, was a threat to any region of the country and was effectively prevented in all but a few cases (Moore 1966, 145–47; J. S. Allen 1970, 66–68; Wright 1978, 161). Consequently, formal freedom through emancipation was not accompanied by substantive freedom through the provision of a means of livelihood, such as land, farm implements, and livestock, to the freed slaves. "Forty acres and a mule" remained merely a campaign slogan never to be realized in practice. The main result of the Reconstruction era was the retention of large landed property and a mere change in titles of ownership (Shannon 1945, 80–81). In fact, not only did the large estates remain intact, but after 1880 the concentration of land ownership increased in all of the Southern states (Saloutos 1960, 1).

With land still concentrated in the hands of the few, it was logical that landowners would want to continue producing agricultural commodities on a large scale. Unlike the decentralized system of family sharecropping, wage labor provided a means of maintaining large-scale operations organized through a more centralized system of control. Consequently, it is quite puzzling as to why family sharecropping, rather than wage labor, came to dominate cotton production in the older regions of the American South.[4]

It appears that this outcome was not the first choice of either freedpeople or landowners (Jaynes 1986, 244). From the ex-slaves' point of view, since the more desirable alternative of land ownership was not forthcoming because of the timidity of federal land reform programs, their options in terms of independence and autonomy in the workplace were restricted (Royce 1985, 287–89). From the vantage point of landowners, the emancipation of the slave labor force left them with acute labor problems. Of foremost priority on the landowners' list of social offenses committed by freedpeople was the latter's refusal to adapt themselves to the landowners' labor market requirements (Jaynes 1986, 102). As one South Carolina planter and agricultural journalist noted in 1871, "no question has so perplexed the southern planter for the past six years as that of labor" (quoted in Jaynes 1986, 191). Hence, even though poor and landless, black labor was still in a position to create serious labor problems for prospective employers, thus also "constricting the possibilities" and the prerogatives of the dominant class (Royce 1985, 288–90).

Historical accounts of these labor problems often document how newly freed laborers engaged in work slowdowns, broke their labor contracts, or refused to enter into contractual arrangements, thus retarding the resumption or continuation of agricultural production (Saloutos 1960, 16; Shannon 1945, 86; Zeichner 1939, 25). Conversely, some landowners embittered by the emancipation frequently treated hired hands in a manner contradictory to their long-term interests by providing food rations of insufficient quantity and quality or reverting to harsh methods of punishment and discipline reminiscent of the slave era. However, despite the protests by some laborers and the excesses of some landowners, there were deeper *structural* problems at the root of the failure of wage labor to adequately substitute for slavery. These problems centered on the inability of landowners to ensure an immobile, stable labor force both on a day-to-day basis and throughout the production cycle (Zeichner 1939, 30; Shannon 1945, 87).

To date, many historians of the postbellum South have discussed how the sharecropping system and its twin—the crop-liens system—helped to control black labor in the face of the emancipation. Under the Southern sharecropping system, the share of the crop appropriated as rent by landowners depended on the amount of land, fertilizer, and farm implements they provided.[5] Moreover, the landowner's control over production was not limited to control over capital assets. Rather, the landowner generally determined what crops were to be planted and exercised close supervision over the actual production process (Shannon 1945, 88; Reid 1975, 428–29). In addition, by tying labor payments to the finished commodity rather than to specified time periods, sharecropping helped to ensure that laborers would remain for the duration of the production cycle. At the end of this cycle, the landowner often took the crop to market and settlement was made on the landowner's reckoning (Rochester 1940, 58). Indeed, a common practice among landowners was to pay croppers the commodity price current on the day of settlement and hold the crop for sale at a later date when the price was higher (Shannon 1945, 220). Thus, in many ways sharecropping entailed stricter landlord control and supervision than did straight tenancy (Wright 1978, 162–63).[6]

The crop-liens system, which grew up alongside sharecropping after the Civil War, was essentially a system of usury whereby farmers in need of credit and supplies during the production cycle obtained advances using their ungrown crops as security. Interest rates under the crop-liens system were exorbitant; charges on loans have been estimated to range from 40 to 110 percent (Shannon 1945, 91). The cumulative effect of this ostensibly short-term indebtedness was to "lock" sharecroppers into existing productive relations by continually reproducing their indebtedness and creating a perpetual state of economic bondage (Ransom and Sutch 1972, 654–55).[7] Consequently, like sharecropping, the crop-liens system served as a barrier to laborers' autonomy and mobility.

Studies on the residential movements of sharecroppers suggest that neither of these institutional barriers to labor mobility was a complete success.[8] Consequently, it is not surprising that additional mechanisms were instituted to further increase control of labor. Among the most blatant abrogations of the ostensibly "free" market in labor was a series of laws—the notorious Black Codes—that incorporated strict regulations over labor. While these laws, which came into effect immediately after the defeat of the Confederacy, were officially repealed in 1867, a number of identical laws remained, under different names, on the books of many Southern states into the 1930s (Zeichner 1940; DeCanio 1974, 32–36). For example, in a number of states it was a crime for persons of color to remain unemployed for any period of time. South Carolina went so far as to require an expensive license for persons of color to engage in any work other than agricultural labor. In short, the passage of such laws gave landowners about as much control over their labor force as was possible in the absence of total ownership (Jaynes 1986, 306 and 311–12).[9]

Along with the nonwage feature of the sharecropping system, these formal and informal controls over labor provide an important basis for distinguishing the noncapitalist mode of labor exploitation in the older cotton-producing areas of the South from developed capitalist forms of production (Wiener 1978, 36 and 69–73).[10] While these noncapitalist institutions eventually came to engulf black and white farmers alike, the focus in this chapter is on the problems faced by freedpeople, since most of these mechanisms of labor control were instituted primarily to deal with the emancipated labor force.[11]

Despite the fact that the terms—share*cropping* and *crop*-liens—refer specifically to farming, historians of the South generally have not considered why the various forms of labor control established in the postbellum South were primarily directed toward *agricultural*, rather than nonfarm, production. Indeed, like the theorists discussed in Chapter 1, historians have ignored the impact the peculiar natural features of agricultural production had on limiting the capitalist development of the South. No doubt, many historians have described the natural problems associated with cotton farming, such as the devastating boll weevil infestation or cotton's lengthy production time. However, only a few scholars have actually related these natural features of agriculture to both labor instability and the failure of wage labor to substitute for slavery.[12] Yet, unlike nonfarm types of production, agricultural production requires an even greater assurance of a stable labor force, because the disruption of any part of the production cycle could mean that the entire year's work was in vain. This was especially true of cotton production, where harvesting had a "certain urgency" because cotton on the boll could be ruined by rainfall (Wright 1986, 91). Below I discuss how class, racial, and gender inequalities played an important role in determining the outcome of planters' attempts to ensure a more stable labor force. I then examine how natural features of agricultural production intertwined with these social factors to foster the establishment of the family sharecropping system.

### *Social Factors in the Rise of Family Sharecropping*

There is much consensus in the literature on the origins of Southern sharecropping that this system arose as a compromise solution to the conflicting interests of landowners and laborers.[13] However, explanations differ as to which class was able to best assert its interests. On the one side are those who focus on the landowners' lack of capital and credit as the primary problem, whereby the shift from wage labor to share payments is viewed as based mainly on the initiative of landowners (Saloutos 1960, 10–11; Zeichner 1939, 27). Here it is argued that landowners benefited from share payments because shares precluded the necessity of borrowing to pay the daily subsistence costs of their laborers. Instead, laborers could borrow on the security of their *own* share of the crop. This not only made the laborer responsible for interest payments, but also it reduced the landowner's risk and liability, since his share of the crop would not be encumbered in the event of a poor harvest.

On the other side are those who argue that the laborers' struggle against the tight control entailed in the wage labor system and their insistence on share payments forced landowners to meet their demands in the face of labor instability and labor scarcity (R. L. F. Davis 1982, 194–96; Mandle 1978, 17–18; Ransom and Sutch 1977, 67; Wiener 1978, 43–46).[14] This latter thesis is sometimes called the black power thesis because it highlights how sharecropping arose as the result of the ex-slaves' victories in struggles for greater autonomy. The following quote captures well the central tenet of the black power thesis: "Here the key determinant was the freedman's refusal to work except in some type of sharecropping system or arrangement. Planters were literally dragged kicking and screaming into the system. Unable to force the freedmen to work for fixed wages in a gang setting, planters accepted sharecropping because they had no choice in the matter" (R. L. F. Davis 1982, 190).

It is possible that these opposing theories of the origins of the sharecropping system can be reconciled if regional differences in labor payments are taken into account. As Gerald Jaynes points out in his superb analysis of the rise of family sharecropping (1986), share payments dominated in those regions where the devastation of property was the greatest and in regions characterized by smaller plantations that would have had far more difficulty acquiring credit to enable landowners to pay wages. Hence, the coincidence of landlords' and laborers' preferences for share payments in these settings is not surprising. In contrast, regions that had some of the finest plantation lands and larger plantations, or suffered less devastation from the war, were more likely to be characterized initially by wage contracts that provided landowners with tighter control over labor (Jaynes 1986, 50–53).[15]

Consider, for example, the work of Ronald Davis, one of the writers who is most insistent regarding the accuracy of the black power theory of the rise of sharecropping. In his study of the Natchez District from 1860 to 1890 (1982), Davis provides convincing evidence that freedpeople preferred share payments to wage payments in opposition to the preferences of landowners. By comparing wage contracts with share contracts, he also showed the extraordinary degree of direct control and hourly supervision of labor entailed in wage contracts.[16] By contrast, share contracts were much more vague and general, including no specific penalties or rules governing work conduct and daily routines (Davis 1982, 104–5). However, the Natchez District, which Davis was examining, was precisely one of the regions that had some of the finest plantation lands, less war devastation, more Northern capital investments, and thus sufficient capital and credit to make regular wage payments (Jaynes 1986, 50–53).[17]

The fact that the wage system dominated only in certain parts of the older cotton-producing areas of the Southeast transforms the prevailing historical understanding of the rise of sharecropping. As Jaynes argues: "The use of the term 'wages' for the method of payment practiced by most planters is one of the true misnomers of the period" (246). He further writes: "In actuality, taking the South as a whole, no general attempt to perpetuate the centralized plantation system on the basis of money wage payments was ever made!" (45). According to his account, the first years of the Reconstruction era witnessed a variety of payment systems, among which payment in shares—not wages—was the most prevalent form (45–49).

This finding undermines the claim of the black power thesis that the primary class conflict in the postbellum South was over the closely supervised wage system versus the more autonomous share system. Rather, as Jaynes points out, since wage payments were rare, it appears that the more fundamental class conflict centered around the issue of whether labor would be organized in family units or in gangs and squads. That is, initially, most laborers, whether working for wages or shares, were organized in gangs and squads, with *family* sharecropping constituting a later stage in the transition of postbellum rural labor organization.[18] Unlike family sharecropping, gang or squad labor gave landowners and their overseers more centralized and direct supervision of labor, as well as the ability to implement and better control a more efficient division of labor in field work (Jaynes 1986, 166). Consequently, family sharecropping was preferred by freedmen for the very reason that it gave them more autonomy than did gang or squad labor.[19]

The use of the term *freedmen*, rather than *freedpeople*, is most appropriate in this context. One of the reasons landowners were eventually willing to shift from gang labor to family sharecropping was because they came to recognize the importance of patriarchal authority within those families for ensuring labor discipline. Unlike landowners who could no longer use the lash on free labor, fathers could legally use corporal punishment to discipline their wives and children in most states in the nineteenth and early twentieth centuries. As one observer noted, "One man, this year, felt obliged to give his own son a tremendous beating, for not performing his share of the labor" (quoted in Jaynes 1986, 185). In some cases, such obligations for disciplining family members were even contractually specified. For example, cropper Thomas Ferguson agreed in his share contract to "control (his) family and make them work and make them behave themselves" (quoted in Jaynes 1986, 185).

It is, of course, possible that personal and emotional commitments, as well as common household interests, also played a role in ensuring labor discipline under family sharecropping, as compared to the impersonal relations between overseers and laborers. However, the disciplinary role of unequal power relations within the family unit was explicitly recognized by landowners in the postwar South and provided an important spur for their willingness to shift to family sharecropping (Jaynes 1986, 185).

Moreover, for landowners, patriarchal and familial relations also provided a means of dealing with the scarcity of labor that accompanied the withdrawal of many freedwomen from field labor after the Civil War.[20] The significance of this withdrawal of female labor has been well documented by numerous historians. Quantitative data suggest that by the 1870s the number of freedmen and -women working in the fields had dropped to one-quarter or one-third of the antebellum level, with the absence of female and child labor accounting for a significant part of this decline (Jaynes 1986, 229; Ransom and Sutch 1977, 232–36; Weiner 1978, 46). Qualitative data in the form of landowners' complaints about the absence of black women from regular fieldwork also suggest that laboring gangs and squads on cotton plantations were overwhelmingly comprised of black men (Jaynes 1986, 188). Family sharecropping and the patriarchal authority it entailed helped to bring more female and child labor back into agricultural production. As one plantation owner remarked, "Where the Negro works for wages, he tries to keep his wife at home. If he rents land, or plants on shares, the wife and children help him in the field" (Jaynes 1986, 187). Other studies of female field labor have also substantiated this claim, particularly in regard to poorer sharecropping households (Bethel 1981, 45–50; Janiewski 1983, 16; Jones 1985, 63).

It is troubling that many historians of the South have ignored the role patriarchy played in bringing black female and child labor back into the fields.[21] It is equally troubling that many social theorists would have incorrectly interpreted this increase in the amount and intensity of family labor in the postbellum South as an example of self-exploitation.[22] Like outright neglect, such an interpretation hides relations of domination, since self-exploitation does not really entail exploitation in the objective sense of the term, that is, how can a person extract surplus labor from his or her own being?[23] By contrast, what happened in the postbellum South was that husbands and fathers used *inter*personal and institutionally legitimated power differentials within their families to control female and child labor.[24] Moreover, since the income from family labor was generally controlled by the male heads of household, this accentuated the structural dependency and potential for abuse internal to family labor enterprises.[25] Indeed, sharecroppers' own voices make clear that domestic abuse was a frequent component of everyday life in the rural South. Based on thousands of pieces of oral and written testimony documenting the interpersonal lives of Southern farm people during the first half of the twentieth century, Kirby concludes: "The corpus of this large, if haphazard, collection of testimony contains far more instances of unhappiness, especially among women. Marriage was a cruel trap, motherhood often a mortal burden; husbands were too often obtuse, unfaithful, drunken, and violent. The collective portrait is less one of bliss than of pathos" (Kirby 1987, 169–70).[26]

The invisibility of patriarchy in the making of the postbellum South goes hand-in-hand with the invisibility of the role of nature. Claudia von Werlhof captures the link between these two realms when she criticizes many theories and histories of uneven development for treating both women and nature as falsely "extra-economic" and promoting a "closet-like existence where all 'inexplicable' and uncomfortable phenomena, such as women's work [and other nonwage work], have so far been deposited" (von Werlhof 1988c, 17).[27] To uncover more of these hidden relationships, I will now examine how various natural features of cotton production exacerbated many of the social conflicts discussed above and thereby helped to foster the rise of the family sharecropping system.

### *Natural Factors in the Rise of Family Sharecropping*

The phenomenon of the "long pay" has been characterized as one of the major causes of the social and economic problems faced by Southern farmers during the Reconstruction era (Jaynes 1986, 46–48 and 224–49). This refers to the fact that immediately after the Civil War, payments to rural laborers—whether in the form of wages or shares—were generally *postharvest* payments. As Jaynes writes: "The quintessence of most financial dealings in southern agriculture [was] waiting. From the poorest laborer to the large planter and merchant, the problem of obtaining cash and credit on the basis of crops which would not be sold until the end of the year proved paramount" (1986, 225).

The "long pay" was a product of both social and natural features of Southern agriculture. As noted above, the general absence of capital and credit in the war-torn economy made it difficult for landowners to pay wages at regular intervals and led landowners to prefer postharvest share payments. Natural features of agricultural production seriously compounded this situation. For example, the natural disasters of 1866 and 1867, which occurred simultaneously with the inauguration of free labor, had a tremendous impact on the Southern economy (Wiener 1978, 66–67; Jaynes 1986, 142).[28] Dr. N. B. Cloud, writing for the U.S. Department of Agriculture, described in detail the disastrous season of 1866: "We had the most unprecedented amount of spring rain through the early summer that has ever been known to the cotton states, culminating in the great flood of June 10, which almost entirely drowned out the cotton plant on the rich river and creek bottom lands. This long-continued, extremely wet weather . . . injured the plant by a surcharge of water in the soil, thereby retarding its growth and rendering the plant more liable to succumb to the ravages of the aphis (plant louse)" (quoted in Jaynes 1986, 141–42).

These problems were merely the beginning of a succession of natural catastrophes. The unprecedented amount of rain was followed by an unseasonable dry spell that turned into drought. After the drought came more heavy rains, the boll worm, and the cotton caterpillar. Together these natural calamities destroyed the few crops that were left. To the utter dismay of Southern farmers, conditions in 1867 were similar, but worse. The crop failures resulting from these recurring natural disasters drove many landowners to shift from wage to share payments. As one Alabama planter put it: "The losses of the year [1866] absorbed all the ready money of the country—actually crippled and disabled many—rendered the payment of wages the next year an impossibility; in consequence the Negroes in 1867 worked for shares of the crops" (quoted in Jaynes 1986, 156).

In the face of such uncontrollable natural forces, the prospect of shifting some of the risks of business onto the laborers through the share system became extremely attractive to landowners (Jaynes 1986, 216; DeCanio 1974, 130; Reid 1975, 430–31). Thus, from the landowner's point of view, one major advantage of sharecropping over wage labor was that the former served as a form of crude insurance whereby the cropper and the landowner shared the risk of natural disasters. Ex-slaves were also quick to recognize the advantages of sharecropping when many wage laborers were thrown off the land so that landowners could avoid meeting wage payments. By contrast, with share payments, even if the season was poor and the laborer's fraction of compensation low, at least compensation would be assured (Jaynes 1986, 145). Moreover, if conflicts arose over the amount of income owed to the laborer, the possibility of some protection based on ownership rights to a share of the crop was preferable to the prospect of arguing over whether wage payments were just in a landlord-dominated civil court (Jaynes 1986, 154).

Conflicts over just compensation were a perennial concern with postharvest payments because laborers had little control over a significant part of their own consumption for long periods of time. In addition, postharvest payments provided many opportunities for corrupt labor practices. For example, in some cases laborers received little or no income at the end of the production cycle as a consequence of the debts incurred throughout the growing season. Since many freedpeople were illiterate, the situation was ripe for distrust and corruption. As one planter remarked: "The Darky don't understand it, he has kept no accounts, but he knows he has worked hard and received nothing" (quoted in Zeichner 1939, 28).

The lengthy production time of the cotton crop exacerbated the already severe problems of lack of capital and increased the necessity of postharvest payments. That is, since the value of the finished commodity (raw cotton) could only be realized after a relatively lengthy time, the acquisition of money to pay labor and production costs also had to await the end of the growing season. In contrast, if landowners or entrepreneurs were producing a commodity that could be quickly finished and sold, they could more easily use their earnings to pay wages on a regular basis throughout the remainder of the year and thereby avoid the credit and labor problems inherent in the "long pay." The problem of a lengthy production time was recognized by Colonel L. Haynes, who noted as early as 1866 the futility of the Reconstruction army's orders for slave owners to replace slavery by wage payments. The colonel maintained that such payments would be difficult to meet because "money can only be realized yearly on a cotton crop." Hence, he argued that it would be far better if the laborer received "his pay at the end of the year"—a point with which many planters agreed (quoted in Jaynes 1986, 48).

The lengthy production time of cotton also contributed to the success of the crop-liens system, since farmers often required credit to carry them through the long production cycle. No doubt, similar credit monopolies, like the company store, have characterized industrial as well as agricultural production. However, in industry they tend to appear only in relatively isolated areas of manufacture where alternative credit facilities are unavailable or in times of serious economic recession (Jaynes 1986, 227). Indeed, the establishment of such credit monopolies seems to be generally associated with two major conditions: those which elongate the interval before the value of a commodity can be realized—such as a lengthy production time—and/or those where credit and financial institutions are either underdeveloped or in crisis. The situation for cotton producers in the Old South was doubly problematic, since both these natural and social conditions existed.[29]

Halting the spread of the crop-liens system through Southern agriculture was extremely difficult due to the existence of the large class of propertyless and illiterate rural producers. The comparatively higher rates of Southern illiteracy compared with other regions of the country increased the difficulties of introducing new forms of money and banking services, like deposit banking. In addition, the virtually propertyless freedpeople had little or no collateral to offer on loans. Consequently, even after Southern banks recovered from the defeat of the Confederacy, most banks shied away from personal loans and loans on real estate or anticipated crop production, leaving a vacuum that was quickly filled by the crop-liens system (Ransom and Sutch 1972, 647–48). As a result, this system of usury had its initial and deepest roots among the poorest sharecroppers, later spreading to engulf both tenant farmers and independent commodity producers.

Along with the lengthy production time of cotton, yet another natural disaster that plagued Southern cotton production for a thirty-year period beginning in the 1890s was the boll weevil—the notorious subject of the famous statement by sharecropper Ned Cobb: "All God's dangers aint a white man" (quoted in Rosengarten 1974, 223). The serious destruction wrought by the weevil is evident in the fact that by 1913 it had reduced the cotton crop in Mississippi by 33 percent. By 1916 it began eating away at the Georgia border with similar devastating results (Daniel 1985, 6–9).

As Daniel points out, this inexorable infestation, more than any other factor at the time, drove Southern farmers to call for government intervention. However, since the government took the less radical route of merely instructing farmers in how to deal with the insect, rather than instituting cotton-free zones to halt its spread, the government's attack on the boll weevil proved ineffective (Daniel 1985, 7–8). Ironically, although the boll weevil did not discriminate by race or class in its conquest of the Old South, government intervention did. Indeed, the struggle against the boll weevil began a process—which would only gain momentum during the New Deal era—whereby government assistance disproportionately benefited the more well-to-do cotton farmers and landowners (Daniel 1985, 16).

The failure to control the evil weevil was to have other significant effects on the Old South. Not only did the boll weevil infestation systematically destroy thousands of acres of cotton, but it accelerated the shift in the westward development of cotton production. As we shall see below, the weevil was just one of many natural factors that fostered the increasing hegemony of cotton production in the younger cotton-producing regions of the Southwest.

### *Regional Differences in the Capitalist Development of Cotton Production*

By 1876, landowners across most of the older cotton-producing areas of the South had instituted family sharecropping (Jaynes 1986, 188). While freedpeople and particularly freedmen gained more autonomy under the family sharecropping system than they had experienced when labor was organized in gangs or squads, landowners fought hard and successfully to keep control over major production decisions, such as crop mix, methods of work, and the marketing of crops. Toward that end, share contracts often specified that the sharecropper was equivalent in status to a hired hand in terms of important production and marketing decisions, and many Southern state laws referred to sharecroppers as wage laborers (Jaynes 1986, 173 and 201; Rochester 1940, 58). However, having similar rights and privileges to wage laborers does not make one a wage laborer. Indeed, the absence of a wage and the presence of both family labor and legal control over a

Table 4-1. Total Number of Cotton Farms, and Number and Percentage of Cotton Farms Hiring Wage Labor, by Region and by State, 1930[a]

| Region and State | Total Number of Cotton Farms | Farms Reporting Hired Labor | Percentage of Farms Hiring Labor |
|---|---|---|---|
| All Cotton Farms in the U.S. | 1,640,025 | 463,697 | 28 |
| Southeast | | | |
| Georgia | 172,395 | 50,942 | 30 |
| Mississippi | 259,198 | 35,947 | 14 |
| Alabama | 206,835 | 46,902 | 23 |
| Louisiana | 115,123 | 40,853 | 35 |
| Southwest | | | |
| Texas | 349,458 | 144,366 | 41 |
| Oklahoma | 86,314 | 39,404 | 47 |

Source: U.S. Bureau of Census 1930a, 66–70.

[a] These data are not available for 1900.

share of the commodities produced placed Southern sharecroppers in a different structural position from wage laborers.[30]

As mentioned at the beginning of this chapter, the inability to use wage labor in cotton production did not uniformly affect all cotton-producing regions in the South. As table 4-1 indicates, there were marked regional differences in the capitalist development of Southern cotton production during the postbellum era. Compared to the older cotton-producing states in the Southeast, the Southwestern states of Texas and Oklahoma showed a relatively high proportion of capitalist cotton farms employing wage labor.

The younger cotton-producing areas of the Southwest were able to utilize wage labor largely because their topography and climate were suitable to the introduction of labor-saving technology. Here irrigation, wheat-growing techniques, and machinery were applied to cotton cultivation. On the broad expanses of level land, cotton growers made use of gang plows, vertical disks, and multirow cultivators (Wiley 1939, 70). While a number of these technologies—the steel plow, seed drills, and cultivators—were pre–Civil War inventions, the scarcity and high price of labor during the war furnished the ultimate impetus to the almost universal adoption of horsedrawn machinery in the Western regions. After 1914, there was a general shift to mechanical power as tractors were used to an increasing extent in soil preparation, planting, and cultivation (Rogin 1931, 91).

By contrast, in the older cotton-producing areas of the Southeast, the rolling terrain and irregular-sized fields were ill suited to the use of such technology (Wiley 1939, 70–71). Here farm implements in general use did not differ greatly from those of antebellum times. Even up until the 1930s, 40 percent of all plows were the one-bottom, one-horse type. Comparatively few disks were used in the preparation of fields, and only about 1 percent of the plows were drawn by tractors (Wiley 1939, 70–71). The major problem, however, was the failure to develop machines that could replace the extraordinary amount of labor necessary for cotton harvesting. Even with the primitive one-mule, half-row equipment, one man could plant and cultivate more cotton than he could pick (Haystead and Fite 1956, 115).

While handpicking prevailed in the Southeastern region, the more efficient methods of hand-snapping and, after 1914, machine stripping dominated the Southwest (Fulmer 1950, 82–87). Studies have estimated that the stripper could do the work of forty-five to eighty-five handpickers, depending on the yield per acre, size of plants, and the amount of weeds in the field. On average, despite the loss of grade associated with machine-stripped cotton, the mechanical stripper resulted in a considerable net profit for the farmer (Christidis and Harrison 1955, 596).

However, unlike cotton picking, snapping and stripping required that the entire boll be removed from the plant. Since cotton does not mature all at the same time (weeks can pass between the appearance of the first ripe boll and the maturation of the last), these methods could only be used in semiarid regions where the open bolls could be left in the fields without damage from rainfall (Christidis and Harrison 1955, 596). Consequently, climatic differences contributed to the Southeast's dependence on hand harvesting, which placed it at a competitive disadvantage with the more mechanized Southwest.

As table 4-2 shows, these variations in the way in which cotton was harvested resulted in major differences in the labor requirements for cotton production by region. Moreover, as in the case of cotton harvesting, other tasks in the cotton production process were also affected by natural factors, such as the climate. For example, next to harvesting, the most time-consuming operations were chopping and hoeing. In the Mississippi Delta, chopping and hoeing required almost as much total labor time as the entire process of planting and harvesting the crop in the regions farther west.

This difference was in part attributable to the fact that in the semiarid regions of the Southwest scarcity of rainfall limited weed growth. In turn, while the Southwestern regions were relatively free of the boll weevil after the turn of the century, the infestation in the Southeast forced cotton farmers to produce a crop in a relatively short season

Table 4-2. Man-Hours per Acre in Cotton Production by Region, 1907–1911, 1917–1921, and 1927–1931

| | All Cotton-Producing States in the U.S. | Eastern Area[a] | Delta Area[b] | Western Area[c] |
|---|---|---|---|---|
| 1907–1911 | 105 | 130 | 122 | 70 |
| 1917–1921 | 95 | 120 | 114 | 62 |
| 1927–1931 | 85 | 113 | 110 | 54 |

Source: J. A. Hopkins 1973, 131. Reprinted courtesy of Da Capo Press, New York.

[a] Eastern Area includes Alabama, Georgia, Florida, Tennessee, North Carolina, and South Carolina.

[b] Delta Area includes Mississippi, Louisiana, and Arkansas.

[c] Western Area includes Texas and Oklahoma.

(Myrdal 1944, 234; Holley and Arnold 1938, 59). Because the effect of thick seeding on the earliness of the crop had been demonstrated, Southeastern cotton was generally planted many times more thickly than would allow the crops to grow to maturity. Consequently, the plants had to be thinned or chopped once they had reached a certain height. In the Southwest, seeding was much wider and some farmers planted only enough seed to ensure a good stand, thus eliminating the thinning process altogether (Holley and Arnold 1938, 59).

The newer Southwestern cotton-producing areas also benefited from richer and less-depleted soils. This advantage is reflected in the regional differences in expenditures on fertilizer. As table 4-3 indicates, the cotton-producing states of Georgia, Alabama, Louisiana, and Mississippi all required much larger expenditures on fertilizer per farm than did either Oklahoma or Texas, thus substantially increasing their relative costs of production. Indeed, the average costs of fertilizer per farm almost follow a direct pattern of decreasing expenditures from the older Southeastern states to the newer Southwestern states.

Together, the greater fertility of land in the Southwest, advantageous climatic conditions, less devastation by the boll weevil, and the increased efficiency of production resulting from the ability to use labor-saving technology enabled these younger cotton-producing areas to be more profitable. As a result, the Southeast was forced to give way to the Southwest in the cotton-growing competition. This is reflected in the increasing proportion of total cotton production attributed to the Western regions. Before the Civil War, most American cotton was grown in the states of the Old South—the Carolinas, Ala-

Table 4-3. Cotton Production 1900 and 1930: Expenditures on Fertilizer per Farm, by Region and by State

| Region and State | Average Expenditures on Fertilizer per Farm in 1930 Dollars | |
|---|---|---|
| | 1900 | 1930 |
| All Cotton Farms in the U.S. | 26.31 | 55.95 |
| Southeast | | |
| Georgia | 68.17 | 119.76 |
| Alabama | 28.30 | 91.98 |
| Mississippi | 7.76 | 36.10 |
| Louisiana | 5.27 | 28.57 |
| Southwest | | |
| Texas | .44 | 12.13 |
| Oklahoma | no listing | 1.02 |

Source: Figures for 1900 calculated from U.S. Bureau of Census 1900, 208–26. Figures for 1930 calculated from U.S. Bureau of Census 1930a, 12–17 and 66–70.

bama, Georgia, Mississippi, and Louisiana. After the war, the centers of cotton production shifted westward, with Texas and Oklahoma together producing half of the nation's crop (Wiley 1939, 67).[31]

While this comparative analysis of the Southeast and the Southwest only focuses on natural constraints on the use of wage labor,[32] these natural factors go some way to explaining the regional differences in the capitalist development of Southern cotton production during the period 1870 to 1930. Although census data on expenditures for wage labor on cotton farms by states are only available for the years 1900 and 1930, table 4-4 shows how some of the regional differences developed over time. In 1900, Georgia had expenditures on wage labor that were above both the national average for all cotton farms and the expenditures in Texas and Oklahoma. By 1930, this pattern had been reversed. By that year, Texas and Oklahoma showed a substantial increase in average expenditures on wage labor per farm. In Texas these expenditures doubled, while in Oklahoma they increased sixfold.[33] By contrast, all of the states in the older Southeast showed expenditures on wage labor substantially below both the national average and the averages for the Southwestern states. Indeed, over these three decades, expenditures on wage labor had been virtually cut in half in all of the Southeastern states, while the number of noncapitalist sharecroppers almost doubled (Rochester 1940, 59).

Given all the factors that weakened the competitive position of cotton production in the Southeast, it is not surprising that in 1920 this

Table 4-4. Cotton Production 1900 and 1930: Expenditures on Hired Labor per Farm and Value of Machinery per Farm, by Region and by State[a]

| | 1900 | | 1930 | |
|---|---|---|---|---|
| Cotton Farms by Region and State | Average Expenditures on Hired Labor per Farm[b] | Average Value of Machinery per Farm | Average Expenditures on Hired Labor per Farm[b] | Average Value of Machinery per Farm |
| Average for All Cotton Farms in U.S. | 57 | 103 | 61 | 170 |
| Southeast | | | | |
| Georgia | 78 | 94 | 38 | 100 |
| Mississippi | 37 | 80 | 18 | 118 |
| Alabama | 50 | 76 | 19 | 116 |
| Louisiana | 44 | 85 | 27 | 112 |
| Southwest | | | | |
| Texas | 57 | 158 | 118 | 293 |
| Oklahoma | 21 | 128 | 124 | 308 |

Source: Figures for 1900 calculated from U.S. Bureau of Census 1900, 208–26 and multiplied by 2.29 to produce equivalent 1930 dollars. Figures for 1930 calculated from U.S. Bureau of Census 1930a, 18–23 and 66–70.

[a] All figures in 1930 dollars.

[b] Expenditures on hired labor per farm calculated by total expenditures on all cotton farms in states divided by total number of all cotton farms in state.

region was in the same position, if not worse off, than it had been in 1890. Cotton monoculture had increased, much more land was ruined or worn, the boll weevil was completing its conquest of the region, and farmers soon were to encounter a price crisis worse than any they had experienced at the end of the previous century (Kirby 1987, xiv–xv).

In addition, although the 1920 census statistically heralded the urbanization of American society, few Southern states participated in this trend. Rather, like in underdeveloped societies, approximately two-thirds of the population of most Southern states was rural (Kirby 1987, 49 and 275). In turn, contrary to the views of such writers as C. Vann Woodward, who maintain that the Southern landowning class was replaced by a "middle-class" with a "capitalistic outlook" after the Civil War (1951, 17 and 20–21), it appears that, despite the abolition of slavery, the older plantation South continued to be dominated by noncapitalist forms of production up until the Great Depression (Kirby 1987, 1; Bartley 1987, 440–42).

## *Conclusion*

In the face of natural and social obstacles to the use of wage labor, landowners were forced to find alternative mechanisms, other than the labor market, to ensure the continuation of agricultural production. Control over labor was most effectively achieved through two separate but integrally related social institutions: family sharecropping and the crop-liens system. I have argued that the establishment of these two noncapitalist institutions reflected attempts not only to deal with class conflicts between landowners and their newly freed labor force, but also to reduce the peculiar risks associated with agricultural production: its seasonal nature, its lengthy production times, and its characteristic of being more subject to unpredictable natural factors.

The effect of these natural factors was particularly acute in the older cotton-producing areas of the Southeast when the absence of capital and credit in the war-torn economy and a succession of poor cotton crops in 1866 and 1867 convinced both landlords and laborers of the hazards of wage labor and the possible advantages of sharecropping. Thus the argument developed in this chapter complements and supplements other analyses that view sharecropping as a compromise solution to the class conflict between freedmen and planters by showing how natural obstacles to the use of wage labor were intertwined with competing class interests and preferences.

The comparative regional analysis shows how landowners in the Southwest faced fewer natural impediments to capitalist cotton production. The more advantageous climatic conditions in the semiarid West, along with its topography and relative freedom from pest infestation, reduced the labor requirements of various production operations and increased the use of labor-saving technology. The greater fertility of the newly opened frontier soils, coupled with the availability of these western lands for expansion, contrasted sharply with the situation in the Southeast, where land was both worn and concentrated in the hands of a few.

Having examined various natural obstacles to rural capitalist development through a comparative analysis of two regions of the American South during the same time period (1870–1930), I will next examine the problem of wage labor in agriculture by comparing the same region—the Southeast—over two different time periods. While from the Civil War up until the Great Depression the Southeast was dominated by family sharecropping, the decades following the Depression witnessed a steady decline in the number of sharecroppers as wage labor came to substitute for sharecropping on an increasing scale. Not only does the next chapter highlight some of the major obstacles capital had to overcome in order to profitably use wage labor in Southeastern cotton production, it also provides a fuller understanding of how capital can subordinate, minimize, or eliminate such natural obstacles to its further development.

# Five

# Hands That Picked Cotton: From Sharecropping to Wage Labor

Millions of farmers displaced from the land . . . how quietly rural people melted away.—Pete Daniel, *Breaking the Land* (1985)

The decades following the Great Depression witnessed a transformation of Southern agriculture that some recent historians view as "the most revolutionary in southern history" and liken in significance to the British enclosure movements (Daniel 1985, 168 and 239; Kirby 1987, 276). As a result of this "Southern enclosure," poor sharecroppers and tenant farmers were forced off the land, and the Southern farm population declined catastrophically by approximately eight million people (Bartley 1987, 438; Kirby 1987, 276). The exodus off the farm has been characterized as "one of the greatest movements of people in history to occur within a single generation" (Fite 1984, 209).

While this great transformation affected many aspects of Southern life, I will focus primarily on the major change that took place in the dominant form of cotton production in the Old South—the demise of sharecropping and the rise of capitalist cotton farms employing wage labor. This unexpected development marked a major reversal of earlier trends in Southern agriculture. Until 1930, the number of share tenants and croppers increased in all of the older cotton-producing states of the Southeast,[1] doubling between 1880 and 1900 and almost doubling again in the subsequent three decades (Rochester 1940, 59). By 1930, sharecropping and share tenancy units comprised almost half (48 percent) of all farms in the Old South (Rochester 1940, 59). Tenancy was highest in those counties with the heaviest black populations and where cotton was the main crop; here tenant farms rose to include as many as 70 to 80 percent of all farms (Fite 1984, 5).

That the depression decade was the crucial turning point in the transformation of the rural class structure of the Old South is visible from the steady decline of sharecroppers that took place after 1930.[2] According to the U.S. census, between 1930 and 1950 the number of sharecroppers was virtually cut in half (see table 5-1). In the single decade between 1950 and 1960, the number of croppers again de-

Table 5-1. Total Number of Sharecroppers in Sixteen Southern States[a] and Missouri, 1920–1959

| Year | Number of Sharecroppers |
|---|---|
| 1920 | 561,091 |
| 1925 | 623,058 |
| 1930 | 776,278 |
| 1935 | 716,256 |
| 1940 | 541,291 |
| 1945 | 446,556 |
| 1950 | 346,765 |
| 1954 | 267,662 |
| 1959 | 121,037 |

Source: U.S. Bureau of Census 1964, 751.

[a] The sixteen Southern states include Delaware, Maryland, the District of Columbia, West Virginia, Virginia, North Carolina, South Carolina, Kentucky, Georgia, Tennessee, Alabama, Mississippi, Louisiana, Arkansas, Texas, and Oklahoma.

creased by one-half. By the 1960s, sharecroppers comprised such an insignificant number of farmers that the census compilers stopped counting them separately after the census of 1960 (Kirby 1987, 208).

As the county and the plantation data in figure 5-1 and table 5-2 indicate, in place of sharecroppers, a class of wage laborers was established. The replacement of sharecropping by wage labor is also reflected in national census data: in 1930 only 28 percent of all cotton farms reported expenditures on wage labor, whereas in 1964 the percentage had increased to 65 (U.S. Bureau of Census 1964, 994–1004).[3] Moreover, since wage laborers often were skilled in the operation and maintenance of complex machinery, there was also an increase in the proportion of skilled to unskilled labor (James 1981b, 4; Kirby 1987, 69).

The purpose of this chapter is to illuminate some of the major events and factors that contributed to this transformation of the class structure of the Old South. To date, much of the existing literature on the demise of Southern sharecropping focuses primarily on developments internal to the United States and to the South as a region. Studies have focused in particular on the impact of New Deal agricultural programs, advances in farm technology, and the labor shortages created by World War II. In contrast, I will supplement a discussion of these domestic factors with an analysis of the effect of both foreign cotton production and the rise of the synthetic fiber industries. As in earlier chapters, I will also highlight how certain natural features of agricultural production intertwined with these domestic and interna-

Figure 5-1. Sharecroppers, 1920–1954, and Hired Farm Workers, 1935–1959, in Selected Cotton Plantation Counties

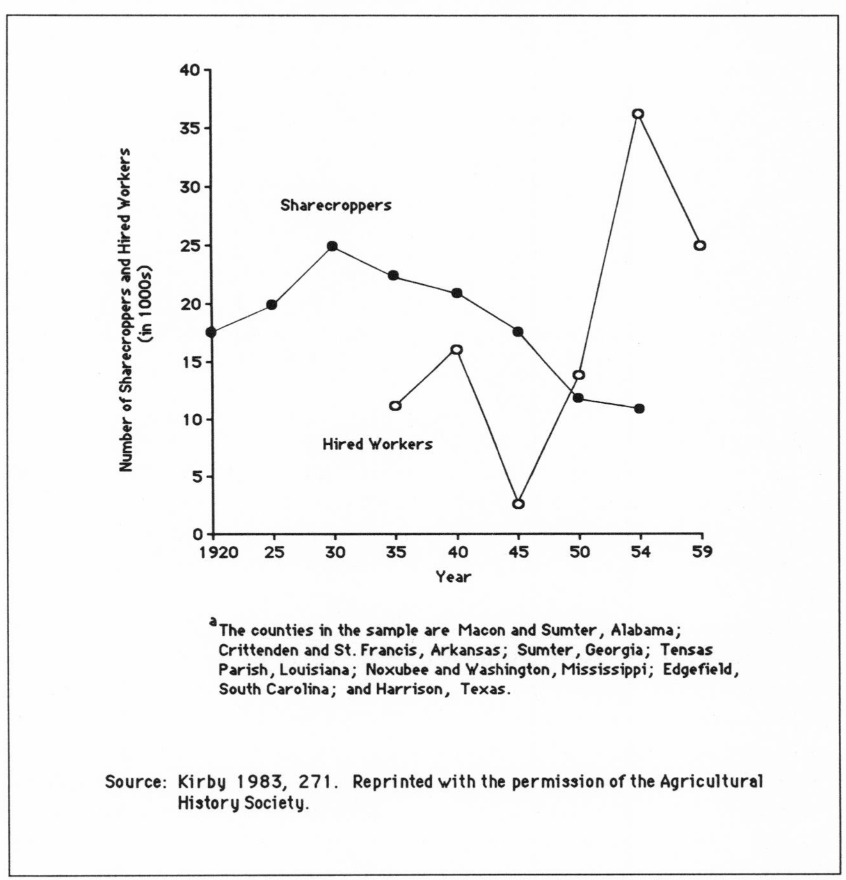


[a]The counties in the sample are Macon and Sumter, Alabama; Crittenden and St. Francis, Arkansas; Sumter, Georgia; Tensas Parish, Louisiana; Noxubee and Washington, Mississippi; Edgefield, South Carolina; and Harrison, Texas.

Source: Kirby 1983, 271. Reprinted with the permission of the Agricultural History Society.

tional social conditions to shape the history of the postdepression South. I will begin chronologically by first focusing on one of the major problems that gave rise to the Great Depression—overproduction.

### *Cotton Overproduction*

Cotton overproduction had been a recurring phenomenon in Southern agriculture since the Civil War. Consequently, it does not in itself explain the demise of sharecropping after the Great Depression. However, overproduction was the root cause of the first direct government

Table 5-2. Percentage of Cropland Operated by Wage Labor, Sharecroppers, and Share Tenants on Twelve Plantations in the Yazoo–Mississippi Delta Region,[a] 1933–1936

| | Percentage of Cropland | | |
|---|---|---|---|
| Year | Wage Labor | Sharecroppers | Share Tenants |
| 1933 | 30 | 52 | 18 |
| 1934 | 40 | 46 | 14 |
| 1935 | 43 | 46 | 11 |
| 1936 | 47 | 43 | 10 |

Source: Langsford and Thibodeaux 1939, 52–53.

[a] According to the U.S. Department of Agriculture, these plantations are representative of trends on plantations in the Yazoo–Mississippi Delta.

interventions in cotton production during the 1930s, which were to contribute significantly to the demise of sharecropping. Since cotton overproduction was integrally related to cotton specialization, let us examine how these twin problems affected Southern agriculture.

As early as 1880, the South ceased to be self-sufficient in basic foodstuffs precisely because most cotton farmers were wed to monocrop production or chose a crop mix that included an excess of cotton. The rapid specialization of production in the decades following the Civil War was particularly surprising, given the virtual stagnation of world cotton demand during this period (Wright 1978, 164–65). Moreover, since the world price of cotton almost directly reflected the costs of producing, handling, and marketing American cotton, this virtual monopoly American cotton held on world markets could have been used to the advantage of Southern farmers (Rochester 1940, 216–17; Wright 1978, 167–68).

Yet American cotton producers did not regulate their supply so as to take advantage of this situation. For instance, downward trends in cotton prices often elicited contradictory responses from cotton producers. Some farmers actually increased their production to make up for low prices by greater volume. Others merely tried to engage in more efficient cotton production to reduce their costs but not their supply. Unlike the norm in other nonfarm branches of production, this increasing specialization of production was not directly related to the economic size of farms. Rather, the relationship between economic size of farm and cotton specialization took on more of a U-shape, with the largest and smallest farms strongly associated with concentration in cotton (Wright 1978, 176).

These peculiarities of cotton specialization in the face of cotton overproduction have been examined by a number of historians. Cost-benefit analyses of cotton as compared to other crops suggest that cotton was usually the most profitable type of production even in the face of declining prices (Fite 1984, 9–10; DeCanio 1974, 13; Ransom and Sutch 1977, 190–91; Holley and Arnold 1938, 110). In addition, debt obligations under the crop-liens system encouraged cotton specialization. Not only was cotton the most valuable use of the land, but also, because it is a relatively nonperishable commodity, it could be stored until the best market conditions prevailed. If the creditor was a merchant, forcing producers to concentrate on cotton increased the demand for food products, which could be sold at exorbitant rates. In turn, the pressure to meet cash payments on debts made producers more likely to abandon the safety-first strategy of self-sufficient food production for specialization in the cash staple (Wright 1978, 169–72; Fite 1984, 84–85; Ransom and Sutch 1977, 159–68; James 1981b, 8).

Cotton overproduction was further exacerbated by the domestic and foreign demand generated by the First World War. In order to expand their production so as to meet wartime needs, a large number of farmers went into debt. After the Armistice, farmers were faced with a dramatic decline in demand and plummeting farm prices. Between 1919 and 1922, prices received by American farmers declined by 40 percent, while rates of bankruptcy, foreclosure, and other signs of economic distress reached record levels. Consequently, for agriculture, the depression began in the early 1920s (Fite 1984, 103–7; Frundt 1975, 44–46).

However, it was not until surpluses reached record figures in 1929 that the government officially admitted the problem of agricultural overproduction. By August 1, 1932, world carryover of American and foreign cotton was sufficient to provide 74 percent of the volume consumed over the next 12 months, while cotton prices fell below the costs of production to less than one-third of their average during the 1920s (Rochester 1940, 218).

In the face of growing social unrest from farmers across the country (Gilbert and Howe 1988), the Roosevelt administration eventually developed and implemented programs specifically designed to stabilize farm incomes and curtail production.[4] This was the beginning of direct government funding of the agricultural sector that was to continue up to the present day and form the core of U.S. agricultural policy. It was also the beginning of what could legitimately be called a "revolution from above" in cotton production in the Old South.[5]

### *The Revolution from Above*

I am using the term "revolution from above" to highlight the fact that the rise of wage labor in the older cotton-producing areas of the South was in part a product of federal government intervention. This revolution from above should also be viewed as a form of "primitive accumulation," because capitalist cotton farming in the Old South did not arise simply as a result of "normal" competitive market activities—rather it occurred through the use of outright force and fraud.[6]

This forced capitalist development was an outcome of the federal government's Agricultural Adjustment Act (AAA), initially implemented in 1932 and later reformulated in 1938. Under the AAA, public funds were provided to farmers who participated in acreage allotments and marketing quotas. Only certain agricultural commodities were included under this legislation, and among these were the South's three major commercial crops: cotton, tobacco, and rice. The AAA also set up the Commodity Credit Corporation (CCC), which was to become the government's principal arm for the acquisition, handling, storage, and sale of surplus commodities. Cash payments made to farmers for surpluses were set at approximately 60 percent of parity (Rasmussen and Baker 1969, 69–88).

While these government programs were ostensibly designed to reduce rather than to heighten social unrest, they had differential effects on farmers, depending on the type of commodity they produced.[7] For cotton growers, particularly in the plantation counties, the AAA enriched well-to-do landowners and displaced or further impoverished the landless (Kirby 1987, 56; Daniel 1985, 109). Indeed, from the very beginning, government support benefits were distributed among cotton farmers almost exactly in proportion to the share of total land each farmer controlled. Consequently, the largest farms received the lion's share of government largess (Schnittker 1970, 90; Daniel 1985, 106, 109, and 175). For example, in one study of 246 plantations in the South, owners received on the average $979 in AAA payments in 1935 and $853 in 1937, or more than 23 percent of their total income. Tenants, on the other hand, received an average of $11 in 1935 and $27 in 1937, only 9 percent of their income (Frundt 1975, 56).

It is not surprising that these federal programs worked in the interests of the Southern landowning class, since the local farmer committees that actually implemented the AAA price-support and acreage reduction programs in the Southern states were dominated by cotton landowners and other large farmers (James 1981b, 3; Fite 1984, 141; Kirby 1987, 59; Gilbert and Howe 1988).[8] Sharecroppers and blacks were excluded from positions of influence on these committees from 1933 until well into the 1960s (James 1981a, 13; Fite 1984, 222–23). Moreover, although the formal regulations of the AAA prohibited the displacement of tenants and required a division of price-support payments between landlords and tenants, with no local enforcement of these regulations, displacement proceeded unchecked.[9]

This displacement of sharecroppers resulted from a number of features of the "Triple A." First, under the acreage reduction program, cotton acreage was virtually cut in half in the decade between 1930 and 1940 (Myrdal 1944, 1246). Since land ownership was highly monopolized in the Southeast, large landowners faced with government demands for acreage reduction simply diverted their least fertile land or withdrew entirely from production farms that had been cultivated by the least efficient croppers (Rochester 1940, 62; Melman 1949, 63).

Second, the benefit payments gave landlords a considerable interest in reducing the number of tenants and croppers or shifting their status to that of wage laborers. Although during the first years of the AAA landlords simply took for themselves the payments that were supposed to be forwarded to their tenants or croppers, in later years they were prevented from doing so by the direct payment of benefits. While this change in the method of payment was designed to improve the situation of small producers, landlords responded by evicting tenants and croppers or shifting them to wage contracts in order to continue receiving the government subsidies (Rochester 1940, 62; Myrdal 1944, 257–59).

Third, the AAA also served indirectly to replace sharecropping with wage labor by accelerating the mechanization of cotton production. Acreage reduction encouraged more intensive types of production, while government subsidies provided the needed capital for such investments. In turn, the substitution of machinery and skilled wage labor for tenants and croppers enabled the landlord to legally receive the total share of government payments (Myrdal 1944, 260 and 1248; Kirby 1987, 52 and 63). As a result, the major beneficiaries of government benefits—owners of large cotton plantations—were the first to let their sharecroppers go, to hire skilled labor, and to invest in labor-saving technology (Kirby 1987, 72). Hence, they were the first major group of landlords in the Old South to be transformed into capitalist farmers.

In some cases, not only did laborers get displaced, but so did landowners. Foreclosures of farm mortgages by banks and insurance companies left many smaller independent farmers in the same landless position as tenants. As early as 1934, it was estimated that banks and life insurance companies owned 30 percent of all Southern cotton land. Another estimate in 1938 showed that insurance companies had increased the value of their land assets ninefold since 1929 and threefold since 1933 (Daniel 1985, 168–69 and 172). These new corporate owners tended to hire wage labor or to rent their land only to farmers who could finance a crop, thus further reducing the number of sharecroppers (Fite 1984, 135).

As a result of all of these developments, not only were new capitalist class relations created, but land became even more concentrated in the hands of a few, and the size of farms actually increased (Daniel 1985, 169).[10] In response to the increasing impoverishment and displacement of sharecroppers, several unions formed to combat evictions, AAA contract violations, and the general mistreatment of tenants. While the Alabama Sharecroppers' Union had dissolved by 1935, the more influential Southern Tenant Farmers' Union (STFU) was created in 1934 specifically to fight the injustices perpetrated by the AAA. Despite a violent backlash from both landowners and local law enforcement officials, the interracial STFU played a significant role in bringing about protections for tenant farmers and sharecroppers under the new AAA of 1938 (Gilbert and Howe 1988). The STFU's organizing efforts, along with the national publicity its spirited and moving protests generated, pressured and embarrassed the Roosevelt administration into taking some measures to help poor farmers through low-interest loans and resettlement programs.

Yet even these minor efforts at reform were attacked by the nation's largest agricultural lobby, the American Farm Bureau Federation, an organization dominated by well-to-do farmers and landowners. Indeed, this lobby not only fought reform legislation, but also helped to purge the U.S. Department of Agriculture of many of its most progressive personnel and agencies (Kirby 1987, 58 and 61; Hooks 1986, 3–5). Hence, the victories for Southern tenant farmers won by union protests were short-lived and limited.[11] Congressional funding of small farm programs benefited only a minute proportion of tenant farmers, and even these scant funds were allocated in a racist fashion (Kirby 1987, 57–58; Fite 1984, 145–49).

As a result, most sharecropping and tenant families found that their long-term situation had not changed for the better. Fite has summed up the failings of the New Deal government interventions: "For these poverty-stricken rural people there was nothing new about the New Deal. . . . If anything, their condition was becoming worse and their future was hopeless" (Fite 1984, 135 and 138). Because it has been argued that the greatest impact the New Deal had on the demise of

Southern sharecropping resulted from its having fostered the mechanization of cotton production (James 1981b, 1), this process is examined at more length below.

## *The Revolution from Within*

As mentioned in the last chapter, the older cotton-producing areas of the Southeast were slow to adopt labor-saving technology. Up until the 1930s, only about 1 percent of plows were drawn by tractors, and the traditional mule and half-row equipment prevailed throughout this region (Wiley 1939, 70–71). Indeed, one observer exaggerated only slightly when he remarked: "Moses and Hammurabi would have been at home with the tools and implements of the tenant farmer" (quoted in Fite 1984, 150).[12]

The intervention of the AAA programs in the early 1930s created new incentives for cotton landowners to mechanize and to invest in farm and land improvement. For example, the acreage diversion programs rewarded landlords for reducing cotton acreage but attached no penalties to increasing the productivity of land on which cotton was produced (James 1981b, 9). Hence, planters began to use increasing amounts of fertilizer and farmed their most fertile land more intensively.

However, there are limits to the level of productivity that can be achieved without any change in the technology employed. Moreover, a reduction in acreage devoted to cotton left large landowners with a significant amount of land that could be used for other purposes. The technology was already available for the capital-intensive production of other crops, while the AAA diversion payments furnished the necessary cash for these investments (Melman 1949, 63). Consequently the acreage of more capital-intensive crops such as rice, corn, and peanuts increased, as did the ratio of noncotton to cotton farms (Fulmer 1950, 48; James 1981b, 10; Kirby 1987, 73–75). Therefore, rather than greater specialization, which one might expect in the industrial sphere of production, diversification accompanied the capitalist development of Southeastern cotton production, just as it did in many other branches of agriculture.[13]

In addition to increasing the capital-intensive nature of Southern agriculture, diversification reduced the nonidentity of production time and labor time by enabling a more efficient synchronization of the labor required for different crops. For example, on one farm, diversification was credited with raising labor time to 212 days per year as compared to an average of 110 days on specialized cotton farms (Kirby 1987, 62). Also, with diversification, much of the machinery purchased by landowners for use on alternative crops could be used in the preharvest operations of cotton production. Consequently, small tractors with multirow equipment suited to use on the rolling terrain and the smaller, irregular-sized farms of the Old South finally began to displace the primitive mule and half-row equipment on cotton acreage (Myrdal 1944, 259–60; Fulmer 1950, 80). In 1919, only 5 percent of the farms in the Mississippi Delta reported the use of tractors; by 1936, 45 percent were able to do so (Holley and Arnold 1938, 58).

While such a technological advance was heralded in circles that advocated scientific agriculture, it had disastrous consequences for Southern sharecroppers. According to one study, each tractor in the South displaced several families, and the 111,399 tractors introduced into cotton-growing states in the 1930s displaced close to a million people (Daniel 1985, 175). In addition, not only did mechanization expedite the replacement of croppers by skilled wage labor, but the increase in yields per acre associated with this more intensive farming also fostered the use of wage labor.[14] As table 5-3 indicates, yields of 350 pounds of cotton or more per acre showed greater net returns from using wage labor than from using sharecroppers.

Nevertheless, before the depression, most Southeastern cotton farmers had been unable to acquire machinery for preharvest operations because of the immense amount of hand labor required for harvesting. To ensure an adequate labor supply for picking the crop, planters considered it economically advantageous to use hand labor throughout the year, rather than invest in the labor-saving technology that was only useful on a seasonal basis (Fite 1984, 151). By contrast, during the depression years, the lack of alternative employment opportunities and the abundance of cheap labor meant that planters could use preharvest technology and still be assured that displaced tenants and croppers would be available in nearby towns and cities to be rehired as needed for the harvest period (James 1981b, 10; Melman 1949, 63).

This situation was soon to change, with America's entry into World War II.[15] Displaced croppers and tenants responded *en masse* to the employment opportunities created by the war (Mandle 1978, 84; Melman 1949, 63). Between 1940 and 1945, the South's farm population dropped by about 22 percent or three million people (Fite 1984, 168). However, it should be emphasized that this large migration from the South was not merely a consequence of the "pull" of increased job opportunities elsewhere, but also reflected the fact that sharecroppers and tenants had already been displaced or forced off the land, only to

Table 5-3. Net Returns per Acre to Farm Operators in Cotton Production with Sharecroppers and Wage Labor, under Different Yield and Price Situations

| Prices and Wage Rates | Yield per Acre | Type of Labor: Sharecropper | Type of Labor: Wage Hand |
|---|---|---|---|
| | | (Net return per acre)[a] | |
| Lint 7 cents/lb. | | | |
| Seed $16.67/ton | 150 | $ 2.34 | $ −0.57 |
| Wage rate $0.50 | 250 | 6.13 | 5.70 |
| per day without | 350 | 9.90 | 11.95 |
| board | 450 | 13.69 | 18.23 |
| Lint 9 cents/lb. | | | |
| Seed $20.00/ton | 150 | $ 4.04 | $ 0.21 |
| Wage rate $0.75 | 250 | 8.96 | 8.09 |
| per day without | 350 | 13.87 | 15.97 |
| board | 450 | 18.79 | 23.85 |
| Lint 11 cents/lb. | | | |
| Seed $23.33/ton | 150 | $ 5.73 | $ 0.96 |
| Wage rate $1.00 | 250 | 11.78 | 10.46 |
| per day without | 350 | 17.82 | 19.94 |
| board | 450 | 23.86 | 29.43 |

Source: Fulmer 1950, 78. Reprinted with permission of the University of North Carolina Press, Chapel Hill.

[a] Prices of fertilizer and ginning, bagging, and ties held constant; other factors omitted.

be reclaimed as needed for the harvest period. Hence their incomes from agricultural labor had been substantially reduced and their former means of subsistence disrupted before the war even began (James 1981b, 3 and 10).

Many historians highlight how the labor shortage generated by the Second World War was the major factor that fostered the mechanization of cotton harvesting (James 1981b, 7; Street 1957, 124; Melman 1949, 64). And indeed, there is little doubt that the availability of a cheap and dependent labor force prior to the war had militated against such innovation. Nevertheless, the fact that cotton harvesters were not in general use until a decade after International Harvester produced the first successful mechanical picker for commercial sale in 1941 suggests that labor scarcity was only one of the major spurs to this technological and social revolution.[16]

Indeed, the full mechanization of cotton production required the combined efforts of a host of scientists from different disciplines attacking the natural foundations of cotton production. First, the cotton harvester had to overcome the difficulties of dealing with the odd physical and external features of the cotton plant. The mechanical spindle-type picker developed by International Harvester accomplished this by using vertical drums equipped with hundreds of revolving spindles that moved along the side of the cotton row, projected into the plant, and engaged the cotton in the open bolls. As they revolved, the spindles with their load of cotton passed through a rubber doffer that removed the cotton and conveyed it to a hopper on the top of the machine.

Second, because cotton bolls do not all mature at the same time, but rather open irregularly over a period of a few weeks, this precluded one single harvest operation. Consequently, for a mechanical harvester to work properly, the plant still had to be transformed internally. This was achieved through genetic innovations that enabled the breeding of a cotton variety on which the bolls would develop higher on the stalk, open in a shorter period of time, and open more evenly (Fite 1984, 86; Goodman, Sorj, and Wilkinson 1987, 36).

Third, machine-picked cotton contained a larger amount of trash than cotton picked by hand. To reduce this trash, chemicals were required not only to control weeds, but also to defoliate the cotton plant before the harvest. The development of herbicides in the 1950s was essential to the removal of the barrier to capitalist development presented by weeding—the second most labor-intensive peak period in cotton production next to harvesting. In some areas flamethrowers had been used as early as the 1930s to reduce this long and arduous process (Holley and Arnold 1938, 59; Day 1967, 429). However, in many places in the Southeast, the climate was too wet to use this "weird by-product of combat" (Kirby 1987, 337–38). Finally, it was also necessary to develop adequate pesticides that could be sprayed efficiently over the crop (Fite 1984, 86). Hence, mechanical, biological, and chemical "warfare" went hand-in-hand in the capitalist conquest of cotton.

These technological advances had a significant impact on the social relations of production. A single-row cotton picker of the spindle type could harvest on the average five 500-pound bales per day. Since the average amount harvested per day by a handpicker was 150 to 200 pounds of cotton, the mechanical picker could replace significant amounts of hand labor (Christidis and Harrison 1955, 590). Cost comparisons between handpicked and machine-picked cotton suggested that substantial savings could be gained by using the machine. Studies done in 1954 estimated costs (including fuel, labor, repairs, and depreciation) at $12.29 per bale for machine-picked cotton. Adding $10.32 per bale for grade loss and $3.15 per bale for field waste, total cost for machine-picked cotton averaged $25.76 per bale. Since at that time handpicking amounted to $45.00 per bale, there was a considerable net saving from using machines (Christidis and Harrison 1955, 603). In turn, the advantages of mechanical harvesting increased over time. Throughout the late 1940s and 1950s ginning plants were becoming better equipped with mechanical devices for cleaning cotton before and after ginning, thus steadily reducing the difference in grade between handpicking and machine harvesting.

Using data from ten counties in the Mississippi Delta generally considered as representative of the Delta region as a whole, Richard Day provides a graphic illustration of how the various advances in cotton technology affected the distribution of unskilled labor requirements throughout the productive cycle. In figure 5-2, Stage 1 represents the most labor- and mule-intensive techniques associated with the sharecropping system. Here, roughly speaking, one sharecropper family and one or two mules provided the power for a fifteen-acre unit. Stage 2 represents the displacement of mule-powered land preparation and cultivation activities by small tractors. In Stage 3, hand-labor requirements are further reduced through the adoption of larger scale equipment (e.g., multirow cultivators) and the use of flamethrowers. Stages 2 and 3, which took place from the 1930s through the 1940s, eliminated much of the hand labor, except for some weeding and the fall harvest. At this level of mechanization, it was possible to push sharecroppers off the farm where they had been maintained on a year-round basis and rely on some skilled labor and transient unskilled harvest labor (Day 1967).

Stage 4 represents the period after the Second World War when the use of mechanical harvesters increased, particularly by large planters. This in turn increased the use of wage labor, as well as the ratio of skilled to unskilled labor. As the graphs in figure 5-2 suggest and other historians attest, all of these developments in the mechanization of cotton production created a more even distribution of labor requirements throughout the productive cycle (Melman 1949, 68–71). Such a reduction of the jagged peaks and gluts in the seasonal nature of labor requirements was a condition that the Mann-Dickinson thesis argued was important for the profitable development of capitalism in agriculture.

Mechanization was particularly rapid during the late 1940s and 1950s.[17] As of 1953, the amount of cotton harvested by machine exceeded that harvested by hand (James 1981b, 18). By 1960, cotton farms in the Delta counties of Mississippi, Louisiana, and Arkansas were nearly 100 percent mechanized (Fite 1984, 188). As a result, the number of tenant and sharecropping units fell. For example, from 1950 to 1955, the number of tenant and sharecropping families on

Figure 5-2. Seasonal Distribution of Unskilled Labor Requirements in Cotton Production by Stage of Technology

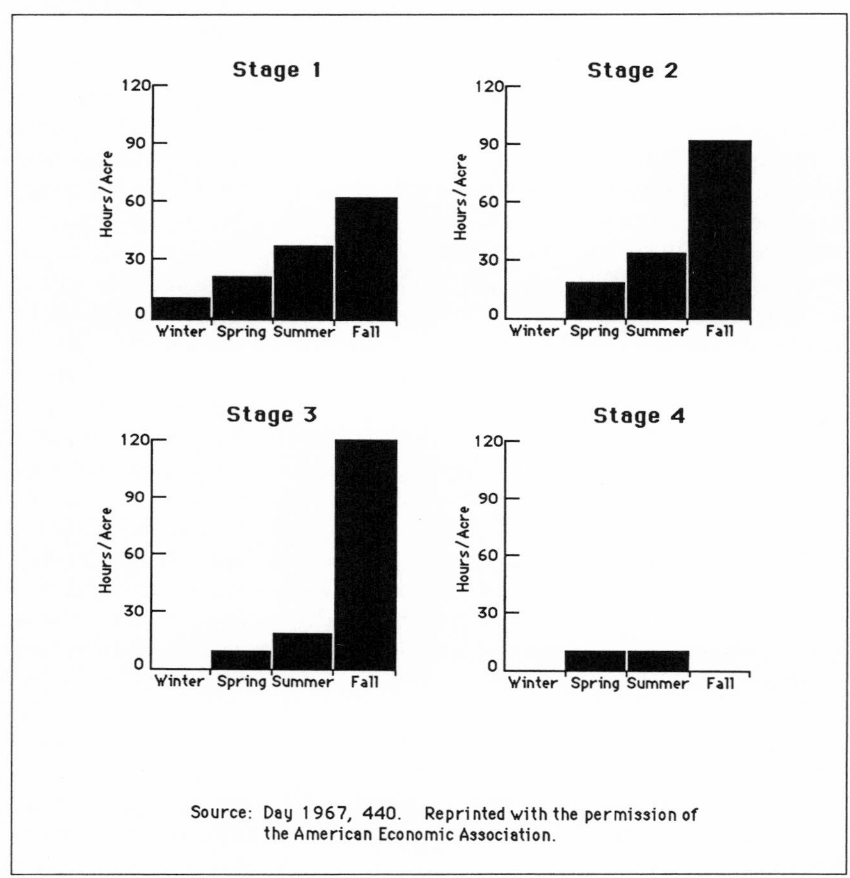


Source: Day 1967, 440. Reprinted with the permission of the American Economic Association.

plantations in the Mississippi Delta region was reduced by 32 percent (James 1981b, 18). In the entire period between 1940 and 1960, the number of black sharecroppers declined by over 75 percent (Mandle 1978, 95).

This "Southern enclosure" not only created the dislocations that eventually erupted in the civil rights movement,[18] but it also eliminated much of the dominant Southern landowning class's economic need for coercive and extraeconomic controls over black labor, since the sharecropping system had generally passed into insignificance in the wake of capitalist development. I shall now examine how this historic transformation of Southern agriculture was fostered by events that took place in the global economy.

### Revolution from Without

A number of modern writers have noted how changes in the global economy, such as the development of foreign cotton production and the rise of the synthetic fiber industries, significantly shaped the modernization of Southern cotton production. For example, Gilbert Fite, who has been called "the preeminent historian of U.S. agriculture writing today"[19] states: "Two key developments hung like a cloud over southern cotton growers. One was the increasing production of cotton in foreign countries . . . which competed with the American product in world markets. In 1941 the United States produced only 38 percent of world production compared to 72 percent back in 1911. In addition, the increased production of rayon was eating into the cotton market. Between 1919 and 1943 the share of the fiber market taken over by rayon rose from 0.3 to 10.6 percent . . . and rayon prices were dropping significantly, making the synthetic fiber a tough competitor" (1984, 175). However, few of the major historians of the postdepression South have given foreign competition and the synthetic fiber industry any serious or lengthy consideration. Even in Fite's most recent book of over 200 pages on Southern cotton production, these "key developments" receive less than two full pages of attention (Fite 1984, 175, 185, and 194). A similar neglect of global developments can be found in the recent and otherwise excellent works on Southern agriculture by Kirby (1987) and Daniel (1985).[20] Indeed, with the exception of Gavin Wright's contributions (1978 and 1986), a global perspective is missing in virtually all of the major historical works examining Southern agriculture after the Civil War.[21]

Yet increased competition from both foreign cotton producers and the synthetic fiber industries placed enormous pressure on American farmers to increase the efficiency of their production units (Fite 1984, 185 and 194). Because of the importance of these developments, I examine each in turn, looking first at the developments in foreign cotton production, which occurred in the underdeveloped or peripheral societies, and then at the rise of synthetic fibers, which were produced in the industrially developed societies.

### *Competition from the Periphery*

Historically, Southern cotton production has been integrally tied to trends in the world economy. Before the Civil War, the dependence of Southern farmers on world markets was greater than for farmers in any other region of the country. In 1860, seven-eighths of all American exports were agricultural, and the bulk of these came from the South. Cotton alone accounted for 60 percent of the country's total exports (Shannon 1945, 110). The disruptions of the war years coupled with massive investments by British capital directed toward increasing cotton production in its colonial outposts had given a stimulus to foreign cotton producers, particularly in India and Egypt (Taylor and Taylor 1943, 15; Todd 1915, 237). As a result of these developments, the percentage share of U.S. cotton in world production suffered a slight, but steady decline, as shown in figure 5-3.

The decline of American output during and after the Civil War did not have as serious an impact as was initially feared, due to the coincident depression in world cotton demand. This drop in demand resulted from the exhaustion of growth potential in the British textile industry, a development that according to Wright, was "largely independent" of the Civil War (1978, 94). While this depression certainly affected the incomes of Southern cotton producers,[22] fears about significant competition from foreign producers in the post–Civil War era were largely unwarranted.[23] Even though foreign cotton production had been given a permanent stimulus, particularly in India and Egypt, where crops tripled between 1870 and 1906 (Taylor and Taylor 1943, 15), for well into the twentieth century the world price of cotton continued to reflect almost directly the costs of producing, handling, and marketing American cotton (Rochester 1940, 216–17; Wright 1978, 90).

With the outbreak of World War I, the share of U.S. cotton in world exports again dropped because the United Kingdom, Germany, and France—the largest and steadiest importers—were all at war (Rochester 1940, 216). The absence of British and German vessels, which normally carried American exports, together with exorbitant shipping rates and wartime interference in export trade, clearly disrupted staple exports from the United States (Saloutos 1960, 238). However, this crisis was relatively short-lived. The entry of the United States into the war gave a boost to Southern agriculture, and American cotton producers benefited from high wartime prices.

For foreign textile manufacturers, the disruptions of the war years once again highlighted their dependence on American cotton. In the period between the two world wars, British capital, which was gradu-

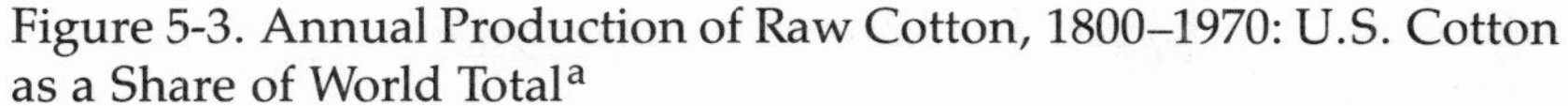

Figure 5-3. Annual Production of Raw Cotton, 1800–1970: U.S. Cotton as a Share of World Total[a]

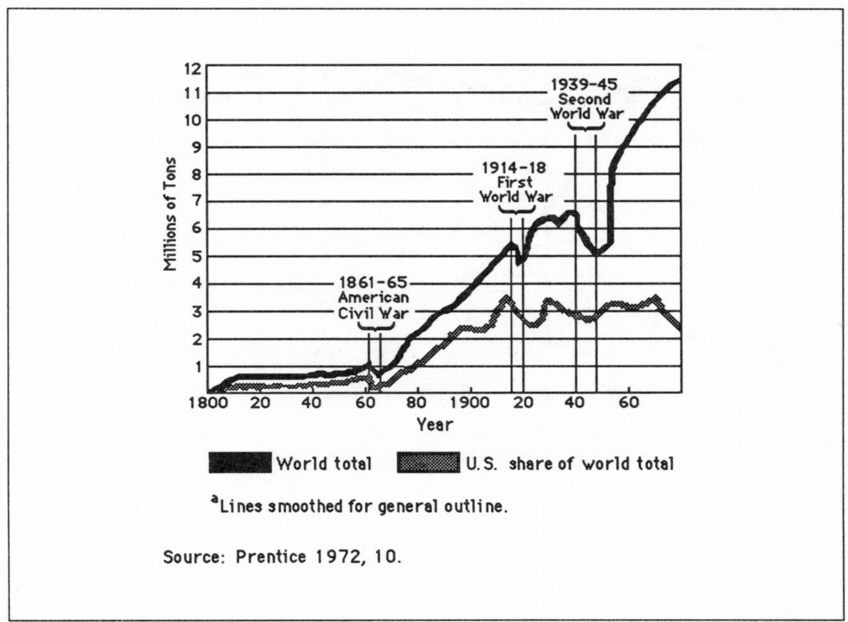


[a]Lines smoothed for general outline.

Source: Prentice 1972, 10.

ally yielding its supremacy in manufacturing to the cheaper textiles of Japan, looked toward greater imperial self-sufficiency by stimulating cotton production in areas of Africa under its control. Notable advances were made, particularly in the Sudan and Uganda, where top-quality cotton was grown on irrigated land (Prentice 1972, 13–14). Brazilian producers, prodded by Japanese capital, also substantially increased their cotton output (Rochester 1940, 217).

Despite the increase in production in other lands, on the eve of the Great Depression, the United States, Egypt, and India still maintained their leadership in cotton exporting. In 1928, these three countries combined accounted for 86 percent of total world cotton exports: Egypt exported practically its entire crop and accounted for 9 percent; India exported over half of its production and accounted for 19 percent; and the United States exported more than two-thirds of its crop and accounted for 58 percent (Taylor and Taylor 1943, 15).

As figure 5-4 indicates, with the onset of the depression, U.S. cotton prices fell precipitously, averaging about six cents per pound or less than one-third of their average price in the 1920s (Rochester 1940, 218). Yet although American cotton prices fell rapidly, this drop was

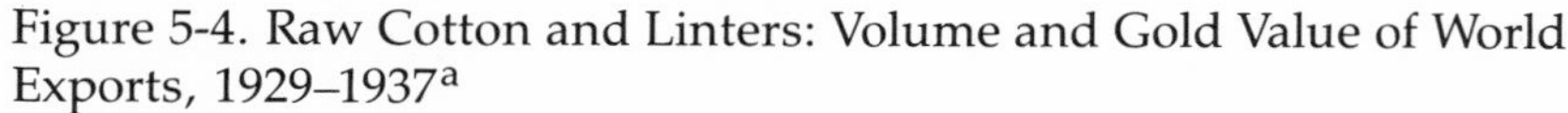
Figure 5-4. Raw Cotton and Linters: Volume and Gold Value of World Exports, 1929–1937[a]

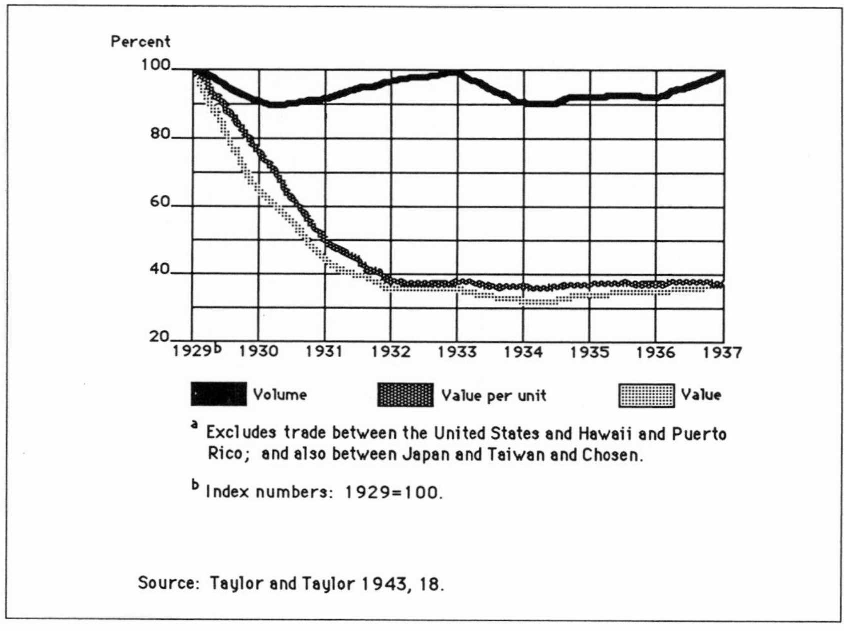


[a] Excludes trade between the United States and Hawaii and Puerto Rico; and also between Japan and Taiwan and Chosen.

[b] Index numbers: 1929=100.

Source: Taylor and Taylor 1943, 18.

not so great as that which occurred in the cases of Brazilian, Peruvian, and, particularly, Indian cotton (Taylor and Taylor 1943, 21).

This price differential, together with attempts by the U.S. government to buttress falling prices by initially holding American cotton stocks off the market and by inaugurating the AAA programs, contributed significantly to America's loss of foreign markets and increased competition from abroad (Rochester 1940, 218–23; Taylor and Taylor 1943, 21; Melman 1949, 61–62). For example, Japan, which by 1930 had succeeded in displacing the United Kingdom as the major importer of cotton, increased its imports of Indian cotton at the expense of the United States. Similarly Germany, which ranked third as a major importing country, began importing much of its cotton from Brazil. Between 1933 and 1938, the volume of total German cotton supplies imported from the United States dropped from 75 percent to 24 percent (Taylor and Taylor 1943, 20). Table 5-4 shows the decline in U.S. cotton exports and the rise in exports from other countries during the 1930s.

That the U.S. government intervention programs were the major factor at the root of this loss of foreign markets is given further substantiation by a similar experiment undertaken by the Egyptian government. In 1929 and 1930, when the Egyptian government followed a price-support policy similar to that of the later AAA programs, its exports, like those of the U.S., dropped sharply. However in 1933 and 1934, when the U.S. instituted strong cotton controls, the Egyptian government reversed its policy in favor of encouraging maximum production with no restrictions on output. Subsequent to this reversal in policy, Egypt's share of world cotton exports showed a general rise (Taylor and Taylor 1943, 22). Indeed, a report by the Egyptian government in 1936 explicitly notes how the American AAA programs aided their cotton exports: "We must acknowledge that our country has been very materially helped by the cotton policy of the American government. . . . We believe that, thanks to the American cotton experiment of the AAA, Egyptian cotton will replace to the maximum the requirements of the industry in medium and long staple cotton" (Taylor and Taylor 1943, 22).

The share of U.S. cotton in world exports dropped from an average of 57 percent in 1929–33, before the AAA controls were implemented, to an average of 42 percent in 1934–38, following the introduction of these agricultural policies (Taylor and Taylor 1943, 24). This marked the first time that U.S. cotton failed to provide more than half of the world's total supply (Rochester 1940, 216). In contrast, the combined exports of India, Egypt, Brazil, and Peru expanded from 28 percent to 40 percent in the same time periods, while total foreign production, excluding that of the U.S.S.R., increased by roughly 40 percent during the 1930s (Taylor and Taylor 1943, 24; Rochester 1940, 217). The Second World War only increased America's loss of foreign markets and the further expansion of cotton production in other areas, since German and Japanese import markets were cut off and Britain stockpiled large supplies of Egyptian, Brazilian, and Turkish cotton (Prentice 1972, 14; Rochester 1940, 223).

I have already discussed how the increased mechanization of American cotton production offset the effects of the U.S. government–enforced acreage reductions. However, mechanization played a dual role, since it also served to reduce production costs so as to keep American cotton competitive with foreign cotton production—particularly foreign production in underdeveloped countries, where relatively low wage rates prevailed and where cotton production had increased during the American cotton famine of the 1930s.

This is illustrated by Robson's comparison of estimates of the average costs of cotton production on mechanized farms in the United States and farms in Pakistan (Robson 1958, 83–85). In 1956, labor rates in Pakistan were approximately forty cents per day or approximately

Table 5-4. World Exports of Cotton by Country, 1909–1913 and 1924–1938 (in thousands of bales)

| Country | Average 1909–1913 | Average 1924–1928 | Average 1929–1933 | 1934 |
|---|---|---|---|---|
| Primary exporters | | | | |
| United States | 8,827 | 8,673 | 8,091 | 6,058 |
| India | 1,965 | 2,938 | 2,583 | 2,869 |
| Egypt | 1,444 | 1,462 | 1,471 | 1,776 |
| China | 240 | 295 | 221 | 97 |
| Peru | 88 | 217 | 231 | 309 |
| Turkey | 88 | 69 | 83 | 60 |
| Brazil | 83 | 69 | 106 | 586 |
| Argentina | 0 | 60 | 115 | 125 |
| Mexico | 0 | 97 | 32 | 18 |
| Secondary exporters | | | | |
| United Kingdom | 586 | 263 | 125 | 134 |
| France | 314 | 115 | 83 | 23 |
| Belgium | 263 | 14 | 51 | 129 |
| Germany | 212 | 254 | 341 | 231 |
| Netherlands | 143 | 0 | 0 | 0 |
| Japan | 0 | 198 | 189 | 157 |
| World | 14,616 | 15,291 | 14,428 | 13,493 |
| Total Exports of Listed Countries as Percentages of of World Exports | 97.5 | 96.3 | 95.3 | 93.2 |

Source: Taylor and Taylor 1943, 26.

one-fifteenth of those in the U.S. cotton belt (Robson 1958, 84). However, cotton farms in Pakistan required an average of 260 man-hours per acre, while mechanization on American farms had reduced the man-hours per acre to about 30, as compared to 160 on unmechanized American farms. Even with the higher price of skilled labor and the increased costs of machinery on the mechanized American farms, this reduction in man-hours per acre reduced the costs of production below the costs of unmechanized U.S. farms and to approximately the same level as the costs of production on Pakistani farms. Average labor costs per pound of cotton in Pakistan were about 6 cents, while the same costs on mechanized farms in the American Delta region were 6.4 cents per pound (Robson 1958, 83–85).

In turn, the virtual absence of expenditures on fertilizers, insecticides, and farm machinery in Pakistan were offset by the higher yields per acre in the United States (Robson 1958, 85). Consequently, total

| 1935 | 1936 | 1937 | 1938 | Average 1934–1938 |
|---|---|---|---|---|
| 6,170 | 5,653 | 6,071 | 4,578 | 5,706 |
| 2,634 | 3,339 | 3,051 | 2,146 | 2,808 |
| 1,777 | 1,616 | 1,844 | 1,645 | 1,732 |
| 145 | 170 | 176 | 630 | 244 |
| 355 | 369 | 374 | 323 | 346 |
| 69 | 101 | 52 | 119 | 80 |
| 639 | 924 | 1,089 | 1,239 | 895 |
| 168 | 227 | 58 | 103 | 136 |
| 123 | 240 | 43 | 102 | 105 |
| 156 | 128 | 125 | 96 | 128 |
| 30 | 19 | 18 | 14 | 21 |
| 142 | 144 | 170 | 177 | 152 |
| 190 | 34 | 0 | 0 | 91 |
| 0 | 3 | 2 | 3 | 2 |
| 194 | 266 | 237 | 19 | 175 |
| 13,775 | 14,361 | 14,846 | 12,566 | 13,808 |
| 92.9 | 92.1 | 89.7 | 89.1 | 91.4 |

costs of cotton production averaged around 18 cents per pound on Pakistani farms and 19.2 cents per pound on American mechanized farms. Both of these figures were lower than the average costs of production on unmechanized U.S. farms, thus knocking these farms and the sharecroppers who farmed them out of the cotton-growing competition (Robson 1958, 83–85).

These comparisons not only indicate the importance of mechanization for increasing labor productivity and keeping American cotton competitive on world markets; they also provide a number of insights into certain hypotheses made by dependency theorists. For example, because dependency theorists see the developed countries as exploiting the peripheral countries through unequal market exchanges, they have argued that the latter would experience their greatest economic development when their ties to the developed societies were the weakest, such as in times of war or depression (Frank 1970, 10).

From a cursory glance at changes in world cotton exports during the 1930s, it would appear that the peripheral producers' increased market shares would substantiate this hypothesis.

However, two factors undermine such a conclusion. First, the rise in the competitive position of peripheral cotton producers only occurred because the demand for cotton from textile producers in certain developed countries increased—a condition that calls into question whether there was in fact a weakening of the ties between the developed societies and the periphery. Second, it could be argued that crisis (in this case, the depression) fostered greater development among producers in the United States than it did among producers in any peripheral society. Indeed, American cotton production became more mechanized and experienced a significant increase in labor productivity. In contrast, peripheral producers only increased their market share but did not transform their labor-intensive, labor-repressive, and low-productivity forms of production. In this sense, many dependency theorists' equation of market shares or market activity with development is erroneous. Rather, as critics point out, changes in labor productivity provide a better indicator of development, which again suggests the importance of focusing on production relations over relations of exchange (Brenner 1977, 91).[24]

Moreover, as a result of the depression and the Second World War, other technological developments were occurring in the developed countries that compounded the problems faced by cotton producers both in the American South and in the peripheral formations. I shall now turn to an examination of these developments.

### *Competition from Substitutionism*

I discussed above how the New Deal agricultural programs and the Second World War had both internal and external implications for the transformation of American cotton production. Alongside the initial internal incentives to mechanize, resulting from acreage controls and subsequent wartime labor shortages, the loss of foreign markets gave an additional external impetus to American producers to increase the efficiency of cotton production through labor-saving technology and the replacement of sharecroppers by skilled, wage labor (Melman 1949, 59–61).

However, mechanization and the biological, chemical, and genetic advances that fostered the full mechanization of cotton production represent merely the social modification or reduction of natural obstacles to capitalist production—what Goodman, Sorj, and Wilkinson term "appropriationism." Far more radical implications for the future of cotton farming arose from "substitutionism," where the actual elimination of the natural rural base of production became at least a possibility, if not a reality, with the substitution of synthetic fibers for cotton (Goodman, Sorj, and Wilkinson 1987, 2–3 and 57–58).[25]

Yet not all fibers lumped under the heading of synthetics are totally devoid of an agricultural base, because these fibers include both vegetable and mineral products. For example, the earliest industrially produced fibers consisted of various types of rayon that all had agricultural roots: rayon viscose is made from wood pulp, while rayon acetate is made from cotton linters. Up until the 1950s, this group accounted for approximately 90 percent of the world's output of manufactured fibers (Hague 1957, 15). It was not until the 1930s that truly synthetic fibers, such as nylon, were developed for commercial use. These fibers were mineral or petroleum products created by a process known as polymerization or making plastics. Here plastic is forced through spinerettes to form a textile fiber.

As might be expected, the earliest developments in the synthetic fiber industry took place in the developed European countries, which were dependent on cotton imports for their textile production. France was first to produce rayon viscose fibers for commercial sale, achieving an output of about one million pounds by 1896. Subsequent developments were most rapid in Germany and the United Kingdom, the world's leading cotton importers at that time. By 1913, Germany accounted for one-third of world production of synthetic fibers, while the United Kingdom accounted for one-fourth, with France following in third place (Robson 1958, 46).

Within each of these countries the process of making synthetic fibers was initially controlled by one firm that not only dominated domestic production but also established subsidiaries in other countries (Robson 1958, 46). Hence, developments in synthetic fiber industries outside Europe were originally based entirely on European patents and generally under the direction of European firms. Even in the United States, which would later become a world leader in synthetic fibers, the first company—the American Viscose Corporation—was established by Courtaulds of France, which held a monopoly over production until its patent expired in 1920 (Robson 1958, 47–48).

Rayon viscose was the first synthetic fiber to compete with natural fibers. However, since silk was more expensive than cotton and because of the continuous nature of rayon threads, rayon producers in the pre-1914 era concentrated on the production of artificial silk (Tisdell and McDonald 1979, 1). The first substantial increase in rayon output occurred in 1912, when rayon was introduced into the hosiery trade ostensibly to compete with silk.[26] The unexpected but actual outcome of this fiber competition was that rayon replaced cotton in hosiery production, leaving the higher-priced silk-based commodities unaffected (Robson 1958, 22).

During the First World War, the acetate process was developed for commercial use. The first use of acetate was for nonflammable coatings for airplane wings and fuselages. Yarn production followed at a greatly accelerated rate with the end of the war: world production of rayon filament textile yarns increased by 45 percent per annum between 1920 and 1925, as compared to a mere 5 percent per annum increase in the five years preceding the war (Robson 1958, 15). This rapid expansion occurred despite the fact that conditions in the postwar era did not encourage the use of rayon on a large scale in textile industries. On the one hand, the postwar slump had reduced cotton prices considerably below their prewar levels. On the other, the quality of synthetic fibers at this time did not pose a serious threat to cotton producers in most branches of the textile industry.

A completely new attack on the natural fiber markets came in the 1930s with the development of both nylon and rayon staple. Nylon was invented in 1927 at the Du Pont plant in the United States and was developed for commercial use by the mid-1930s. Its strength, elasticity, and fineness made it especially suitable for hosiery, and it almost completely displaced silk by the end of World War II (Robson 1958, 32).[27] However, on the cotton-spinning system—the principal outlet for raw cotton—rayon staple became the major synthetic fiber used (Robson 1958, 33). This synthetic fiber was developed in Britain in the mid-1920s and experienced a major increase in production and consumption during the 1930s, when the U.S. government introduced cotton acreage controls.[28]

As table 5-5 shows, world rayon staple production was 27 times greater in 1935 than in 1929 and increased again almost tenfold between 1935 and 1938. The expansion of rayon staple production was particularly great in Germany, Italy, and Japan, mainly owing to their policies of increasing self-sufficiency by reducing their dependence on foreign cotton imports (Robson 1958, 23). By 1939, these countries accounted for more than 60 percent of the world's production of both filament and staple rayon and 80 percent of world rayon staple fiber production (Robson 1958, 24–25). Total world production of both filament and staple rayon yarns increased from 35 million pounds in 1923 to 1,000 million pounds in 1935 and doubled to almost 2,000 million pounds between 1935 and 1938 (Moncrieff 1954, 430). As might be expected, this enormous expansion in production was accompanied by a decline in the price of rayon. In both the United States and the

Table 5-5. Average Yearly World Production of Rayon Staple Yarn

| Year | Average Production of Rayon Staple Yarn (in millions of pounds) |
|---|---|
| 1929 | 5 |
| 1935 | 138 |
| 1936 | 300 |
| 1937 | 625 |
| 1938 | 930 |

Source: Moncrieff 1954, 430. Reprinted with permission of Butterworth & Company (Publishers) Ltd.

United Kingdom, rayon prices were more than halved between 1930 and 1939 (Moncrieff 1954, 436).

Another boost to the synthetic fiber industries came with the outbreak of World War II. Up until the late 1930s, these fibers had been used almost entirely for apparel and household textiles. However, during the war years, synthetics proved their adequacy in the face of wartime shortages and the needs of military procurements. In particular, nylon production increased dramatically during and immediately following the war: production increased by 600 percent between 1940 and 1944 and increased by another 400 percent between 1945 and 1950 (Moncrieff 1954, 432). Major innovations also occurred in the rayon industry with the development of special high-tenacity types of rayon viscose, which had twice the strength of standard viscose. This enabled rayon to invade the industrial markets where strength and durability were important. In particular, the advantages of this high-tenacity rayon viscose for tire yarn were so marked that by 1956 rayon had virtually replaced cotton in tire production (Robson 1958, 26–28).

The rise in the price of natural staple fibers during the war, coupled with a decline in the relative costs of producing higher quality synthetic fibers, only served to increase the competitive strength of the rayon staple. Table 5-6 presents a comparison of average cotton and rayon prices from 1930 until 1954 and documents the importance of the war years for rayon's transition to competitive price superiority. As a result of these developments, firms that had introduced rayon into their yarns or fabrics during the Second World War, when high cotton prices prevailed, did not substantially reduce the percentage of synthetic fibers they used even in the face of subsequent reductions in the price of cotton (Hague 1957, 219).

The war years also witnessed a reversal in the prewar pattern of foreign domination of the synthetic fiber production. Since American industries escaped the war damage experienced in other countries,

Table 5-6. Average Cotton and Viscose Rayon Staple Prices

| | Annual Averages in Pence per Pound | |
|---|---|---|
| Year | American Middling Cotton[a] | Viscose Rayon Staple[b] |
| 1930 | 6.0 | 36.0[c] |
| 1931 | 5.5 | 30.4 |
| 1932 | 5.3 | 26.6 |
| 1933 | 5.5 | 23.2 |
| 1934 | 6.1 | 18.0 |
| 1935 | 6.8 | 14.5 |
| 1936 | 6.8 | 11.0 |
| 1937 | 6.4 | 11.0 |
| 1938 | 5.1 | 10.9 |
| 1939 | 5.9 | 10.2 |
| 1945 | 12.4 | 14.0 |
| 1946 | 13.8 | 14.0 |
| 1947 | 20.3 | 14.8 |
| 1948 | 22.8 | 16.5 |
| 1949 | 25.0 | 18.0 |
| 1950 | 35.9 | 18.5 |
| 1951 | 46.4 | 24.9 |
| 1952 | 39.2 | 26.8 |
| 1953 | 31.9 | 25.5 |
| 1954 | 33.0 | 24.0 |

Source: Calculated from data in Hague 1957, 37, and Robson 1958, 88.

[a] Spot Liverpool—allow 2 pence for delivery to mill.

[b] Delivered to mill.

[c] The excise duty of 6 pence per pound on rayon staple was imposed in 1925, reduced to 3 pence per pound in 1934, and abolished in 1935.

the production of American synthetic fibers doubled. In contrast, production remained virtually stationary in the United Kingdom, whereas in Germany, Italy, and Japan production was reduced to approximately one-tenth of previous levels. By 1946 the United States accounted for over one-half of world production of rayon compared with only 18 percent in 1939 (Robson 1958, 36). As early as 1951, the U.S. dominated world nylon production, boasting more than 85 percent of total world production. In addition, during and immediately after the war, there was a dramatic change in the ownership of synthetic fiber industries with the important interests of American-based European firms being taken over by U.S. citizens. At the same time, American corporations began to develop nylon subsidiaries in other countries, also reversing the prewar pattern of neocolonialism and multinational development (Robson 1958, 48–49).

Table 5-7. Rayon Production by Country, 1951[a]

| | Rayon Production (in millions of pounds) | | |
|---|---|---|---|
| Country | Continuous Filament | Staple Fiber | Total |
| U.S. | 951 | 336 | 1,294 |
| Germany | 154 | 618 | 772 |
| United Kingdom | 217 | 167 | 384 |
| Japan | 138 | 231 | 369 |
| Italy | 144 | 145 | 289 |
| France | 126 | 109 | 229 |
| Austria | 3 | 91 | 94 |
| U.S.S.R. | 50 | 40 | 90 |
| Netherlands | 54 | 25 | 79 |
| Poland | 25 | 40 | 65 |
| Belgium | 27 | 37 | 64 |
| Czechoslovakia | 12 | 50 | 62 |
| Canada | 40 | 17 | 57 |
| Spain | 22 | 30 | 52 |
| Brazil | 40 | 9 | 49 |
| Switzerland | 21 | 20 | 41 |

Source: Moncrieff 1954, 431. Reprinted with permission of Butterworth & Company (Publishers) Ltd.

[a] Many other countries produce smaller quantities.

Despite these setbacks for foreign producers, in the initial postwar era the production of rayon increased most rapidly in Germany, Italy, Japan, and France (Moncrieff 1954, 431). During the 1950s, the rate of increase in the production of other synthetic fibers was also much greater in Western Europe and Japan than in the United States (Robson 1958, 36–38). Table 5-7 shows the leading synthetic fiber–producing countries in 1951. In terms of continuous filament production, the United States accounted for more than the other five leading countries combined. However, in the case of staple fiber production, which served as a direct substitute for cotton, Germany produced almost twice as much as the United States, with Japan and the United Kingdom following in the third and fourth positions respectively—the greater interest of these foreign countries in staple fiber production, of course, reflecting their greater dependence on cotton imports.

Once relative price and quality turned in favor of rayon staple fibers, as they did during the war years, major advantages were derived from substituting synthetic fibers for cotton. These advantages reflect the serious natural obstacles that certain crops present to capitalists' ability to efficiently manipulate and control the production process so as to make adequate profits. For example, with synthetic fibers it is possible to produce a fiber with constant staple length—a condition not met in the case of either cotton or wool (Hague 1957, 217). This greatly enhances the ability of capitalists to standardize production processes and to save on costs. Also, because all natural fibers are mixed with dirt and other impurities, many of the operations in cotton spinning mills have to be concerned with cleaning the fibers. Since synthetic fibers were neither dirty nor closely packed, their production resulted in further savings (Hague 1957, 221).

In addition, while the nonidentity of production time and labor time creates numerous problems for cotton farmers in terms of the underutilization of labor and machinery, the synthetic fiber industries are based on continuous production. Indeed, both the higher capital costs and the nature of the process of spinning synthetic fibers from a solution or melt require continuous processing. In the 1950s, if the production process was stopped for any period of time, it would take an entire day to start it up again. Thus, maximum productivity demanded that labor be continuously applied in production by shift work and the absence of night or weekend stoppages (Moncrieff 1954, 435). Contrast this to the situation faced by Southern sharecroppers in the early 1930s, when average labor requirements on specialized cotton farms were only 110 days of work a year (Kirby 1987, 62).

Still other obstacles are presented by the climatic and spatial requirements of land-based agricultural commodities and are reflected in the fact that many natural fibers can be grown only in certain locales. In contrast, synthetic fibers can be produced in close proximity to textile mills, thereby reducing transportation costs. For example, in the 1950s, importing raw cotton to the United Kingdom from the United States or western Africa cost approximately 4 pence per pound or almost one-seventh of the cost of the cotton itself—a cost that could largely be avoided when fibers are industrially produced (Robson 1958, 86).

Natural fibers are also far more susceptible to the vagaries of the weather or pest infestations that can affect regularities in supplies and precipitate violent price fluctuations. By contrast, the prices of synthetic fibers were much more stable (Moncrieff 1954, 428; Tisdell and McDonald 1979, 39). Such price stability presented a significant advantage to yarn and fabric producers, who could plan their future output with greater precision and guarantee prices farther in advance of purchase (Hague 1957, 217–18).

Price stability has also been attributed to the fact that the synthetic fiber industries are organized in an oligopolistic fashion and hence could be better regulated and controlled than a multitude of small producers (Prentice 1972, 17). By the 1950s, of the eight leading rayon-producing countries, only one country—Japan—had more than ten companies involved in rayon production (Robson 1948, 49–51). By 1974, the major companies involved in synthetic fiber production were among the leading corporations in the world—the top seven synthetic fiber industries ranking among the top fifty corporations in terms of sales (Tisdell and McDonald 1979, 38).

The oligopolistic nature of the synthetic fiber industry is in part a product of monopolies on patents (Tisdell and McDonald 1979, 37). However, even more important in explaining the high degree of concentration and centralization found in this industry are the immense capital costs required for research and development, plant and equipment, and marketing. For example, in the development of nylon, the American company Du Pont spent $45 million on research, $21 million on sales investigation, and $196 million on plant equipment (Moncrieff 1954, 435).

While synthetic fiber production has been vertically integrated primarily by petrochemical companies, there has been virtually no vertical integration of those fibers which rely on natural raw materials for their productive base. In the case of Southern cotton, there has been little or no integration of cotton farms and textile mills. Even in the case of rayon viscose, which is made from wood pulp, vertical integration proved both rare and unprofitable. These failures were attributed to the lengthy production time of trees, the immobility of production sites, the high costs of land, and the underutilization of labor (Robson 1958, 65).[29] Hence, the organizational structure and the competitive success of the synthetic fiber industries were in part due to the fact that these industries mitigated or transcended certain natural impediments to capitalist accumulation that characterize land-based fiber production.

Moreover, as figure 5-5 indicates, the timing of the major expansions in synthetic fiber production—particularly the expansion of rayon staple production, which served as a direct substitute for cotton—coincided with the various social and economic problems faced by American cotton producers in the 1930s. From small beginnings in the predepression era, the synthetic fiber industries expanded at an astonishing rate in the following decades. The development and commercial production of acrylic fibers and polyesters in the 1950s only heightened the competition presented in earlier decades by nylon and rayon.[30] All of the synthetic fiber industries spurred cotton producers to increase the efficiency of their productive units in order for them to remain competitive in a world economy where domestic and foreign producers were developing adequate substitutes for cotton. Yet even

Figure 5-5. World Production of Man-Made Fibers, 1900–1960

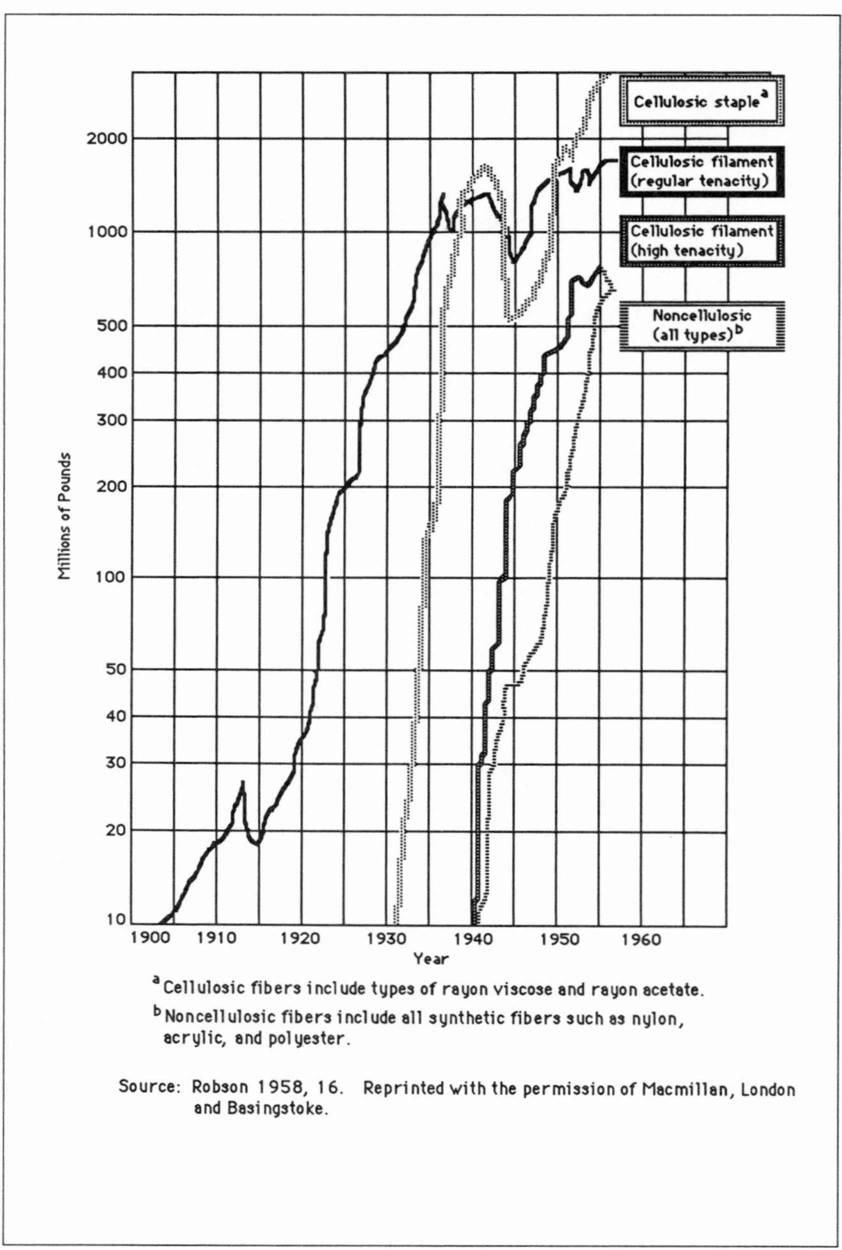


[a] Cellulosic fibers include types of rayon viscose and rayon acetate.

[b] Noncellulosic fibers include all synthetic fibers such as nylon, acrylic, and polyester.

Source: Robson 1958, 16. Reprinted with the permission of Macmillan, London and Basingstoke.

with mechanization and the employment of skilled wage labor, natural fibers could not keep pace with the new industrial substitutes. While world cotton production rose in absolute terms in response to increased world consumption, synthetic fibers supplied a sixth (by weight) of world textile needs in the early 1950s, a third by the mid-1960s, and had taken over the lead from cotton in the 1970s (Prentice 1972, 17).

## *Conclusion*

Historians have used a variety of terms to capture the essence of what has been called the "quiet revolution" in Southern agriculture (quoted in Fite 1984, 220). As I noted above, writers like Kirby (1987) and Daniel (1985) highlight its features as a "Southern enclosure," while Wright describes the economic transformation of the region as primarily a result of the "effective destruction" of the formerly isolated "low-wage southern labor market" (Wright 1986, 16). In my view, however, these disparate descriptions simply apply to various stages of the development of capitalism in Southern agriculture, from its early stage of primitive accumulation through enclosure and displacement of tenants, to its hegemony as the Southern labor market became more fully incorporated into the dominant mode of production following the revolutionary shift from nonwage to wage labor.[31]

This chapter has examined the integral relationships between the domestic and international factors that contributed to this historic economic transition in the South. It highlighted how the transformation of social class relations in Southern cotton production could not be analyzed independently of developments in the world economy—particularly since American cotton played such a dominant role in world fiber production and consumption. By doing so, it underlined the limitations of many existing studies of the postdepression rural South that use the nation-state as the unit of analysis.

I also argued that existing studies of the postdepression rural South are limited by their failure to understand the capitalist development of Southern cotton production within the context of landowners' abilities to minimize, reduce, or transcend certain natural obstacles to capitalist development. Indeed, the conquest of the natural foundations of cotton production required the combined force of mechanical, biological, and chemical advances. Most importantly, the development of a viable mechanical harvester required surpassing the natural barriers established by the peculiar external and internal features of the cotton plant. In turn, major advances in herbicides and pesticides reduced many of the problems associated with weed and insect control.

Together, all of these technological advances resulted in a more continuous use of labor throughout the productive cycle, smoothing out the jagged peaks and valleys of unskilled labor demand that had plagued the former sharecropping system. In addition, problems arising from the nonidentity of production time and labor time were further reduced by crop diversification. Diversification better synchronized the labor requirements of different agricultural commodities, increased total labor time, and resulted in the more efficient employment of labor and machinery throughout the year. Hence, as in the case of Southwestern cotton production, mechanization in the postdepression Southeast was accompanied by the replacement of family labor by wage labor—a finding that further undermines those theories that view labor-saving technology as the savior of family labor farms (Nikolitch 1969; Dovring 1965, 136).

The "quiet revolution" in the Old South also illustrated how certain social obstacles to capitalist development were modified, reduced, or eliminated. In particular, this chapter showed the important role the state can play in fostering or impeding social change. In the predepression era, local state governments impeded capitalist development by helping to maintain a number of repressive and regressive controls over black labor. They also serviced the noncapitalist landowning class by failing to break the back of the usurious crop-liens system, which tied laborers to the land. In contrast, governments in other regions and countries successfully eliminated credit monopolies hindering rural development.[32] It took the initiative of the federal government to begin the process of capitalist development in the Old South by providing capital incentives to mechanize and to shift to wage labor. However, the federal government achieved these revolutionary outcomes by allying with large landowners rather than alienating them—an alliance that is typical of patterns found in comparative studies of modernization and development resulting from "revolutions from above" (Moore 1966). Hence, the landowning class was the true beneficiary of the "quiet revolution" in Southern agriculture, even though in the process this rentier class was itself transformed into a class of capitalist farmers. The rise of these capitalist farmers, along with the replacement of sharecroppers by wage labor, more fully incorporated the rural South into the capitalist mode of production.

Social obstacles to capitalist development were also transcended through disruptions in the international cotton trade. The Civil War and, to a greater extent, the depression and both world wars fostered cotton production in areas outside of the United States and put pressure on Southern farmers to increase the efficiency of their production units. These disruptions of American cotton exports also spurred foreign textile producers to develop synthetic substitutes for cotton, adding pressure to the fiber competition. The Second World War, in particular, gave an immense boost to technological developments in fiber production—both natural and synthetic—if the advances in the production of synthetic fibers are considered alongside the advances in Southern agricultural technologies. That these crises fostered more economic development in developed countries than in peripheral countries contradicts certain predictions made by dependency theorists.[33]

Moreover, the competitive advantages of synthetic over natural fibers illustrates yet again how the unpredictability of nature can present problems to capitalist production. With synthetic fibers, constant staple length, the absence of dirt and impurities, the continuous nature of production, and greater price stability all served to reduce costs and to increase capitalists' ability to plan, predict, augment, or curtail production with more precision and less risk. The fact that natural fibers could not keep pace with these industrial substitutes in the world fiber competition reflects the contradictions between the predictability and standardization required by capitalism and the unpredictability and capriciousness of nature.

Externally, competition from both synthetic fibers and low-priced foreign cotton increased the pressure on Southern landowners to replace sharecropping with machinery and skilled wage labor, a process already initiated internally by the U.S. federal government controls on cotton production and the labor shortages created by World War II. Indeed, it appears that breaking the back of the well-entrenched Southern sharecropping system and transcending the social and natural obstacles to capitalist development required the historical conjuncture and combined force of all of these factors.

# Six

# The Civilization of Nature

> The moral of history . . . is that the capitalist system works against a rational agriculture, or that a rational agriculture is incompatible with the capitalist system . . . and needs either the hand of the small farmer living by his own labor or the control of associated producers.
> —Karl Marx, *Capital* (1894)

Capitalist development is neither invincible nor inevitable. Indeed, contrary to the expectations of many nineteenth- and twentieth-century social theorists, characterizations of capitalism as a mode of production that can easily sweep aside all obstacles to its expansion have little validity in the light of the uneven development of the modern world. Throughout this book I have argued that when capital is unable to modify or transcend certain natural barriers to its development, these spheres are left in the hands of petty commodity producers or other nonwage forms of production. In this sense, the survival and revival of nonwage forms of production in the modern era are "anomalous necessities" that often reveal industrial capitalists' inability to subordinate nature to their own production requirements.[1]

The root of this contradiction between capitalism and nature is social and lies in the characteristics of the commodity form. The commodity is the most elementary form of the product of labor in capitalist society, and it is for this reason that Marx began *Capital* with an analysis of commodities. He then went on to discuss how each commodity has an exchange value that is realized on the market and a use value that is realized in either personal or productive consumption (1967a, 43–87). While most analyses of the new sociology of agriculture recognize these basic features of commodity production, many still do not recognize the implications of this analysis for spheres of production centered in nature.

I have already discussed Marx's views on how the form a commodity takes as an exchange value can affect the ease of marketing and, thereby, influence the realization of profits. Here, perishable produce and the oddly shaped products of nature present different problems to commodity producers as compared with producers who are simply engaged in production for use. Indeed, the wonder of nature where no two objects are alike contrasts sharply with the standardization of commodities preferred by the market. While these problems have been minimized over the last century by developments in the food-processing, food preservation, and transportation industries, any capitalist or noncapitalist commodity producer confronts these problems in the sphere of circulation.

Yet, while these marketing concerns plague all commodity producers, what is distinct about capitalist production is the existence of *generalized* commodity production, where all means of production have become commoditized. Consequently, unlike nonwage forms of commodity production, capitalism entails "the production of commodities by commodities" (Kloppenburg 1988, 22–23). Here the form the commodity takes in production is as much a concern as the form it takes in marketing. This is where capitalist production and nonwage forms of commodity production diverge. Indeed, it is this integral relationship between the form of the commodity produced and the full and efficient productive consumption of the use values of all means of production, including labor power, that can present obstacles to the capitalist development of agriculture.

Yet even after private property and private profits are abolished, socialist modes of production still entail commodity production. Consequently, the question also arises as to what role natural obstacles play under socialist modes of production. Marx implies in the quote at the beginning of this chapter that socialism or "the control of associated producers" could overcome natural impediments to rural modernization. Similarly, I have argued in a previous work that once the rate of profit is no longer the major objective determinant of socioeconomic organization, these natural obstacles "need not play a role in fostering the uneven or unequal relations among people" (Mann 1982, 262).

On the one hand, such deductions seem reasonable because under socialism, political decisions, rather than private profit and/or market determinations, can govern production. Therefore, a change in the social organization of a particular branch of agriculture could take place for social or political reasons, irrespective of the profitability of that change, so long as this transformation could be subsidized (if necessary) by another sector of the economy. It is in this way, for instance, that the Soviet Union kept the price of bread low for decades after the Second World War, despite changes in the market situation.

On the other hand, socialist economies are not oblivious to market determinations or to issues of efficiency and productivity. Moreover, many commodities produced in these economies compete on world markets with commodities produced by capitalist and noncapitalist producers. Since these commodities are subject to world market determinations, the question arises as to what role natural features of the agrarian production process play, both domestically and in terms of global economic relations for socialist modes of production.

This question is even more intriguing because the early debates over the collectivization of agriculture were premised not only on the greater social equality that would arise from the abolition of private property in land, but also on the greater efficiency that could be derived from replacing family labor enterprises with large-scale units of production based on wage labor. It was argued that these larger collective units could introduce a more highly specialized division of labor, make better use of labor and machinery, and thereby increase agricultural productivity. However, in practice these arguments about the superiority of collectivized agriculture failed in many cases to be realized. Moreover, in theory, these arguments mirror some of the same assumptions about the superiority of large-scale, factory-style production that guided many social theorists in their claims about the superiority of capitalist enterprise. Consequently, I am questioning whether the debates over the collectivization of agriculture also failed to consider seriously Marx's writings about the problems generated by the natural features of certain branches of agriculture—particularly since these natural obstacles preclude the specialization and the continuous use of labor and machinery that can operate in other spheres of large-scale production.

Contemporary data on agriculture in socialist economies suggest the coexistence of a variety of forms of production. For example, in some Eastern European countries, family farms still make up a sizable proportion of the agrarian sector. Moreover, the socialized sector of agriculture often receives considerable subsidies from other sectors of the economy, which also suggests problems with the efficiency and economic viability of collective farms (Goodman and Redclift 1982, 21–23). While there certainly could be social and political reasons for the maintenance of family farming in these socialist countries, it would be interesting to examine the role natural features of the production process play under this very different mode of production.

It is also interesting to consider the implications of the Mann-Dickinson thesis for societal institutions other than the economy. Toward this end, I shall briefly examine how this theory could be used to enhance our understanding of both the household and the state in developed capitalist societies. Since the triumvirate of institutions embodied in the household, the economy, and the state constitute the productive and reproductive moments of capitalist society as a totality, the analysis below, while only suggestive, should significantly broaden the parameters of future research on nonwage labor.

## The Household

Along with agriculture, the other major sphere of nonwage labor in developed societies is the labor carried out on a daily basis in individual households. Household or domestic labor is responsible for the production and reproduction of labor power at the *individual level*. This has two distinct moments. The first is the intergenerational replacement of members of society through childbearing and child rearing. The second is the day-to-day rejuvenation of the labor force through preparing meals, providing emotional support, and maintaining a household environment sufficiently secure and sanitary for both the physical and psychological renewal of labor power.

Although almost everyone has performed some of this labor, prior to the rise of the modern feminist movement in the 1960s and 1970s, this sphere of *nonwage labor* remained virtually "hidden in the household." Indeed, the famous "domestic labor debates" of the late 1960s and early 1970s were concerned primarily with how capitalism intersected with the household, much in the same way that the Marxist-Narodnik debates had been concerned with how capitalism intersected with agriculture (Benston 1969; Seccombe 1973 and 1975; Gardiner 1975; Silveira 1975; Fox 1980). Yet outside of the field of women's studies, few theorists of nonwage labor paid attention to these developments. Even today, only a few writers in the new sociology of agriculture have made any links between these two important spheres of production (Blumenfeld and Mann 1980; Flora 1981 and 1985; Long 1984; von Werlhof 1985; Rosenfeld 1985; Friedmann 1986; Mies, Bennholdt-Thomsen, and von Werlhof 1988).

Prior to the feminist movement, it was common for mainstream sociology to portray the modern household primarily as a unit of consumption.[2] In contrast, feminist writers pointed out how the household was also a unit of *production* that placed women in a structurally different and unequal position to men (Benston 1969; Rowbotham 1973). It also placed some women in a different structural position from other women, since certain households are wealthy enough to hire domestic servants. However, because our interest is in nonwage forms of production, the analysis below only focuses on households in which family members perform the majority of domestic labor, and these nonwage domestic production units comprise most of the households in modern society.

Feminists also pointed out how the "modern" household was, in fact, not so modern, but rather had many traditional or "preindustrial" characteristics that fostered inequalities between men and women. For example, the absence of direct wage payments places housewives or homemakers in a structurally dependent position on persons (usually husbands and fathers) employed outside of the home.[3] The absence of a highly specialized division of labor means that domestic laborers perform innumerable petty, nonspecialized, and overlapping tasks—none of which are considered "real work" because they are outside of the market. As under petty commodity production, family members often own their domestic means of production, such as stoves, refrigerators, and other household appliances, and they also provide the labor for this production unit. That is, even though women perform the greatest part (approximately 70 percent) of domestic labor,[4] there is still a division of labor by sex and age in most households, where men and children perform certain domestic tasks. Moreover, like preindustrial laborers, homemakers' production is often for immediate use rather than for exchange, because under capitalism's pervasive market economy the commodities produced by the household are increasingly reduced to one—labor power (Blumenfeld and Mann 1980, 278 and 281).

However, this one commodity—labor power—is the most important commodity in capitalist production precisely because it is the only commodity that produces surplus value. Hence, capitalism is faced with a "profound contradiction," since the commodity upon which capitalist accumulation is predicated continues to be produced noncapitalistically within the confines of individual households (Blumenfeld and Mann 1980, 302). Moreover, the fact that women have primary responsibility for the production and reproduction of this most valuable commodity suggests even further contradictions. As Simone de Beauvoir writes: "It is outrageously paradoxical to deny women all activity in public affairs, . . . to assert her incapacity in all fields of effort, and then to entrust to her the most delicate and the most serious undertaking of all: the molding of a human being" (de Beauvoir 1952, 494).

As these contradictions within contradictions became more apparent to feminist readers and writers, a number of feminist theorists focused their attention on why capitalism had not penetrated the household and what economic roles domestic labor played under capitalism. A variety of answers were given to these questions. Most answers coming from both Marxist and feminist perspectives are reminiscent of the dependency theories discussed above, because they view nonwage forms of labor—in this case domestic labor—as functional to capitalism and as providing an alternative means of extracting surplus value. Here, for example, capitalists are portrayed as extracting value or "superprofits" from domestic labor's unpaid contribution to the value of labor power, and domestic laborers are considered part of the unemployed "reserve army" that keeps wages low and the capitalist system functioning in times of war or crisis (Benston 1969; Gardiner 1975; Fox 1980; Mies, Bennholdt-Thomsen, and von Werlhof 1988).

By contrast, Emily Blumenfeld and I offered a different, but complementary, argument that used the Mann-Dickinson thesis to explain why many of the tasks that make up domestic labor had not been taken over by capitalist enterprise (Blumenfeld and Mann 1980). We argued, for instance, that household tasks like cooking, housecleaning, and washing or drying laundry involve noticeable gaps between production time and labor time, because none of these tasks are done on a continuous basis throughout the entire day. Just as in the case of farm machinery, household appliances are employed on an irregular or sporadic basis and, hence, are used inefficiently. In turn, household labor, like farm labor, must shift from task to task in order to be fully utilized throughout the day.

To better understand these problems, consider the gap between production time and labor time involved in the transformation of raw or frozen foods into edible meals. During actual cooking time, food is "abandoned to the sway of natural processes," and labor is only used sporadically to check on the progress of the meal.[5] In recent years, this gap has been reduced by new technological advances. For example, the attraction of microwave ovens and the new self-regulating "crockpots" that reduce heat or turn on and off automatically reflect the normal inconvenience of waiting for or constantly supervising the cooking of foods that require relatively lengthy production times, such as stews or roast beef (Blumenfeld and Mann 1980, 294).

Yet even with such advanced technology, the continuous use of labor and machinery in cooking is also precluded by the social and physiological rhythms of the human eating cycle. Unlike in commercial stock production, there are no shortcuts such as forced feeding or fast-fattening processes developed for the human species. Rather, our eating habits are temporally structured, both by our physiology and by such social factors as work and culture. The intervals between meals introduce a sporadic and noncontinuous nature to the production process of food, which does not encourage capitalist development that actually *competes in terms of relative prices* with domestic food preparation. That is, while there are many capitalist restaurants existing in the modern world, few of these restaurants have actually reduced the socially necessary labor time needed to produce edible meals below the costs of petty-producing domestic labor (Blumenfeld and Mann 1980, 294).

The exceptions to my argument are the new and cheap fast-food chains. Not only have such fast-food giants as McDonalds or Burger King minimized the gap between labor and production time by producing foods that have a very short production time, but they also produce only certain foods, such as hamburgers, fries, and salads, that are more amenable to being eaten at any time of the day.[6] In short, what McDonalds has accomplished under the guise of "doing it all for you" is reducing the unproductive gaps that the normal housewife experiences in the intervals within and between meal production. Future projections suggest both a widening and a deepening of the capitalist development of fast foods, with increased capital investments in fast-food operations; competitive advertising shifting its focus to the nutritional quality of fast foods; and production branching out into new areas, such as ethnic specialties.[7] These developments indicate that capital has conquered many obstacles to competing with household food preparation. However, the relative youth of the fast-food industries, in terms of being only a few decades old, is testimony to the relatively problematic nature of this sphere of production (Blumenfeld and Mann 1980, 294–95).

And how about the production of people—the ultimate source of labor power? Only a few decades ago one would likely have said that the reproduction of the human species is so circumscribed by nature that prospects for the social transformation of this production process are severely limited. However, the new developments in reproductive technology, first used in livestock production, are now being used for human infertility problems. Such developments as artificial insemination, in vitro fertilization, surrogate mothering, and gender preselection, portend all kinds of new possibilities in this arena.

However, whatever scientific developments occur in the sphere of childbearing, there is still a qualitative and inalienable aspect to child rearing, which is an intrinsic part of the process of becoming human, even though this process is often distorted.[8] This qualitative and inalienable aspect of child rearing involves the affective or emotional relations between adult and child that preclude either machinery or the impersonal cash nexus of the labor market from substituting for specific or "significant" human agents in this process.[9]

Nevertheless, the very fact that such affective relations, such "labors of love," are part and parcel of domestic labor also suggests how the petty and disparate tasks that comprise domestic labor contradict, yet are necessary to, one another. That is, in domestic labor, as contrasted to work outside the home, it is far more likely for intimate relations with people to interrupt relations with things, and each requires a different mode of reaction. A plate can be smashed to the floor in a moment of frustration and anger with little consequence, but not so a child. Such interruptions of emotions and human relations at every turn not only help make the household a major arena of violence in our society, they also create obstacles to replicating the impersonal, continuous, task-oriented nature of capitalist production (Blumenfeld and Mann 1980, 300–301). Eli Zaretsky recognized this when he wrote: "The family attuned to the 'natural' rhythms of eating, sleeping, and childcare can never be wholly synchronized with the mechanized tempo of industrial capitalism" (Zaretsky 1973, 49).

In sum, Blumenfeld and I argued that the gaps between production time and labor time, the difficulties with synchronizing the petty and sporadic tasks entailed in domestic work, the absence of a specialized and nonoverlapping division of labor, and the essential requirement of affective relations for human health and well-being create innumerable obstacles to the full incorporation of domestic labor into capitalist commodity production. While rudimentary, this analysis presents an entirely new way of looking at the relationships between the household and the economy, as well as the relationships between men and women. Ironically, as in traditional analyses of gender, where biology is destiny, nature again plays a role in determining gender differences in our analysis. However, it is no longer the nature of body and soul, but rather the nature in different modes of work that is the critical issue.

## *The Capitalist State*

The analysis of the household above shows how capitalism is faced by a major contradiction, given the continued production of its most valuable commodity in a noncapitalist fashion. Similarly, an analysis of the state also reveals a significant contradiction involving nonwage labor. Here, however, the contradiction is slightly different. That is, in one of the most highly developed capitalist societies to date—the United States—a sector of the economy marked by an inordinately large number of noncapitalist forms of production—agriculture—receives a disproportionately large share of largess from the capitalist state.[10] As one observer notes: "Farming probably has received more special government solicitude over the last fifty years than any other sector of the economy" (Chapman 1979, 16–17).

Moreover, this "special government solicitude" was practiced long before the rise of the expensive agricultural price-support programs established during the New Deal. Consider the following examples:

- The U.S. Department of Agriculture, established in 1862, was the first government agency created specifically to serve the interests of a special clientele (J. O'Connor 1973, 67).
- Government-sponsored agricultural research had a very early history, dating from the Morrill Land Act of 1862, which authorized federal land grants for agricultural colleges, to the Hatch Act twenty-five years later, which secured federal matching funds for state experimental stations and authorized expenditures for a federal research organization (later known as the Agricultural Research Service).
- Public appropriations for research purposes have almost doubled in each decade since the initiation of these nineteenth-century policies to the present (McCall in Hadinger and Browne 1978, 78; Busch and Lacy 1983).
- No other sphere of the economy has received the wealth of government subsidies provided by the New Deal agricultural price-support programs and continued up until the present day (Chapman 1979).

A number of writers in the new sociology of agriculture have tried to make sense of this seeming anomaly by showing how government agricultural policies actually work in the interests of capitalist farmers. For example, studies have shown that, from 1933 to the present, government price-support programs have been distributed to farms almost exactly in proportion to the share of total production each farmer has controlled, whereby the largest farms are the largest beneficiaries of government support (Schnittker 1970, 90 and 96; Frundt 1975, 55–56; Gilbert and Howe 1988). Similarly, if the predictions by the government's Office of Technology are correct, the appropriational and substitutional innovations developed by agricultural research and development are likely to increase the role of vertical integration, contract farming, and other means whereby capitalism increases its control over the countryside (U.S. Congress 1986, 9 and 12). In light of such findings, it has been correctly argued that the recurring inequalities resulting from farm policies indicate a divorce between the government's formal claim to be supporting and protecting the family farm and the impact of its actual farm policies and programs, which disproportionately benefit large enterprises.

However, rather than looking at the role of the capitalist state in agriculture as mechanistically working in the interests of capitalist farmers, it would be more valuable to supplement such analyses by viewing the state's role in agriculture through a broader lens, relating the state's activities to two fundamental concerns, the collective reproduction of labor power and capital's inability to conquer certain spheres of production for social or natural reasons. The first concern centers around the issue of food as a major commodity entering into the value of labor power in all sectors of the economy. The second concern centers around the more specific issue of agriculture as a production process. Below I shall briefly note how these two concerns could be integrally interrelated.

I discussed above how the reproduction of labor power at the *individual level* is usually undertaken by households. By contrast, the reproduction of labor power at the *collective level* is the responsibility of the state and is undertaken through a mixture of authority, ideology, and force. Such reproductive activities include the maintenance of households through various unemployment, health, and welfare programs often funded through redistributional income tax programs. They also include attempts by the state to standardize the quality of individual labor power in the face of the variable particularities of individual households through the creation of compulsory social services such as education, or in the case of social "deviants," mental hospitals and prisons (Mann 1986, 225; Dickinson and Russell 1986, 5–12).

These particular functions of the capitalist state are part and parcel of its more general role in providing those conditions of production that cannot be provided by individual capitalists alone. This role of the state as the "ideal total capitalist" is necessary for a variety of reasons (Engels 1969, 330). First, conditions of production may require a level of generality that is beyond the limited purview of any individual capitalist. For example, individual capitalists will be concerned about the reproduction of those particular laborers they employ, but not necessarily about the reproduction of the proletariat as a class. Second, the scale of enterprise required to ensure certain general conditions of production may exceed the resources of any one capitalist, as in the case of the state's role in highway construction. Third, if an individual capitalist gained control of certain spheres of production, such as the postal system or currency production, the possibility of monopoly control of such infrastructural services could undermine the very workings of society. For such reasons, the separation of administration from property allows the state to act as mediator and protector of the fundamental aspects of property relations. In this sense, ironically, it is in the interests of capital as a whole that the ruling class not be synonymous with the class that rules (Mann and Dickinson 1980, 284–85).

As James Dickinson and I have argued (1980), if this view of the state is coupled with our theory of natural obstacles to agrarian capitalist development, then even more sense can be made of the inordinate amount of government intervention in agriculture. For example, if capital itself is unwilling or unable to enter certain fields of food and fiber production due to low profitability and uncontrollable natural risks, then state subsidies to agriculture can be seen as just one of the numerous instances where the state functions to secure those very conditions of production that cannot be assured by private capital alone. Similarly, the state's role in agricultural research and development can be seen as paving the way for capital through its appropriational and substitutional innovations.[11]

In turn, the natural obstacles faced by capitalists in the sphere of agricultural production are exacerbated by the peculiar role food plays as a major part of the socially necessary subsistence level of laboring classes. As noted in any introductory economics text, while people require a certain minimum of food each day, once they have consumed a given amount they are unlikely to want significantly more, regardless of the price. This phenomenon creates barriers to market expansion and exacerbates the tendency to overproduction and low product prices, which in turn heightens the need for state intervention.[12] Through intervention in the rural economy, the state's role in the collective reproduction of labor power serves capital's interests as a consumer of labor, just as its role in the sphere of agriculture serves capital's interests as a producer of food. Hence, while individual capitals may be in conflict over whether or not cheap food serves their particular interests, "the state, in short, is charged with reconciling the conflicting effects of continued productivity growth associated with advances in appropriationism on rural incomes and rural social structures" (Goodman, Sorj, and Wilkinson 1987, 162).

The various ecological crises facing modern industrial societies give rise to yet another way in which the capitalist state must reconcile conflicting interests if it is to adequately serve as the "ideal total capitalist." That is, because people not only live off nature, but *in* nature, the capitalist state must deal with the contradictions between the destruction of the environment in the short-term interests of private profit and the maintenance of the environment in the long-term interests of reproducing the very basis for private profit—future generations of labor power.

Insight into these ecological crises also suggests the need for an alternative view of the relationship between nature and society from that which has dominated the modern industrial era. Under the current appropriational and substitutional strategies of modern industry, nature is viewed primarily as an object of human domination to be worked upon, shaped, and transformed into commodities. Correspondingly "progress" is viewed as either the domination, subjugation, and appropriation of nature or the "liberation" from nature and its constraints. In both cases, nature is viewed as antithetical, rather than integral, to society. Such views of nature are "far from natural." Rather, they are historically specific social creations that arose during the so-called "age of discovery" and the rise of a world market (von Werlhof 1988a, 96 and 111).

Seen in these various ways, state intervention in the field of agriculture is "far from being an anomaly" or simply the direct product of specific ideological or social class forces or pressures.[13] Rather, the role of the state in various appropriational and substitutional trajectories becomes a precondition for the role of capital in agriculture, because of the peculiar nature of agrarian production—centered as it is in nature. In turn, state intervention also becomes a precondition for the reproduction of labor power as a whole, given the peculiar role food plays in people's means of subsistence and the peculiar role nature plays as the universal "home" for the human race.[14] Such an approach better links producers and consumers, agriculture and industry, as well as nature and society, in an analysis of the role of the state in modern society.

## *Conclusion*

What about the future? Will capitalism's current "incompatibility" with agriculture be short-lived? Is it possible that capitalists are only just beginning to obtain the means by which to transcend the barriers presented by the natural foundations of rural production? In other words, it seems clear that the industrial revolutions of the late eighteenth and nineteenth centuries, while sufficient to industrialize industry, were not sufficient to industrialize many spheres of agriculture. By contrast, the petrochemical and green revolutions of the post–Second World War era and the current advances in biotechnology witnessed in the last two decades are attacking the natural foundations of agriculture in a totally different manner.[15] In terms of appropriationism, whereas mechanization only dealt with the external features of agricultural production, these new technologies modify plants and animals internally, transforming their intrinsic characteristics, such as their productive or growth capacities, their gestation and maturation periods, and their ability to hold nitrogen or to resist frosts and insects. In terms of substitutionism, these new technologies portend the possibilities of industrially produced substitutes replacing many agricultural commodities, as well as the agricultural inputs used in the process of making these commodities. Since these new methods have much more serious implications for bringing the natural foundations of agricultural production under social control, perhaps we are only now witnessing agriculture's "industrial revolution."[16] If so, these new technologies could "mark the end of the pre-history of the food industry,"[17] and, thus, the end of the major contradictions between capitalism and agriculture.

Unless or until this civilization of nature occurs, the modern agricultural landscapes of even the most highly industrialized societies will continue to be characterized by the coexistence of wage and nonwage forms of production. Moreover, advances in science and technology directed toward subordinating natural obstacles to capitalist development are most likely to take place in and be developed for use in industrialized societies where capital-intensive and energy-intensive agricultural systems prevail. Consequently, such advances are likely to exacerbate the already gross inequalities between developed and underdeveloped societies and, thus, further inhibit the generalization of capitalist relations of production on a global scale. As contradictory as it may seem, such uneven and distorted development is in the last instance created by capitalism's own logic and lust for private profits. In this sense, Marx has at least been correct to date in arguing that: "The *real barrier* of capitalist production is *capital itself*" (Marx 1967c, 250 [his emphasis]).

# Appendix 1

# Conceptual Dilemmas Presented by the Modern Agricultural Landscape

A major trend in modern American agriculture has been the decline in independent, medium-sized family farms and the emergence of a "bi-modal farm structure" characterized by extremely large (in terms of volume of sales) and extremely small farms (Buttel 1983, 92). A number of these large and small farms have presented conceptual dilemmas in the new sociology of agriculture because they appear to hold ambiguous or "contradictory" class positions (Mooney 1983).

For example, some of the larger farms utilize more wage labor than family labor, but they do not fit our general conception of capitalist factory farming. Rather, they are family-owned, family-managed, and they hire on average only eight wage laborers. Moreover, because they hire so few workers, they lack a complex and highly specialized division of labor like that found in the modern industrial factory. Nevertheless, these farms play an extremely important role in modern American agriculture and have increased both in number and in their proportion of total farm sales.

To date, the apparent confusion in designating the class position of these farms is captured in the ambiguous term used to describe them: "larger-than-family farms" (Goss, Buttel, and Rodefeld 1980, 114–15). In my view this ambiguity only arises from the failure to recognize that surplus value is not enhanced merely because of the number of wage workers, but rather by the productivity of wage workers. Therefore, a farm with eight workers could have a higher rate of profit that another enterprise that hired twenty or thirty workers. Hence, I have no problem classifying these farms as capitalist farms.

Unlike other writers,[1] I also have no problem categorizing small farmers who are in debt as simple commodity producers, so long as their production is primarily based on family labor and they have not formally or legally lost ownership of their means of production and/or the commodities they produce. Indebtedness certainly can indicate the process of finance capitalist accumulation at work, since value is siphoned off in the form of interest payments. However, this does not in itself transform indebted farmers into a proletariat. Rather, people in a variety of different social classes pay interest on debts and this does not affect their class position unless debts become so serious as to result in a loss of their income-producing property.[2]

By contrast, another type of small family farmer making up the current bimodal farm structure are farmers who in fact hold a dual class position by virtue of their reliance on off-farm employment (Wimberley 1983; Swanson and Busch 1985). Though current agricultural census data do not provide precise enough measures, these farmers should be considered simple commodity producers only so long as their farm income is greater than their income from other sources. Otherwise their class position, as well as their occupation, should be determined by their off-farm employment. The plight of many of these part-time farmers is becoming an increasingly serious issue in American agriculture today. Indeed, it has been estimated that 1.7 million of America's 2.6 million farms had farm incomes inadequate for an acceptable standard of living and whose survival was "squarely premised on access to significant off-farm income" (quoted in Goodman, Sorj, and Wilkinson 1987, 173–75).

Two new forms of production that only arose in the post–World War II era—contract farming and a modern form of sharecropping I call ex-capitalist sharecropping—present more difficult conceptual problems to class analysis. Currently, data on both of these new forms of production are sketchy. However, it is estimated that ex-capitalist sharecropping is prevalent only in certain locales (Wells 1984, 4–5), while contract farming is more prevalent nationwide, currently affecting about 30 percent of American farms. Moreover, contract farming is particularly pervasive in certain spheres of agriculture, such as poultry and floristry, where it can account for as much as 90 percent of total production (J. E. Davis 1980; Wilson 1986). Since contract farming is predicted to become an even more dominant feature of the future agricultural landscape (Wilson 1986; Goodman, Sorj, and Wilkinson 1987, 177–84; U.S. Congress 1986, 9 and 12; Kloppenburg 1988, 283), it deserves more attention in the new sociology of American agriculture than it has currently received.

These new forms of production share some common features. First, both contract farming and ex-capitalist sharecropping are nonwage, family labor forms of production, where producers maintain formal ownership of the commodities they produce. For these reasons, they represent variations of simple commodity production. Second, close supervision and strict guidelines govern the production process under these new forms of production. Here farmers are told not only what commodity is to be produced, but precisely how it is to be produced. Third, it appears that both of these types of production are fostered by market blockages, such as underdeveloped or tightly controlled credit and/or labor markets. However, in the case of contract farming, oligopolistic commodity markets play a more significant role than they do under ex-capitalist sharecropping (Wilson 1986, 58–61). Finally, contract farmers and modern sharecroppers both exist in a subordinate relation to another class—a class which has a capitalist orientation to production.

Here, however, the similarities end, because these social class relations are quite different. Contract farmers exist in a subordinate commodity market relation to a class of capitalist entrepreneurs who are generally involved in food processing or capitalist farming. In contrast, modern sharecroppers exist in a subordinate land market relation to a class of landowners who serve mainly as collectors of ground rent, even if these landowners were previously capitalist farmers, hence the term—ex-capitalist sharecropping.

Nevertheless, because of the capitalist orientation of these dominant classes, advanced technology is more likely to be used in these modern forms of production, than, say, in more traditional sharecropping units. In turn, the commodities produced need to be tailored or standardized to meet the requirements of industrial food processing or capitalist factory farming. Hence, the contracts or rental agreements are more likely to mirror the Taylorization of modern industrial factories, where planning is separated from execution and the craft nature of farming is broken down into relatively unskilled components. Indeed, the producer's loss of control over production appears to be even greater under modern contract farming and ex-capitalist sharecropping than under the traditional sharecropping system, since these modern contracts and leases are more likely to entail extremely detailed instructions about how production must be carried out.

This loss of control over the production process, coupled with the ostensible piece-rate nature of these forms of production, has led some modern writers to characterize contract farmers and modern sharecroppers as a new rural proletariat and, hence, as victims of capitalist exploitation. For example, J. E. Davis (1980), Mooney (1983), and Wilson (1986) all discuss contract farming as a new form of capitalist development in American agriculture, while Wells makes similar claims in regard to ex-capitalist sharecropping (1984, 24).

Despite these similarities, these writers claim different theoretical roots for their conceptual schemes. Wells views her own analysis of ex-capitalist sharecropping as a critique of Marx's theory (Wells 1984, 1–2 and 6), while J. E. Davis (1980), Mooney (1982), and Wilson (1986) argue that their analyses of these new forms of production are grounded in Marxist theory. In fact, however, all of these new conceptual schemes are representative of the unequal exchange theories I discussed in Chapter 1—theories more akin to the writings of Ricardo or Weber than to those of Marx. As I discussed in this earlier chapter, Marx took great pains to distinguish capitalist exploitation (the extraction of surplus value at the point of production) from other forms of exploitation, such as rent or unequal market exchanges—a distinction these new conceptual schemes ignore.

To examine such distinctions at more length, let us first look at contract farming. Since wage labor is the basis of the capitalist extraction of surplus value for Marx, it is important to note a number of significant differences between contract farmers and wage laborers. First, even though contract farmers lose control over production, they still formally own their farms and often use family labor in their production processes. Second, unlike wage laborers, contract farmers maintain formal ownership of the commodities they produce. This makes this form of production quite different from piece-rate production proper, where hired labor is paid for the amount it produces but cannot claim property rights over these commodities. Moreover, the contract farmer's ownership of the commodities he or she produces provides the very basis for the contract, since this is a market relation where entrepreneurs are not purchasing the farmers' labor power, but rather the commodities the farmer produces with it. These commodities often serve as raw materials for the entrepreneurs' own industry and, hence, constitute commodities that Marx called circulating capital.

The oligopolistic nature of circulating capital commodity markets may no doubt foster price-fixing and increased control over production, but this is a limited form of vertical integration, nonetheless. Since labor is not hired, there is no basis for capitalist exploitation proper and even unequal exchange is dubitable because these capitalists must pay the prevailing market price for their contracted commodities. Indeed, if unequal exchange is occurring, it is a product of the oligopolistic nature of these markets, not an intrinsic feature of exchange or market contracts. Moreover, such market issues are more relevant to an analysis of merchant capital than industrial capital—a form of capital which existed long before the rise of modern capitalism.

Yet another way of looking at this peculiar form of production might be to consider that contract farmers have been relegated to a particular niche in the circuit of commodity capital. In some cases, contract farmers only produce part of a finished commodity, such as when hatcheries distribute chicks and collect the broilers after a number of weeks (Kirby 1987 356–57). Empirical analyses often ignore these distinctions by mistakenly lumping together these different stages in the circuit of commodity capital under one general farm-type heading, such as poultry production. However, not only can these different stages represent physically different commodities, but these commodities can also operate on different markets. Moreover, in the example mentioned above, contract farmers may have even lost ownership rights and control over the commodities they produce, since the chicks are delivered to them, as contrasted to certain contract farmers who produce the entire commodity (Pfeffer 1982, 77; Kloppenburg 1988, 283). These distinctions between types of contract farmers should also be addressed, because they could reflect different social class positions.

Usually such niches for either completed or partially completed commodities entail relatively higher risks than other forms of commodity production. As Wilson writes: "Most production contracts, while transferring control to the processor, leave most of the risk of loss in the hands of the farmer" (Wilson 1986, 56). These risks can result either from the intrinsic natural features of the particular commodity produced or from external sociopolitical conditions. For example, many commodities produced by contract farmers today are labor intensive but entail the inefficient, noncontinuous use of labor time. In these cases, this is the only way capital can extend its control progressively over the countryside when its own wage labor processes prove unamenable to the natural features of these types of production (Wilson 1986, 55).

In spheres of production that are less naturally problematic, it appears that contract farming substitutes for wage labor under specific sociopolitical conditions, such as when previous sources of labor have dried up or where unionization endangers capitalists' access to cheap labor (Wilson 1986). In these latter cases, contract farming is a reactionary response to sociopolitical developments—in terms of both a reactionary retreat to more traditional forms of production and also a political reaction against the progressive development of unions or adequately compensated wage labor.

A similar conservative reaction by capital is visible in the rise of ex-capitalist sharecropping, since this form also appears to flourish under specific conditions where wage labor, for whatever sociopolitical reasons, has become particularly problematic (Wells 1984). Here again, specific crop characteristics also can make some forms of production more amenable to ex-capitalist sharecropping. However, as was the case with contract farming, these natural features of production alone are "not a reliable guide to the choice of contracts in agriculture" (Wells 1984, 8). Indeed, as I have argued elsewhere in this book and analysts of contract farming and ex-capitalist sharecropping agree, the particular commodity has to be viewed within the social and historical context of specific relations of production (Wells 1984, 8; Wilson 1986, 52).

Yet analysts who tend to focus on labor market conditions as the primary factor in the development of these new forms of production also need to ask why capitalists in these particular spheres of agriculture cannot deal with unionization or more adequate wage labor compensation, when capitalists have been forced to do this in the industrial sphere without retreating or reverting to more traditional family labor forms of production. Addressing such differences in the responses of capitalists in agriculture and industry would provide a more complete understanding of the peculiar risks associated with capitalist accumulation in agriculture.

Despite the similarities between the conditions that give rise to these two new forms of production, ex-capitalist sharecropping is most basically distinguished from contract farming because it is not predicated on market exchanges but rather on the payment of rent in kind to a class of landowners, which constitutes a distinct form of class exploitation, as I noted above. Moreover, such modern sharecropping forms are also distinct from more traditional sharecropping units, where rent is paid to a noncapitalist, rather than an ex-capitalist, landowning class. A more detailed analysis of this peculiar modern form of production should address the differences between precapitalist, noncapitalist, and capitalist forms of rent in order to further distinguish ex-capitalist sharecropping from its predecessors.

While the conceptual analyses above are brief, they should at least provide an understanding of some of the major analytical features of contract farming, ex-capitalist sharecropping, and small family farms where farmers are in debt and/or employed in off-farm labor. To summarize, perhaps the major features of these forms of production that preclude their forming a rural proletariat are the absence of wage labor and the fact that these family farmers generally maintain ownership over the commodities they produce. This unity of labor and capital suggests that these farms represent subtypes of simple commodity production and, therefore, provide yet further examples of the peculiar noncapitalist forms of production that inhabit the modern American agricultural landscape.

# Appendix 2

# A Reconsideration of Patrick Mooney's Critique of the Mann-Dickinson Thesis

In the literature on the new sociology of American agriculture, Patrick Mooney was the first to challenge the empirical validity of the Mann-Dickinson thesis.[1] In the introduction to his article, "Labor Time, Production Time and Capitalist Development in Agriculture: A Reconsideration of the Mann-Dickinson Thesis" (1982) Mooney writes: "Mann and Dickinson's proposed explanation has hitherto met with little, if any, critical reflection. The validity of their propositions has often been presumed without subjecting them to either critical thinking or empirical verification" (279–80).

To address this shortcoming in the literature, Mooney used U.S. census data from selected years between 1944 and 1974 to examine whether two of the natural obstacles identified in our thesis—perishability and the nonidentity of production time and labor time—affected the employment of wage labor in a number of different agricultural commodity groupings. His findings are presented in tables A-1 and A-2 below, where he uses "labor variance" as a measure of the nonidentity of production time and labor time.

As compared to my empirical analysis in Chapter 3, Mooney's study resulted in substantially different findings regarding the role played by the nonidentity of production time and labor time. Whereas I found that commodity groupings experiencing the greatest gaps between production time and labor time tended to be less capitalistically developed, Mooney found "very little support for the thesis that posits the non-coincidence of labor time and production time as an obstacle to capitalist development" (288). Indeed, his findings almost suggest the reverse—that low labor variance is often associated with less capitalist development (285–88).

I would argue that these conflicting results arise from Mooney's misinterpretation of what is meant by the nonidentity of production time and labor time. This confusion is apparent in his operationalization of this concept, where monthly variations in labor requirements, or what he calls the "seasonal variance in demand for both paid and family labor," are used to measure the nonidentity of production time

Table A-1. Monthly Labor Variation and Capitalist Development for Selected Commodities, 1944–1974

| | Variance in Monthly Labor Requirements | | Hired Labor as Percentage of Value of Product | | | Non-Household Hired Labor as Percentage of Labor Required | Hired Labor as Percentage of Cost of Production |
|---|---|---|---|---|---|---|---|
| Commodity | 1944 | 1964 | 1950 | 1964 | 1974 | 1964 | 1974 |
| Cash Grain[a] | 20.1 | 7.4 | 6.6 | 4.2 | 2.9 | 15.8 | 5.1 |
| Tobacco | 33.3 | 21.4 | — | 9.7 | 7.9 | 29.9 | 14.7 |
| Cotton | 55.7 | 15.5 | 19.7 | 11.0 | 10.0 | 54.2 | 13.2 |
| Other Field Crops | — | 6.7 | 13.1 | 15.2 | 8.5 | 59.4 | 13.9 |
| Vegetables | — | 13.0 | 27.7 | 26.2 | 18.8 | 80.7 | 25.6 |
| Fruits and Nuts | 7.7 | 12.9 | 30.8 | 22.2 | 21.0 | 79.2 | 27.7 |
| Poultry[b] | 1.0 | 1.4 | 5.8 | 4.3 | 3.9 | 33.2 | 4.2 |
| Dairy | 1.3 | 1.8 | 9.5 | 6.0 | 4.8 | 11.7 | 6.4 |

Source: Mooney 1982, 284. Reprinted with permission of *Sociologia Ruralis*, Assen, Netherlands.

[a] In 1944 this referred to all food and feed grains.

[b] In 1944 this referred to chickens.

and labor time (Mooney 1982, 282). However, while the nonidentity of production time and labor time is reflected in the seasonal nature of labor requirements, these two phenomena are not synonymous.

To illustrate this distinction, some earlier critics of Mooney's work, Singer, Green, and Gilles, point out how two branches of production could have very similar seasonal variations in labor demand, but entirely different production times. Mooney's study would have detected no differences between these two branches of production, precisely because it includes no measure of total production time. As these critics correctly conclude, if there is no measure of production time, there is, indeed, no measure of the gap between production time and labor time (Singer, Green, and Gilles 1983, 281–82).

Mooney's misunderstanding of the nonidentity of production time and labor time can be visually appreciated using the graph in figure A-1. This graph represents a poultry farm in 1913 where there was little seasonal variation in labor demand. According to Mooney's measure, this poultry farm would have entailed a close identity of production time and labor time. However, in fact, this farm represented a

Table A-2. Summary Table: Levels of Labor Variation and Capitalist Development for Selected Commodities, 1944–1974

| High | | Medium | | Low | |
|---|---|---|---|---|---|
| Labor Variance | Capitalist Development | Labor Variance | Capitalist Development | Labor Variance | Capitalist Development |
| Tobacco | Fruit/Nut | Vegetables | Cotton | Dairy | Dairy |
| Cotton | Vegetable | Fruit/Nut | Tobacco | Poultry | Poultry |
| | | Cash Grain | Other Field Crops | | Cash Grains |
| | | Other Field Crops | | | |

Source: Mooney 1982, 285. Reprinted with permission of *Sociologia Ruralis*, Assen, Netherlands.

significant excess of production time over labor time, since only about two hours a day of labor time were required, even though clearly the chickens continued to grow the entire day.

It is for this reason that the graphs I used in Chapter 3 to examine the relationship between production time and labor time measured both daily and seasonal labor requirements. When both of these measures are taken into consideration, a poultry farm, like the one represented in figure A-1, would only represent a close identity of production time and labor time if flocks could be large enough to utilize labor the entire day. In 1913, this was not possible, primarily because another natural obstacle—disease—presented too high a risk for farmers to place large numbers of poultry in close proximity.

This example, where a closer identity of production time and labor time could give rise to a different natural obstacle—disease—illustrates yet another problem with Mooney's analysis. That is, by restricting his study to only two of the natural obstacles identified in our thesis, Mooney also missed this type of overlap or relationship between different natural impediments. Consequently, this reduced his ability to see either the cumulative effect a number of natural obstacles could have on a given type of farming or how some natural advantages could be offset by certain natural disadvantages. What I am suggesting here is the need for a more holistic approach in which various natural obstacles are seen as interrelated, rather than a mechanistic approach, where each obstacle is seen as separate and autonomous.

In addition, despite Mooney's claim that our thesis should be submitted to "critical reflection" (1982, 279), he does not submit his own

Figure A-1. Distribution of Labor Requirements in the Production of Poultry, 1913

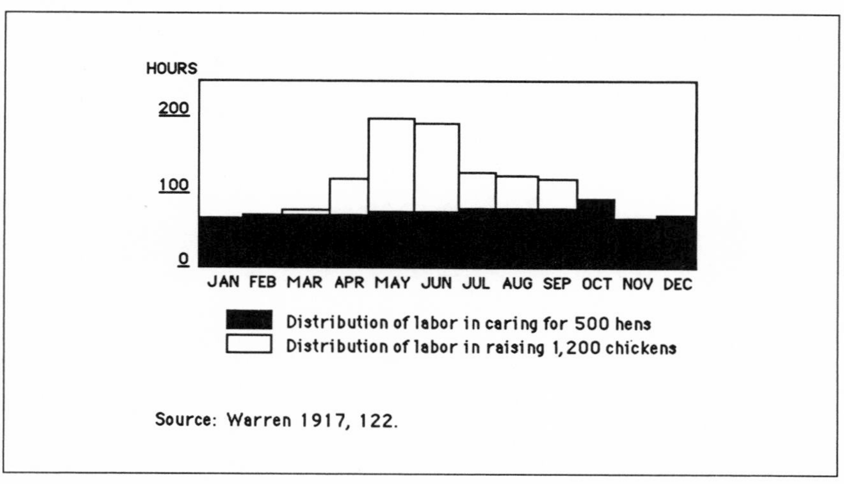


findings to serious reflection. For example, his study, like my own, found that the most perishable commodities—fruits and vegetables—were also the most capitalistically developed. However, the conclusions we derived from these similar findings were quite different. He concluded that perishability did not serve as an obstacle to capitalist development, while I suggested the need for a more historically specific approach that considered how various advances in food processing and preservation may have affected the impact of perishability. Indeed, using such a historical approach one would expect that Mooney's study of post–World War II data would be even less likely than my study of data from 1900 and 1930 to find perishability serving as a major obstacle to agrarian capitalism, given the significant developments in substituting manufactured products for fresh produce that were provided by the quick-freezing techniques introduced in the 1930s.

Finally, there are a number of problems with the way in which Mooney measured capitalist development. For example, two of these measures—"hired labor as a percentage of the total costs of production" and "hired labor as a percentage of the value of the product"—yield totally different results from his third measure—"hired labor as a percentage of labor required." Looking again at his findings for poultry production in table A-1, one can see that this commodity grouping ranks medium in terms of capitalist development relative to other commodities in 1964—the only year in which his third measure was available—but ranks very low in terms of capitalist development in the other census years, when the first two measures are used. How does Mooney account for these differences? The answer is—he does not.

In contrast, I would account for these differences by pointing out that his first two measures are incorrectly conceived and interpreted. According to Mooney, a low rating on these measures would indicate a low level of capitalist development. However, in fact, a low ratio of the value of labor to the value of other capital inputs into the production process could represent a very high degree of capitalist development, where a firm had developed to the point of being able to invest heavily in machinery to increase labor productivity. Indeed, Karl Marx viewed this as a sign of the more advanced development of capitalism in his discussion of the increasing organic composition of capital in modern industrial production—a process that he thought would eventually lead to a falling rate of profit. In contrast, Mooney fails to address the whole issue of what is meant by the organic composition of capital—a failure that is particularly puzzling given his attempts to ground his work in Marxist theory.

Ironically, Mooney's mistake here might be salvageable precisely because of the natural differences between agricultural production and industrial production that he attempts to deny. As I noted in Chapter 2, one of the peculiarities of agriculture as contrasted to industry was that a high organic composition of capital (i.e., a high ratio of constant capital to labor) might in fact represent earlier, rather than later, stages of capitalist development because of the heavy investment in constant capital (particularly land and livestock) required by extensive forms of agricultural production. Nevertheless, salvaging Mooney's mistake in this manner merely points out that the problems of extensive as opposed to intensive types of production are just one of many issues in need of clarification if the first two measures Mooney uses are to reflect in any way accurately different degrees of capitalist development.

Clearly his best measure of capitalist development is "hired labor as a percentage of labor required"—a measure which unfortunately was only available in the census year 1964. However, if we just look at his findings for this census year, they are in fact very similar to my own findings and predictions. That is, the commodity groupings that are the most intensive, that have the shortest production times and the closer identities of daily and seasonal production time and labor time are the most capitalist developed—the fruits and vegetables. In contrast, the commodity groupings that are the most extensive, that have the lengthiest production times (at least in the case of grain production) and the largest gaps between both daily and seasonal production time and labor time are the least capitalist developed—dairy and grain production. Poultry production falls in the middle range, reflecting its mixed blessing of low seasonal variations in labor demand, but problematic daily labor requirements.[2]

In sum, given the fact that the compilers of the census frequently are not using conceptual and operational definitions that accurately reflect the complex theories we might be addressing, great care has to be taken in our operationalization choices, particularly since different measures often result in different theoretical implications, as we have seen above. Closer attention to the relation between theory and research can only enhance the field of American rural sociology—a field that historically has been weak in both theory and critical analysis (Buttel, Larson, and Gillespie 1989; Falk and Gilbert 1985).

# Appendix 3

# Aquaculture: A Nonfarm Application of the Mann-Dickinson Thesis

Given the focus of this book on an analysis of agrarian capitalism, the implications of the Mann-Dickinson thesis for the nonfarm economy are not apparent. Yet, our theory of natural obstacles to capitalist development should be applicable to any sector of the economy—agricultural or nonagricultural—where nonwage labor prevails. While there are few sectors of the nonfarm economy that have not been fully incorporated into the capitalist mode of production in developed societies, there are some relatively new areas of production that are confronting some of the same problems faced by agricultural entrepreneurs.[1]

One obvious sphere of production similar to agriculture in terms of being literally *centered in nature* is aquaculture.[2] By aquaculture I do not mean fishing, raking, or netting finfish, shellfish, and other seafood. Such activities are more akin to hunting and gathering in the sense that fishermen and -women only gather or catch what nature provides; they do not replenish the sea. By contrast, aquaculture means that the producer is actually raising or producing seafood. Here the difference between a "wild" and a "domesticated" catch captures well this distinction and my argument that capitalist development in aquaculture, as in agriculture, is predicated on the necessity of "civilizing" nature.

Compared with the appropriational and substitutional technologies developed in agriculture to combat nature, aquaculture is still in its infancy. However, over the last two decades in the United States, intense interest has been generated in the business of aquaculture for a number of reasons. In particular, commercial fisheries in the U.S. are not meeting the demand for fish. In the two decades between 1950 and 1970, fish imports had increased significantly from 25 percent to 65 percent of total supply. In turn, because fish are better feed converters than land-based animals and because their cold-blooded nature means they do not expend calories maintaining a constant body temperature, a pound of fish generally can be produced more cheaply than a pound of red meat. Since fish are also a valuable source of protein, they could potentially provide tough competition for livestock producers (Bell 1978, 282).

However, numerous natural and social obstacles preclude the profitable production of many species of fish and seafood. Some of the more serious social obstacles include aquatic pollution and the expense of acquiring rights to shoreline property suitable for aquaculture. Some of the more serious natural obstacles to the expansion of aquaculture include finding species that have fairly wide temperature tolerances, few breeding problems, and relatively fast growth rates (Bell 1978, 283–84 and 293–94). In some cases, aquaculturalists are facing similar problems to those that have plagued livestock producers. For example, as in livestock production, one of the most serious problems currently facing redfish farmers in Louisiana is disease—but far less is known about redfish diseases than livestock diseases. Fish farmers are also facing problems that make animal husbandry look relatively simple. Consider, for example, the difficulties inherent in trying to raise redfish in their natural habitat, rather than in artificial ponds, and having to construct cages strong enough to withstand hurricane-force winds and tides. Presented with such serious obstacles, it is not surprising that aquaculture in the United States today is devoted primarily to the production of luxury foods or high-value output, such as shrimp and salmon (Bell 1978, 282–83).

Moreover, because type of commodity is an important issue in the success of profitable aquaculture, as in agriculture, generalizations about natural and social obstacles are difficult. For example, the social problem of acquiring shoreline property noted above is eliminated with species of seafood that can be "farmed" on low-value land—such as ravines, swampland, or marsh—that is not well suited to other uses. Hence, in future studies of aquaculture, a species-specific commodity analysis would be as important as the "type of farm" commodity analysis was to this book.

Given the similarities between aquaculture and agriculture in terms of being spheres of production "centered in nature," it is not surprising that the commodities derived from both sea and field often continue to be produced by petty commodity producers.[3] Moreover, many petty producers who make their living from the sea share the "peculiar" class positions discussed in Appendix 1, like indebtedness, contract production, and/or part-time employment. This brief examination of aquaculture, therefore, should indicate not only the potential use of the Mann-Dickinson thesis in nonagricultural spheres of the economy, but also the broader social implications of the knowledge being generated by the new sociology of agriculture.

# Notes

## *Introduction*

1. See Durkheim (1964), Marx (1967a, 714–15), and Weber (1968a, 223).

2. For example, see John Naisbitt's *Megatrends* (1982), in which much importance is given to the recent rise of small nonfarm businesses, but little care is taken in defining what is meant by a "small business." For example, Naisbitt reports that self-employment increased 25 percent between 1972 and 1979, after two decades of decline, but whether these self-employed entrepreneurs hire labor or use family labor is not discussed. One of the few places where this issue is even partially addressed is where he notes that two-thirds of the new jobs created between 1969 and 1976 were generated by businesses that had twenty or fewer employees. He further notes that the major rise of new businesses has been in the area of high-tech firms. Given the nature of this high-tech work, it is highly unlikely that these are family labor enterprises. Moreover, one of the major factors Naisbitt uses to explain these developments is the "abrupt increase in venture capital money"—a factor which has more to do with the state of modern finance capital than any inherent advantages of family labor enterprises (Naisbitt 1982, 146–47).

3. The Mann-Dickinson thesis has been cited in several recent overviews of literature on the development of capitalism in agriculture. See for example Perelman (1979), J. E. Davis (1980), or Mooney (1982) for critical views of this thesis and Glavanis (1984) or Buttel, Larson, and Gillespie (1989, chap. 4) for positive appraisals.

## *Chapter 1*

1. For a history of American rural sociology, see Buttel, Larson, and Gillespie (1989, chap. 4) or Gregory Hooks's article (1986).

2. For a comparison of Marxist economics with neoclassical economics, see Gordon (1977, 1–15). Gordon points out that along with the more individualistic market orientation of neoclassical economics, there is also an assumption that individual actions combine to produce stable, harmonious, social equilibriums. This is also very different from the class conflict–oriented approach of Marx. In turn, such equilibrium-oriented analyses share more in common with the writings of Chayanov than with those of Weber.

3. Originally, the concept "family farm" referred to units of production in which all labor was provided by family members. Over time this concept has been redefined to include increasing amounts of wage labor. A recent definition used by the U.S. Department of Agriculture includes any commercial en-

terprise (i.e., farms with sales of $2,500 or above) using less than 1.5 man-years of hired labor (Armstrong 1969, 39; Foote 1970; Nikolitch 1965, 84). This definition is at least compatible with Marx's concept of simple commodity production, since 1.5 man-years means that family labor still constitutes at least 50 percent of the farm's labor. For a discussion of other conceptual schemes used to examine rural forms of production, see Friedmann (1980b) and Goodman and Redclift (1982, chaps. 2 and 3).

4. For example, see Goss, Buttel, and Rodefeld (1980); Mooney (1982); and Wells (1984).

5. Such deductive determinations are possible only with forms of production integrally dependent on markets for both their farm inputs and their farm outputs. Forms of production that can revert to production for use, such as many peasant farms, do not meet these criteria. This is one of the reasons why the peasantry have proven so difficult to conceptualize and integrate into theoretical analyses (Friedmann 1980b).

6. See also Poulantzas's (1975) political analysis of petty commodity production.

7. See also Shanin's (1971) very interesting analysis of the peasantry as a political factor and its need for guided political action.

8. See in particular Marx's discussion of the Russian *mir* in Laski (1948, 108–9). For a contemporary analysis of how the different structural conditions in which rural producers live have given rise to different political behaviors, see Paige (1975, 59–66) and Shanin (1971). The role of modern mass communications in breaking down the isolation of peasant life should also be considered when trying to apply Marx's theory to the modern world.

9. As Lenin writes: "Fractionalized, individual, petty exploitation binds the toilers to a particular place, disunites them, prevents them from appreciating their class solidarity. . . . Large-scale capitalism, on the contrary, inevitably severs all the workers' ties with the old society . . . it unites them, compels them to think and puts them in conditions which enable them to commence an organized struggle" (quoted in Rochester [1942, 21]).

10. Consider the following quote: "Both logic and history teach us that the petty-bourgeois class out-look may be more or less narrow and more or less progressive, just because of the dual status of the petty bourgeois. And far from dropping our hands in despair because of this narrowness and stupidity of the muzhik or because he is governed by prejudice, we must work steadily to widen his outlook and to help his judgement triumph over his prejudice" (Lenin, quoted in Rochester [1942, 35]).

11. For various conceptual schemes and analyses of peasant forms of production in the new sociology of agriculture, see Wolf (1966), Shanin (1971), Bernstein (1979), Friedmann (1980b), Goodman and Redclift (1982), and Roseberry (1983).

12. Consider, for example, the early writings of Lauren Soth—a recent recipient of the American Rural Sociological Society's Distinguished Service to Rural Life Award: "Marxist critics of the American economic system long have talked about the disappearance of the family farm. . . . Marxists are not interested in preserving the family farm of course. They are interested in fanning

dissent and creating dissatisfaction. But their misinterpretation of the effects of economic development in this country is swallowed by sincere anti-socialist agricultural leaders" (1957, 24). See also Mitrany (1951, 10–12) and Nikolitch (1962).

13. Systematic Marxist explanations of the dynamics of agriculture only began to receive serious scholarly attention in American rural sociology during the 1970s. For example, the official journal of the American Rural Sociological Society, *Rural Sociology*, did not publish any articles based largely on Marxist theory until 1972 (Buttel, Larson, and Gillespie 1989, chap. 4).

14. Russian narodism is, perhaps, the first ideological expression of the social and economic position of backward, largely agrarian societies faced with the problem of modernization in the context of the adverse conditions created by coexistence with more highly developed capitalist nations. In this sense, the Narodniks were the first to postulate the possibility of a noncapitalist/nonsocialist road to development for underdeveloped societies.

15. Given the positivistic nature of American sociology at this time, the quantitative, empirical focus of these studies helped to legitimate Marxism in American rural sociology. Moreover, while these writers did not extend Marxist theory, they at least introduced readers to this theory and developed concepts that greatly improved studies of rural stratification.

16. This shift is evident in the current use of the terms "noncapitalist" or "nonwage" forms of production, as contrasted to Marx's and Lenin's tendency to call petty commodity production a *pre*capitalist form or, as Marx wrote, a "prelude to the history of capital" (1967a, 714).

17. Not only did these studies transform the traditional macro-level unit of analysis from individual societies to a world system, but also they viewed the world system as both the "site" and the "source" of social change (McMichael 1987c). Such works as Theda Skocpol's study (1979) of the role of agrarian classes in social revolution, Gavin Wright's analysis (1978) of the postbellum American South, and Philip McMichael's book (1984) on the agrarian transformation of the Australian frontier have revolutionized the conceptual framework of debates over these major historical events and processes.

18. See in particular Wallerstein (1973 and 1974b). For an overview of this literature, see Goodman and Redclift (1982, chaps. 2 and 3).

19. Weber's multidimensional analysis of stratification is often viewed as an improvement on Marx's analysis of class because it provides a better understanding of empirical cases where wealth, power, and status do not overlap; it deals more adequately with noneconomic forms of power; and it introduces a social-psychological dimension to stratification through its focus on people's subjective assessment of status or prestige (Zeitlin 1981, 159–63). For a comparison of Marx and Weber on social class, see Mann (1984a).

20. For example, Weber defines capitalism as the "rational" pursuit of profit, highlighting how capitalists use mathematics, accounting, and the science of economics to assess rates of profit and to guide investment decisions (1972, 66–68 and 331). See also Weber (1968a, 85), Albrow (1970, 63), and Freund (1968, 20).

21. Marx recognized that under certain conditions, such as monopoly con-

trol, unequal exchange could occur. However, for him this was not the primary source of capitalist profits.

22. For a more detailed discussion of contract farming see Appendix 1.

23. For example, see Ryan (1986, 50–51 and 162–65), who documents how most American families today are indebted. This indebtedness cuts across class lines and tells us nothing about the labor processes or social relations of production in which these people are engaged.

24. J. E. Davis, for example, views dependency and world-systems theories as "a reaffirmation of Marx's notion of the universality of capitalism" (1980, 134). However, when Marx writes about capitalism spreading across the globe, he focuses not merely on the rise of a world market but on changes in the mode of *production* (Marx 1970, 39 and 1967b, 36).

25. The idea that the economic behavior of simple commodity producers is sufficient to constitute a separate and distinct *mode* of production can be found in Chayanov (1966). For debates over this issue, see Bernstein (1977), Friedmann (1979), Goodman and Redclift (1982), and Roseberry (1983).

26. For a discussion of how Weber "actually spent little time" on micro-level, subjective analyses, see Ritzer (1983, 126–27, 132, and 134).

27. For a more detailed discussion of these contradictions in Weber's work, see Mann and Dickinson (1987a and b).

28. Chayanov's writings have been revived today by the notable efforts of such scholars as Teodore Shanin, Basile Kerblay, and the late Daniel Thorner. See for example Chayanov (1966a and b), Shanin (1973, 1974, and 1986), Kerblay (1971), and Thorner (1971).

29. In his recent assessment of Chayanov's influence on rural sociology, Teodore Shanin argues that it is incorrect to interpret Chayanov's writings as substituting psychological or idealist explanations for materialist explanations (1986, 5). However, from my reading of Chayanov, his subjectivist analysis is central to his explanation of the persistence of family labor farms. See in particular Chayanov (1966b, 233–39).

30. Because of these inconclusive empirical findings, Teodore Shanin suggests that this aspect of Chayanov's theory is one of the "least substantiated" and "least useful" components (1986, 2–5).

31. In pre-market, kin-based production systems, economic activity is closely bound up with the family life cycle (Meillassoux 1983). Although developed markets do not eliminate demographic forces, they tend to reduce available survival strategies so that demographic and subjective factors take a backseat to objective market conditions (Friedmann 1980b; Meillassoux 1983; Seccombe 1986).

32. In the literature on family farms there is seldom a discussion of the internal economic behavior of these units of production that does not utilize the idea of self-exploitation. See, for example, Long (1984); de Janvry (1980); and Buttel, Larson, and Gillespie (1989). For a critique of various contemporary writers who fail to recognize the patriarchal dimension of family labor farms, see Welty (1987), Friedmann (1986), and Mann (1987b, 1988, and 1989).

33. For a detailed critique of what I term eclectic or "mix and stir" theories

that try to synthesize Marx and Weber, see Mann and Dickinson (1987a and b).

34. The term "reproduction" simply refers to the ability to renew or initiate another cycle of production. Hence, successful reproduction would require that the necessary raw materials, energy, technology, and labor power were available to maintain the continued operation of a given form of production.

35. For debates over the distinction between modes and forms of production, see Bernstein (1977), Goodman and Redclift (1982), Friedmann (1979 and 1981), and Roseberry (1983).

36. While self-exploitation, or what she calls the "flexibility of personal consumption," is integral to Friedmann's theory (1981, 17), she recognizes that family farms are differentiated by gender and age. Thus, unlike many of her gender-blind predecessors, she discusses patriarchal domination as a feature of simple commodity production (1986).

37. The quotation "a remarkable similarity of the laws of evolution" is from Lenin (1974, 102).

38. Goodman, Sorj, and Wilkinson (1987) also recognize that their quote is relevant to modern writings in the new sociology of agriculture. However, when they note that the terms of the debate were "frozen," they are referring specifically to the Lenin-Narodnik debates. I discuss contemporary writers who have analyzed various problems associated with the natural features of agricultural production in Chapter 2.

## *Chapter 2*

1. See, for example, Wiley (1939, 70). The issue of how topography can affect the use of farm machinery is also discussed in Chapter 4.

2. The organic composition of capital refers to the value of land, rather than the amount of land. Consequently, while a high organic composition of capital is likely to be accentuated in extensive types of farming, it may also be a problem in intensive types of agriculture, where improved acreage can result in high land values even when the amount of land is small (Lenin 1974, 52; Warren 1917, 152).

3. It should also be kept in mind that Marx (1967a) argued that if all other conditions were equal and no countervailing tendencies were present, a high organic composition of capital could lead to a falling rate of profit. That is, since only labor power creates value, a high ratio of constant to variable capital can present a problem. Nevertheless, applying this tendency for a falling rate of profit to an individual enterprise is not without problems.

4. Marx's analysis of absolute rent, since it is predicated on a higher organic composition of capital in industry than in agriculture, appears difficult to reconcile with my argument about a relatively high organic composition of capital in extensive types of agriculture. However, since I also argued that the high capital expenditures in agriculture did not necessarily reflect enhanced labor productivity, these two seemingly contradictory theses can be reconciled if

one views Marx's understanding of the differences between industry and agriculture as actually rooted in differences in labor productivity. For more discussion of Marx's notion of absolute rent, see note 5 below.

5. If, by contrast, the landowners are capitalists and they obtain a surplus from differential rent, this could serve to attract capitalist investments to agriculture. It should also be noted that because Marx's notion of differential rent does not include any explanation of how the most marginal land also has a rent, Marx developed his concept of absolute rent. Here Marx argued that landed property presented a barrier to the free mobility of capital in agriculture. This meant that agriculture was insulated from the equalization of the rate of profit and, hence, prices of agricultural commodities would continue to reflect their value rather than postequalization prices of production. This difference between price and value formed the basis of absolute rent. In turn, if agriculture, as Marx argues, has a lower organic composition of capital than industry, the excess profit arising from a lower organic composition of capital is maintained in the sphere of agriculture and enters into this equation as absolute rent.

6. Contreras's article (1977) discussed many of the same "limits" to capitalist development that we discussed, such as perishability, the lengthy production times of many agricultural commodities, the nonidentity of production time and labor time, and difficulties farmers have with quickly augmenting or curtailing production. One major difference between our two approaches is that he presents an unequal exchange theory between town and country, similar to those of the world-systems and dependency theorists, which we reject.

7. For example, although I have reviewed much of the literature on the new sociology of agriculture, the first and only references I have seen to Contreras's work in any English-language publication appeared in Goodman and Redclift (1982), and Goodman, Sorj, and Wilkinson (1987).

8. This quote is from Gartrell and Gartrell (1980, 524). In addressing the "ecological suitability" of agricultural innovations, Gartrell and Gartrell argue for a "broader sociological interpretation" of the relationship between natural and social factors affecting the adoption of innovations. Similarly, we argue that nature takes on different meanings in different social contexts, despite the fact that our theory has been misinterpreted as a biological determinist theory (Mooney 1982, 281). Some critics, like Perelman (1979) and Mooney (1982), also argue that because all forms of production strive to minimize the natural impediments to rural production, natural obstacles play no special role under capitalism. However, these critics ignore how some forms of production can adapt more easily than others to natural restrictions on production. In particular, they ignore the difference between simple and expanded reproduction and how capitalism is predicated on the latter, unlike family labor forms of production. They also ignore the differences natural factors play in the production of exchange values as contrasted with the production of use values.

9. I would argue that many of the unequal exchange theories derived from dependency and world-systems theory implicitly suggest that nonwage forms of production are functional to capitalism because they provide adequate al-

ternative mechanisms of capitalist accumulation. See, for example, J. E. Davis (1980), Mooney (1983), and von Werlhof (1985).

10. In the original Mann-Dickinson thesis, we incorrectly used the term "socially necessary labor time" when distinguishing production time from labor time (Mann and Dickinson 1978, 471). As Singer, Green, and Gilles (1983) correctly point out, so as not to confuse value terms with the specific conditions of a concrete production process, a more accurate distinction is between actual labor time expended (which may or may not approach the social average) and production time. These writers prefer "working period" to my term "labor time." I have chosen not to use their terminology, since the concept of the "nonidentity of production time and labor time" is so frequently used in the current debates that switching the terminology at this point would likely generate more confusion than clarification. Nevertheless, in keeping with their correct observation, throughout this book I have attempted to use "labor time" consistently to refer to actual labor time expended, as distinct from "socially necessary labor time," which entails an analysis of value.

11. Some critics of our thesis pointed out that spheres of production entailing lengthy turnover periods are today effectively being penetrated by capital, due to advances in the development of credit systems, an increasing presence of the state in directing the flow of credit, and various other mechanisms that foster long-term over short-term investments (Singer, Green, and Gilles 1983, 282–83). A similar point was made by McMichael for earlier historical eras in which finance capitalists established particular types of credit systems to reduce the problem of a lengthy turnover time (1984, 108–18). These insights better highlight the relative and historically specific nature of this particular natural impediment to capitalist development.

12. For example, Perelman (1979) argued that, given the equalization of profit, a lower than average turnover rate for capital would be compensated by a higher than average profit rate. My response to Goodman, Sorj, and Wilkinson's critique would also apply to this criticism by Perelman.

13. This issue of the spatial constraints of land and, hence, the need for more maneuverable farm machinery is further discussed in Chapter 3.

14. For a more detailed discussion of larger-than-family farms, see Appendix 1.

15. In an article a few years later, James Dickinson and I also discussed the role of the state in research and development projects and in taking over spheres of production with extraordinarily lengthy production times, such as timber growing as contrasted to its harvesting or processing (Mann and Dickinson 1980). This analysis complemented some of the modern Marxist theories of the state which view the state as providing those necessary conditions of production that cannot be assured by private capital alone (Mandel 1975, 476–80).

16. For example, writers who correctly pointed to the necessity of viewing our discussion of natural obstacles as historically specific or "relative" include Singer, Green, and Gilles (1983, 284). Also, those who correctly recognized that we viewed capitalism's "selectivity" as the basis for the persistence of family labor farms include Long (1984, 4); Buttel and Newby (1980, 19); and

Buttel, Larson, and Gillespie (1989, chap. 4).

17. See, for example, Mooney (1982). Similarly, our theory was incorrectly lumped together with neopopulist theories that stressed the permanent role of family farms in the farm economy (de Janvry 1980, 158).

18. Although only about 1 percent of U.S. cattle are involved in embryo transfers, it has been predicted that such transfers will increase rapidly due to their obvious potential for upgrading the quality and productive efficiency of livestock (U.S. Congress 1986, 36). However, a reviewer of this book noted that because of the high cost of embryo transfers, it is questionable as to whether their use will ever extend beyond purebred livestock and transferring disease-free germ plasm across international borders.

19. An earlier book by Goodman and Redclift (1982) discusses how natural features of agriculture serve as obstacles to capitalist development. However, these natural obstacles are not given a central role in their analyses. By contrast, the 1987 book by Goodman, Sorj, and Wilkinson focuses entirely on agro-industrial capitals' conquest of nature. Consider the following quote from the introduction of this later book: "The key to understanding the uniqueness of agriculture, we would argue, lies neither in its social structure nor in its factor endowment. Rather agriculture confronts capitalism with a *natural production process*" (1 [their emphasis]).

20. For example, some writers maintain that real subsumption can occur even when nonwage farmers hold legal property rights over land or other means of production (J. E. Davis 1980; Goodman, Sorj, and Wilkinson 1987, 150). In contrast, I would argue that such legal property rights over means of production and the commodities produced seriously affect the internal logic of units of production and usually preclude the real subsumption of nonwage forms of production by capital. Hence, such controversies have not been resolved simply by the creation of these new concepts.

21. The history of advances in food preservation, such as safe canning, dehydration, refrigeration, and quick freezing, also illustrates attempts at substitutionism, in that they substitute industrial products for rural products. However, such methods of food preservation are still dependent on fresh foods, and, hence, on land-based agriculture. By contrast, the creation of synthetic fibers and foods completely eliminates the need for land and farming (Goodman, Sorj, and Wilkinson 1987, 63–79 and 94–97).

22. While the new biotechnologies were based on advances in molecular genetics made in the 1950s and 1960s and later developments in genetic engineering in the early 1970s, they were not spawned merely by developments in science. Biotechnologies were given a major boost by both global and domestic sociopolitical events. The formation of the OPEC cartel and the oil crises of the 1970s exposed the marked dependence of developed economies on nonrenewable fossil fuels and their derivatives, such as the oil and nitrogen central to advanced farming technology and fertilizers. This, coupled with the rise of domestic ecology movements demanding stricter controls on pollution, toxic substances, and the wasteful consumption of energy, gave even more momentum to the rise of these new agricultural technologies (Goodman, Sorj, and Wilkinson 1987, 99–100).

23. When Goodman, Sorj, and Wilkinson (1987) do discuss class conflict, they tend to focus on conflict between different fractions of capital, particularly within agribusiness. While these discussions are too brief, even less attention is given to the role of noncapitalist classes.

24. See Singer, Green, and Gilles (1983, 284–85). These authors point to other ways in which natural obstacles can be reduced, such as countering nature's negative effects on the rate of profit by increasing the rate of exploitation through the use of marginalized and exceedingly cheap wage labor. Interestingly, their analysis here was originally directed as a critique of the Mann-Dickinson thesis for being a technological determinist argument. However, as this book should make clear, their analysis is totally in keeping with our views. Moreover, some of the issues they raise are concretely dealt with in Chapters 4 and 5.

25. For a detailed discussion of Mooney's empirical critique of the Mann-Dickinson thesis, see Appendix 2.

26. Much of the empirical analysis presented in the next chapter was originally written for my doctoral dissertation; see Mann (1982).

## *Chapter 3*

1. This notion of an earlier "Golden Age" of family farming was resurrected in the 1970s, when American farmers were demanding that parity payments provide the same purchasing power their predecessors had experienced between 1910 and 1914 (Chapman 1979, 16–17).

2. For example, specific agricultural commodities, such as tomatoes and cabbages, are lumped together into commodity groupings, such as vegetables.

3. See, for example, Goldschmidt (1947), Lenin (1974), or Rochester (1940). For critical analyses of whether tenancy, off-farm employment, and/or indebtedness provide good indicators of proletarianization, see Goss, Buttel, and Rodefeld (1980) and Mooney (1983).

4. The empirical analyses by both Lenin and Rochester did present data showing how different degrees of capitalist development were associated with different types of farms (Lenin 1974, 72–78; Rochester 1940, 86–87). However, while this data could have suggested important variations in the production processes of different agricultural commodities and, thereby, provided a clue to certain natural obstacles to capitalist development, neither Lenin nor Rochester pursued this line of inquiry.

5. There are some problems of comparability between the commodity groupings used in the 1900 and the 1930 censuses. In 1900, the cash-grain grouping included hay farms but excluded rice farms, whereas in 1930, rice farms were included and hay farms were excluded. In addition, while both the 1900 and the 1930 censuses included livestock commodity groupings, the groupings were organized differently in each of these census years and do not enable comparisons over time. The implications of these changes will be noted when they are relevant.

6. It is possible that the inclusion of rice farms and the exclusion of hay farms in the 1930 census's cash-grain category may have affected the comparison of wage labor expenditures per farm in this commodity grouping between 1900 and 1930 (see the preceding note). Hay farms tended to be small, under a low state of cultivation, and less likely to hire labor. In contrast, rice farms required a much more intensive type of production and were generally associated with relatively high expenditures on wage labor (U.S. Census 1900, lxiii and cxxviii). However, since the comparison in table 3-2 between 1900 and 1930 shows a decline, rather than a rise, in expenditures on wage labor *per acre*, this adds even greater credibility to the thesis that the more extensive types of grain production presented serious problems to capitalist development.

7. The organic composition of capital refers to the value of land, rather than the amount of land. Consequently, while a high organic composition of capital is likely to be accentuated in extensive types of farming, it may also present a problem in intensive types of agriculture, because land values, particularly on improved acreage, can be high even when the amount of land is small (Lenin 1974, 52; Warren 1917, 152).

8. Along with controversy over the relationship between price and value (J. Wayne 1981, 81–83), one reviewer of this book correctly pointed out that there are also problems with applying Marx's argument that a high organic composition of capital can lead to a falling rate of profit to an individual enterprise. For these reasons, the index of capital composition used in table 3-5 must be taken as a limited measure of Marx's predictions regarding the organic composition of capital.

9. The significance of these developments is suggested by the fact that 75 percent of U.S. beef was fattened on feedlots by 1972 (Murray 1978, 21).

10. Even today, disease is the major problem affecting the efficient, large-scale, capitalist production of livestock and poultry. For some producers, this problem has led to the further mechanization of livestock production through the use of computer programs to assess the well-being of individual animals and to keep detailed records on health-related concerns (U.S. Congress 1986, 40–41).

11. The use of automation currently is also restricted to these high-density, rapid-turnover horticultural crops. In terms of field crops, it has been predicted that automation and robotics are most likely to be introduced into high-value, labor-intensive crops, particularly in orchards, where trees can be uniformly spaced and more compactly arranged than other field crops (Goodman, Sorj, and Wilkinson 1987, 120–22; U.S. Congress 1986, 67).

12. The weeks to economic maturity of different agricultural commodities are not synonymous with production time, since, for example, land preparation takes place before and harvesting after crops are planted and mature. However, this measure does give an indication of the natural constraints on production time, which was the major point at issue in the Mann-Dickinson thesis.

13. This weak relationship is not surprising, because there are a number of industrial commodities, such as ships, that have a relatively lengthy produc-

tion time but have been produced successfully along capitalist lines. The more fundamental issue appears to be the gap between production time and labor time—a problem that does not plague most industrial commodities.

14. While the graphs in figure 3-1 provide a rough basis by which to make comparisons between different types of agricultural commodity production, they are not without problems. For example, there is no uniformity in the economic size of each type of farm represented. Graph A represents twenty-one acres of winter wheat, which is not comparable in acreage or in terms of value of produce to the farm in graph D, which represents cabbage production. Nevertheless, the blackened portions of these graphs, which represent work fixed as to time, do provide some indication of the nature of labor requirements in relation to the entire productive cycle. Hence, while the vertical axis, which represents labor intensity or man-hours per day, might vary if all of these farms were of uniform size, it is doubtful that the gaps on the horizontal axis, which represents the seasonal nature of labor requirements, would vary proportionately. Moreover, since crops continue growing throughout the productive cycle, labor time as measured on the vertical axis would have to cover the entire working day in order to provide a close identity of production time and labor time.

15. The fact that poultry production in the early 1900s showed less capitalist development than fruits and vegetables despite its more continuous production has in part been attributed to the risk of disease, particularly if large flocks were assembled together to increase the coincidence of production time and labor time (Rochester 1940, 283). By contrast, as a result of advances in vaccines and antibiotics, poultry operations of 100,000 or more birds are common today. However, such large flocks are viewed as high-risk ventures because infectious diseases can still have devastating effects (U.S. Congress 1986, 40–41).

16. In his empirical critique of the Mann-Dickinson thesis, Patrick Mooney (1982) fails to note this distinction between seasonal labor requirements and the nonidentity of production time and labor time. For a detailed discussion of this problem, see Appendix 2 of this book and Singer, Green, and Gilles (1983, 281–82).

17. The role of diversification in reducing the gap between production time and labor time is also illustrated by the historical example of capitalist wheat farms in the small-grain area, where wide variations in labor employment were reduced by maintaining a large number of livestock alongside wheat production (Elwood et al. 1939, 53).

18. In the 1930 census, farms that did not receive at least 40 percent of their income from any particular commodity were categorized as "general farms" and made up 16.6 percent of all farms. In the 1900 census, such farms were categorized as "miscellaneous farms" and made up 18.5 percent of all farms. However, some types of farms, like nurseries, were included in the 1900 census, while in 1930 they were lumped together under a new category "unclassified farms," whether or not they were specialized or diversified. (U.S. Census 1930a, 12; U.S. Census 1930b, 4 and 5; U.S. Census 1900, cxxviii).

19. For a more lengthy discussion of this, see U.S. Census (1930b, 2–7).

Here the census compilers note: "Were the classification repeated it would probably be desirable to change the method of classification somewhat so as to recognize more adequately these specialized, combination types. This could be accomplished by using two percentages—one to segregate highly specialized farms, and the other to apply to the combination types."

20. The graphs in figure 3-4 represent price fluctuations during the period from January 1954 to December 1956. Unfortunately, such informative graphs could not be obtained for the period 1900 to 1930.

21. The U.S. Bureau of Labor Statistics found a general tendency for frequency of price change to be inversely related to the degree of durability in their study of 1,789 industrial and agricultural commodities (U.S. Bureau of Labor Statistics 1959, 7 and 32).

22. In order to determine whether data calculated from annual price averages (as in table 3-9) may have obscured price fluctuations throughout the year, I also examined data on monthly ten-year average wholesale prices for the same crops. Again, potatoes, the most perishable crop, had the highest mean deviation, with prices deviating from the ten-year monthly average by approximately plus or minus 4.9 cents (Mann 1982, 92–93).

23. The eleven farm products included in Shepherd's price comparison were: eggs, butter, hogs, corn, lambs, cattle, oats, potatoes, wheat, flax, and cotton. Prices in each case were average monthly prices at the most important terminal market for the commodity concerned (Shepherd 1941, 71–72).

24. Shepherd attributed the relatively high cost of egg storage to their bulky and fragile nature, as well as to the fact that eggs had to be stored under refrigeration at comparatively low temperatures (Shepherd 1941, 77).

25. These twentieth-century advances in food processing and food preservation may also explain why Mooney's (1982) critique of the Mann-Dickinson thesis did not find perishability to be an obstacle to capitalist development. For more discussion of this critique, see Appendix 2.

26. For example, today in tomato production, roughly 70 percent of the American crop is processed, which clearly reduces the importance of perishability as a natural impediment to agrarian capitalism (Goodman, Sorj, and Wilkinson 1987, 108).

27. For studies that focus primarily on market relations between farms and agribusinesses see, for example, J. E. Davis (1980) and Frundt (1975). See also Goodman, Sorj, and Wilkinson (1987) for a description of the impact food-processing industries had on certain natural features of agricultural production. While their book presents a wealth of information, it does not provide sufficient documentation of changes in the rural class structure to show specifically how the expansion of food processing affected the capitalist development of farming.

28. An analysis of census data alone cannot adequately explain variations in the degree of capitalist development *within* any particular commodity grouping, e.g., why certain cotton farms were capitalist, while others were based on family labor. This is another reason why the historical-comparative analyses in Chapters 4 and 5 enrich this study.

*Chapter 4*

1. The U.S. census definition of the South is used here and includes: the South Atlantic states of Delaware, Maryland, the District of Columbia, West Virginia, Virginia, North Carolina, and South Carolina; the East South Central states of Kentucky, Georgia, Florida, Tennessee, Alabama, and Mississippi; and the West South Central states of Louisiana, Arkansas, Oklahoma, and Texas. However, since there is a good deal of diversity in this region, when I use the term "Old South" I will be referring to what Kirby (1987, 25-50) calls the "plantation south" to distinguish it from other "rural souths." Later in this chapter I will compare these older plantation areas with the younger cotton-producing areas of Texas and Oklahoma.

2. The term cotton belt generally refers to the strip of land lying 300 miles north to south between the twenty-fifth and thirty-seventh north latitudes and spreading 1,600 miles from the Carolinas to western Texas. It includes the cotton-producing areas of the Carolinas, Georgia, Alabama, Louisiana, Mississippi, Texas, Oklahoma, and Arkansas.

3. The emancipation not only resulted in a significant reduction of the wealth that slave owners could directly appropriate from the products of slave labor, but also it reduced their access to credit, since human property could no longer be offered as collateral on loans (Ransom and Sutch 1977, 4; Jaynes 1986, 34–35).

4. It has been argued that cotton plantations organized on the basis of wage payments were more efficient, in terms of productivity, than comparable plantations organized on the basis of share payments. For example, based on a sample of cotton plantations from the 1880 census, Jaynes has estimated that wage plantations were approximately 35 percent more efficient than share plantations (1986, 242–43 and 326–41). Hence, as Jaynes writes: "Why would planters and laborers voluntarily forsake such a large percentage of their income?" (1986, 244).

5. Sharecropping arrangements were generally made in terms of "halves," "thirds," or "fourths." For example, the cropper working on "halves" furnished mainly his labor and some farm provisions. The landowner provided the land, seed, fertilizer, and some farm implements. At the end of the year, the crop was divided in half. The arrangements based on "thirds" and "fourths" involved variations on the same theme, in which the landowner would provide even greater amounts of capital assets and reap a greater proportion of the crop (two-thirds or three-fourths respectively) (DeCanio 1974, 278–86).

6. Consider the following description by the Georgia Supreme Court in 1872: "There is an obvious distinction between a cropper and a tenant. One has possession of the premises exclusive of the landlord, the other has not. The one has a right for a fixed time, the other has only a right to go on the land to plant, work and gather the crop" (quoted in Wright [1986, 102]).

7. The crop-liens system also fostered specialization in cotton production, which led to severe problems of cotton overproduction and low cotton prices (Jaynes 1986, 245; Ransom and Sutch 1977, 159–68; Wright 1978, 169–76).

8. For example, see data on the terms of occupancy for share tenants in 1910, which show that about 45 percent of share tenants in the older cotton-producing areas of the Southeast stayed on farms for less than one year (Wright 1986, 93).

9. Alongside these formal or legal controls over labor, informal mechanisms such as agreements between landowners to limit labor competition, planter collusion with the Freedmen's Bureau, and the outright use of terror served as further controls over black labor (Du Bois 1975, 670–728; Wiener 1978, 35–69).

10. Friedmann (1980a) argues that both the sharecropping and the crop-liens systems in the American South were similar to precapitalist institutions. She likens the crop-liens system to a precapitalist form of credit because it was based on factor monopolies and coercion rather than market competition. She further argues that, along with these credit monopolies, the immobility of land and labor meant that Southern sharecropping was comparable to a peasant form of production because the reproduction of sharecropping farms was not based on direct market relations. For other writers who view sharecropping as similar to a "precapitalist" form of labor exploitation, see Lenin (1974, 25), Moore (1966, 111 and 147), and Rochester (1940, 63).

11. As early as 1900, white sharecroppers outnumbered blacks (Rochester 1940, 59–60; Shannon 1945, 99). However, not only was Southern sharecropping developed primarily to deal with the problems of controlling the newly freed black labor force, but also white sharecroppers were far less likely to experience racially motivated terror or barriers to education, credit, and occupational advancement—all of which contributed to the semi-free nature of black labor under the American sharecropping system.

12. Some notable exceptions here are Jaynes (1986) and Wright (1986). Although Wright devotes less of his analysis to these issues than does Jaynes, Wright gives a high priority to natural factors in his explanation of why wage labor failed to substitute for slavery in postbellum cotton production. He captures the essence of this problem when he writes: "Tenancy was the price planters paid for the certainty of harvest labor" (1986, 235; see also 91).

13. There are other writers who argue that family sharecropping arose from mutual agreement between landowners and laborers. According to these theories, this compromise was not the result of class struggles, but rather of the workings of the "hidden hand" of the market, which eventually demonstrated that the economic interests of both classes were most rationally and best served by the family sharecropping system (Reid 1973; Shlomowitz 1979). For a critique of this view see R. L. F. Davis (1982, 194–96) and Royce (1985, 289–90).

14. Laborers' preferences for share payments shifted with different historical conditions. After the Panic of 1873, there were attempts by some rural laborers to replace share payments with wages paid on a regular monthly basis. Historians often overlook this later rejection of share payments and the fact that shares were often only preferred by laborers to *postharvest* wage payments, not necessarily to wages paid on a regular basis. Indeed, there is a good deal of documentation that laborers in a number of Southern states preferred day labor or regularly paid wages to share payments, particularly after

experiencing the limitations of the sharecropping system (Jaynes 1986, 220–23).

15. Because of these regional differences, when black power thesis advocates are discussing the rise of sharecropping they tend to be documenting a slightly later period in the chronology of the emergence of family sharecropping. For example, R. L. F. Davis argues that family sharecropping replaced wage labor as the dominant mode of agriculture in 1889 (1982, 58), while Jaynes argues that family sharecropping was well established by 1876 (1986, 188).

16. For example, under wage contracts laborers often were docked pay for any activities resulting in loss of time from the job, such as tardiness or insubordination (R. L. F. Davis 1982, 104–5).

17. The Natchez District suffered less war devastation because of the early and relatively easy taking of Natchez and the surrounding countryside by Union forces in 1862. The ease of this occupation has been attributed to both the Confederate decision to concentrate its strength at Vicksburg and to the pro-Union sentiments held by numerous planters in the Natchez District (R. L. F. Davis 1982, 59).

18. By examining samples of share contracts in the years 1867 and 1868, Jaynes provides convincing documentation of the fact that these labor contracts were made to groups that were too large and contained too many diverse surnames to constitute family units, thus suggesting squad or gang labor (1986, 169–73). See also the description of the "through and through" method of sharecropping, described in Paige (1975, 59) or Wright (1978, 163).

19. While advocates of the black power thesis are incorrect in regard to their argument that class conflict arose primarily over the wage system versus the share system, they were correct to highlight how autonomy in the workplace was a major issue.

20. Many factors contributed to this decline in female field labor. There is some evidence that blacks (both male and female) held the traditional view that women's place was in the home (Jones 1985, 63 and 78; Rosengarten 1975, 120–21; Woloch 1984, 226). Jones also suggests that withdrawing from field labor was one way of removing black women from physical and sexual abuse by white landowners and overseers (1985, 60). Jaynes argues that more important factors included the extremely low wages women received for cotton field labor (regardless of their individual productivity) and the significant economic contributions women's domestic labor and subsistence gardening provided to black households (1986, 231–32).

21. Jaynes's (1986) is the only work I have seen that explicitly discusses the major role played by patriarchal authority in bringing female and child labor back into the fields. Indeed, there exists some controversy as to whether sharecropping households were patriarchal. For example, even some feminist historians are hesitant to characterize sharecropping households as patriarchal because of the interdependence of family labor and the virtually propertyless nature of these households, where male croppers controlled little economic and political power (Jones 1985, 104–5). For a detailed discussion of these and other writings on sharecropping and patriarchy, see Mann (1989).

22. See, for example, Weber (1972) or Chayanov (1966a and b). For a discussion of various theories of the role of self-exploitation in family labor enterprises, see Chapter 1.

23. Welty (1987) has a more detailed discussion of these and other problems associated with the concept of self-exploitation.

24. For a more detailed discussion of how unequal interpersonal relationships within sharecropping households were politically and institutionally buttressed by the state, churches, and ruling class hegemony, see Mann (1989).

25. As Ruth Allen observed from her analysis of women in Texan cotton production in the 1920s, "It is practically a universal situation that the money received from the sale of the crop is the man's income" (1931, 147). See also Sachs (1983, 26).

26. For a more detailed discussion of domestic violence in sharecropping households, see Mann (1989).

27. Von Werlhof presents an intriguing thesis about the relationship between nature, nonwage labor (particularly peasant production), and women's work. Her link between agriculture and women is particularly interesting, given the fact that, historically, women's social roles have so often been defined by their natural or biological capacity to bear children, just as I am arguing that social relations in agriculture are often defined by nature. See her interesting coedited book, *Women: The Last Colony* (Mies, Bennholdt-Thomsen, and von Werlhof 1988).

28. Jaynes argues that the natural disasters of 1866 and 1867 could have been offset by adequate government policies. More adequate levee construction could have mitigated the effect of flooding, while government financial assistance could have fostered earlier land preparation and planting, which could have reduced the effect of the cotton worm (1986, 244–45).

29. Consider in contrast, the wheat-producing areas of the West, where farmers faced an even longer production time for wheat, but where the rapid growth of state mortgage and deposit banks crushed local credit monopolies. Not only were these wheat farmers more literate than most Southern rural producers, but also they tended to be property-owning simple commodity producers, rather than sharecroppers, so they had assets to offer as collateral on loans. This comparison suggests that the problem of a lengthy production time is not an immutable barrier to development, but that it can be modified, reduced, or offset by social factors.

30. There are a number of other important distinctions between sharecropping and wage labor. Because Southern sharecropping was organized on the basis of family labor, croppers were not hired as individuals. Rather land was allocated on the basis of the size, as well as the gender and age composition of the family unit, with less land being allocated for females and children than for males (Shannon 1945, 88). Here the value of labor power not only was blurred by family labor, but also by the fact that labor was tied to the production of a finished commodity, rather than to specified time intervals. Moreover, the more isolated nature of family sharecropping also contrasts with the more cooperative nature of either wage or share work when laborers are orga-

nized in gangs or squads. As noted above, Southern sharecropping also entailed a number of formal and informal restrictions on labor mobility that were more reminiscent of precapitalist than of capitalist forms of labor control. For more discussion of these issues, see Mann (1984b) and Friedmann (1980a).

31. The regional imbalances in the profitability of cotton production were also reflected in the fact that the newer cotton-producing areas were able to pay higher wages and hence attract and maintain a more stable labor supply. For instance, in 1867, laborers in North Carolina were paid on average $104 per year, and in Georgia, $125 per year. In contrast, in Texas they were paid on average $139 per year, and in Oklahoma, $158 per year (Zeichner 1939, 29).

32. While this regional comparison only focused on natural factors, certainly the close proximity of Texas to underdeveloped Mexico provided an alternative source of abundant and cheap labor (DeCanio 1974, 69; Myrdal 1944, 1249; Fulmer 1950, 83). Landowners in the Southeast tried unsuccessfully to attract immigrant labor to solve their labor supply and management problems. Their plans to import labor met with fierce opposition from small white farmers and from ex-slaves, since such cheap labor would place both of these groups at a competitive disadvantage (J. S. Allen 1970, 72; Saloutos 1960, 19; Zeichner 1939, 26).

33. Cotton production was only introduced into the new irrigated cotton lands of California, New Mexico, and Arizona after 1914, in response to the demands of World War I. However, in a short fifteen years all of these states in the Far West showed extremely high average expenditures on wage labor per farm, surpassing both the Southeast and the Southwest (U.S. Bureau of Census 1930b, 15–17 and 66–70).

## *Chapter 5*

1. The U.S. census did not count sharecroppers separately from other share tenants until 1920. However, during the decade between 1920 and 1930, sharecropping farms increased from 17.5 percent to 24.1 percent of all Southern farms. By 1930 they made up 36.2 percent and 27.9 percent of all farms in the Delta and Eastern regions respectively, but only constituted 18 percent of all farms in Texas and Oklahoma (Rochester 1940, 59; Fulmer 1950, 74).

2. There was a back-to-the-farm movement in most regions of the country during the 1930s, including most areas of the South. However, despite this movement, the Southern plantation counties lost population during this period (James 1981b, 14; Rochester 1940, 69). For example, in the Mississippi Delta region, the farm population decreased by 13.4 percent between 1930 and 1935 (Melman 1949, 63). Both black and white sharecroppers were victims of this Southern enclosure (Fulmer 1950, 74–75).

3. Prior to 1954, the U.S. agricultural censuses tended to underestimate the number of hired workers because the counts were often taken in months when labor requirements were especially low, such as months following the peak harvest period (Kirby 1987, 67–68).

4. There is currently a debate over whether the state played a "neutral" and

class "autonomous" role in regard to the New Deal agricultural policies or whether the state developed its farm policy in response to pressure from rural class forces. For a discussion of this debate, see Gilbert and Howe (1988), Hooks (1983), Skocpol and Finegold (1982), Finegold (1981), and Skocpol (1980). I share the view of Gilbert and Howe that the state was responding to class forces, that it was itself an arena of class struggle, and that the New Deal state policies served the interests of specific social classes.

5. For a discussion of different forms of "revolutions from above," see Moore (1966, xv–xvi and 433–52).

6. Marx used the term "primitive accumulation" to refer to the initial accumulation of capital that occurred through mechanisms other than market activities and that fostered the origins of modern capitalism. As he writes: "The so-called primitive accumulation, therefore, is nothing else than the historical process of divorcing the producer from the means of production" (1967a, 668).

7. In both tobacco and rice farming, the AAA stabilized farm incomes and did not disrupt traditional tenure arrangements (Daniel 1985, 109).

8. A notable example of the domination of AAA committees and agencies by large farmers is provided by Oscar Johnston, finance director of the AAA in 1933 and later vice-president of the AAA's Commodity Credit Corporation. Mr. Johnston was also the manager of the largest cotton plantation in the United States (Rochester 1940, 64). For more discussion of local farmer committees that implemented the AAA programs, see James (1981c, 243–328).

9. There were also strong links between the Southern landowning class and the Democratic party. For a discussion of these links and their effects on local politics, see Bloom (1981).

10. Between 1934 and 1937, the average plantation size increased from 955 acres to 1,014 acres (Daniel 1985, 169).

11. By the late 1930s the STFU had been substantially weakened as a result of splits within its ranks and changes in the Southern economy that undermined its membership and the sharecropping system in general (Kirby 1987, 259–71; Fite 1984, 145).

12. Friedmann argues that factor monopolies and the relative immobility of labor resulting from the sharecropping and crop-liens systems militated against both technological innovation and certain types of market responses (1980a, 174–75).

13. For a more detailed discussion of various ways in which agriculture and industry differ in terms of the specialization of production, see Chapter 2.

14. In many cases controls on acreage were offset by increasing yields per acre. For example, in 1938, when the AAA provided payments to farmers who participated in acreage allotments for corn, wheat, rice, and cotton, yield per acre began to show an upward trend for all four crops. By the 1960s, it was estimated that the intensification of land use had reduced the overall impact of production controls by one-half (Rasmussen and Baker 1969, 76; Paarlberg 1964, 297).

15. Despite the fact that racism restricted blacks from many wartime jobs, the number of black men in the principal war industries, such as iron and

steel, machinery, aircraft, and shipbuilding, tripled in the four years between 1940 and 44 (Mandle 1978, 86). Along with causing a rural labor shortage, the war also generated demands for certain types of foods and oils that furthered the diversification of Southern agriculture and moved farmers into types of farming that could more easily be mechanized. In addition, the prosperity during the war provided many farmers with profits to invest in more capital-intensive farming of all types (Fite 1984, 164–67).

16. It is argued, for example, that the basic principle on which the first commercially viable mechanical harvesters were eventually based was discovered in 1927, but little interest was generated by this discovery because of the availability of a cheap and dependent labor force (James 1981b, 7; Street 1957, 124; Melman 1949, 64). Rather than using natural impediments to explain the delay in the widespread use of the mechanical pickers after International Harvesters' commercially viable invention in 1941, it has been argued that during the war years the shift to mechanical harvesting, though often desired by planters, was not always feasible due to the shortage of materials (Mandle 1978, 91). For more discussion of these issues, see also Fite (1984, 188) and Haystead and Fite (1956, 116).

17. Along with the government subsidies that disproportionately benefited well-to-do farmers, the high costs of mechanization and the fact that harvesters were economically viable only on landholdings of a certain size also contributed to the process whereby mechanization took place first on the largest farms. For example, in 1945 a cotton picker cost $2,674 and a tractor $1,250. According to Fite, with "only slight exaggeration" a South Carolina farmer reported in 1949 that a picker would cost as much as a hundred acres of land (1984, 186).

18. As Bartley points out, the rural roots of the civil rights movement have not been fully appreciated even by scholars of Southern history: "During the second half of the 1960s, ghetto riots in northern cities spurred occasional journalistic interest in the 'southern roots of the urban crises,' but rarely did scholars demonstrate concern or understanding of the southern enclosure" (1987, 440).

19. Jack Temple Kirby, quoted on the jacket of Fite's book on Southern agriculture, *Cotton Fields No More* (1984).

20. Daniel argues that competition from Western cotton producers in the United States provided a much greater threat to Southern farmers than competition from either synthetic fibers or foreign cotton producers, which may account for his failure to examine these global factors in any detail (1985, 22).

21. There are other notable exceptions here, such as the writings of Street (1957) and Rochester (1940). However, even though these writers mention the impact of global factors, their discussions tend to be brief and descriptive, rather than analytical. That is, these global factors are not examined within the context of a larger theoretical framework that explains uneven development.

22. Wright argues that the decline in world cotton demand contributed to the slow growth of Southern incomes for decades to come. To buttress his

argument, he shows the remarkable correspondence between world demand for cotton and Southern per capita income from 1860 until World War I (1974, 634).

23. American cotton had a number of advantages over cotton produced in other countries. Indian cotton was of extremely short staple, which yielded less yarn per machine. It also broke more easily and produced cloth whose quality diminished with washing (Wright 1974, 618–19). Brazilian cotton was of long staple, which was not well adapted to the requirements of the British textile industry. It also was of such high quality that it was largely peripheral to trends in world demand. Similarly, Egyptian cotton was of such high price and quality that it was devoted to fine uses for which the American staple did not compete, although later improvements in cotton varieties increased its competitive position in world markets (Wright 1974, 622; Shannon 1945, 111).

24. For a more detailed discussion of the problems that arise from focusing on exchange as opposed to production, see Chapter 1, as well as Brenner (1977), Goodman and Redclift (1982, 29–51), and Mann (1987c, 228–29).

25. For more discussion of appropriationism and substitutionism in relation to the major theses of this book, see Chapter 2.

26. Prior to this, due to the weakness and luster of rayon, it had been used primarily for embroideries, for which there was a limited market (Robson 1958, 22).

27. Since nylon could be rapidly knitted on warp knitting machines, it also began to displace natural fibers in the production of knitted fabrics (Robson 1958, 32).

28. German manufacturers had tried unsuccessfully to produce rayon viscose of short staple length as early as World War I (Moncrieff 1954, 355).

29. For example, attempts were made in the 1950s to vertically integrate timber production with rayon viscose production. The unprofitability of these attempts was primarily attributed to the fact that even the smaller softwood species of trees had a lengthy production time of about ten years. This together with the costs of land and labor made such vertical integration economically prohibitive (Robson 1958, 65).

30. Acrylics and polyesters were particularly successful in replacing natural fibers in the knitted fabric and smaller woolen industries as early as the 1950s (Robson 1958, 31–34; Tisdell and McDonald 1979, 5).

31. The different focuses of Kirby, Daniel, and Wright also explain their different timings of this transformation of Southern agriculture. Kirby and Daniel, who focus on the Southern enclosure, both highlight the earlier period between the 1930s and the 1940s. In contrast, Wright, who focuses on the incorporation of the Old South into the national labor market, dates this development as occurring after World War II (Bartley 1987, 442).

32. I have mentioned in Chapter 4 how the rise of state mortgage and deposit banks in the American West crushed local credit monopolies. Another example is provided by the Egyptian government's initiatives in 1910, which were designed to undermine local moneylenders and merchants. These measures included government-provided seed, government posting of cotton prices on a daily basis, attempts to develop savings banks, and laws that pro-

hibited the seizure of small holdings under mortgage (Todd 1915, 296–98).

33. It should be noted that a corollary to Frank's hypothesis that the underdeveloped societies would experience their greatest development when their ties to the developed countries were the weakest is that once the developed countries recover from their crises, the previous development of the periphery would be choked off or channeled into less promising areas of development (Frank 1970, 11–12). Despite this addition, his theory still does not explain why the developed countries witnessed greater development than the peripheral countries during periods of crisis.

## *Chapter 6*

1. In his study of unfree types of labor in the modern era, Miles mentions social and natural obstacles to capitalist development, but tends to do so primarily in a descriptive rather than a theoretical fashion. He also coined the term "anomalous necessity" to refer to conditions "where either capitalist relations of production cannot develop or where their development is obstructed" (1987, 221).

2. For a discussion and critique of this, see Benston (1969).

3. Even though many women work outside the home today, they often are still in structurally dependent positions, because of unequal pay by gender, women's greater likelihood of having part-time work, and the frequent interruption of women's career paths through childbearing and rearing.

4. See Coverman (1989). She summarizes findings from a variety of empirical studies that show how women still do the vast majority of domestic labor, whether or not they work outside of the home.

5. The quote is from Marx's analysis of agriculture (1967b, 242).

6. Breakfast foods were a later addition.

7. Blumenfeld and Mann (1980, 295 and 305). The negligible nutritional value of many fast foods still poses a problem for adequately competing with domestic food preparation.

8. I am referring here to both physical and psychological abuse in families, as well as the findings of distorted child development in many studies of children raised in institutional settings. See also Blumenfeld and Mann (1980, 296–98).

9. See, for example, Ritzer's discussion of Mead's or Cooley's analysis of the development of the self (1983, 298–324).

10. This anomaly is also true in the case of government subsidies to help maintain the nonwage household production and reproduction of labor power.

11. See Mann and Dickinson (1980) and Goodman, Sorj, and Wilkinson (1987, 156–62) for similar insights into the nature of the modern capitalist state.

12. The increase in agricultural productivity fostered by many state programs has the contradictory effect of fostering more government intervention. Hence, taxpayers become part of an endless cycle of subsidizing the chaos

created by the anarchic market. Moreover, the questionable use of farm surpluses from overproduction for imperialistic goals and purposes abroad also has negative effects on different classes in American society. For more on these issues, see Mann and Dickinson (1980, 309–15).

13. Goodman, Sorj, and Wilkinson (1987, 156–57). These writers also make the important point that a view of the state as simply the "guarantor of appropriation and substitution" should not replace other analyses.

14. For a discussion of alternative views of the relationship between nature and society, including this view of nature as the "home" of the human race, see Moltmann (1984).

15. Buttel does not view the advances in biotechnology as constituting a new revolution in agriculture, but rather as an extension of the petrochemical and green revolutions that took place after World War II. In discussing these developments, he points out how the earlier technologies alone resulted in a compound annual growth rate of world agricultural output of 2.43 percent or roughly a 150 percent increase from 1950 to 1985 (1987, 21).

16. For a discussion of revolutions in agricultural production throughout world history, see Lipton with Longhurst (1985). These writers include the neolithic revolution (3500 to 700 B.C.); the medieval agricultural revolution (A.D. 600 to 1200); the eighteenth-century agricultural revolution in Northwest Europe, and the green revolutions in the advanced industrial societies after World War II and in the Third World after 1960. See also Buttel (1987, 20).

17. See Goodman, Sorj, and Wilkinson (1987, 189) for more discussion of these issues.

## *Appendix 1*

1. See, for example, J. E. Davis (1980, 145).

2. Empirical evidence suggests that most American families are indebted today, regardless of whether they are engaged in farm or nonfarm occupations (Ryan 1986, 50–51 and 162–65).

## *Appendix 2*

1. James Dickinson and I responded to some of Mooney's criticisms in Mann and Dickinson 1987a and b. For an earlier critique of Mooney by other authors, see Singer, Green, and Gilles (1983).

2. Mooney's writings are often inconsistent and contradictory in regard to defining capitalist development. According to the definitions used in his 1982 study, poultry production is considered to be very low in terms of capitalist development, even in his latest census year—1974. Yet in another study, he characterizes contract farming as "a specifically capitalist form of exploitation" (1983, 573). Consequently, one would assume that poultry production was highly developed along capitalist lines, given that approximately 90 percent of American poultry was produced by contract farmers in 1970 (J. E. Davis 1980,

144). Moreover, that Mooney uses one definition to critique our thesis empirically (1982, 284–85) and another definition to critique our thesis theoretically (1982, 280 and 288–90) is confusing, to say the least. Even more problematic, however, is the fact that his empirical analysis contradicts his *own* theoretical analysis.

## *Appendix 3*

1. While aquaculture is relatively new to the United States, it has a long history in other societies and is quite developed in the Far East and in Eastern Europe. For example, Hungary and Czechoslovakia derive over 75 percent of their fishery protein from aquaculture (Bell 1978, 295).

2. In some cases, aquaculture is treated as a branch of agriculture, such as in library references and in some government agencies. However, in precise terms it is clearly a nonfarm form of production.

3. Because aquaculture is so underdeveloped, I am referring here to the fact that even in highly industrialized societies there are a multitude of petty commodity producers who make their living from the sea by gathering, raking, or netting shellfish and finfish, such as shrimpers or fishermen and -women.

# *Bibliography*


Albrow, Martin

1970 *Bureaucracy*. New York: Praeger.

Allen, James S.

1970 *Reconstruction: The Battle for Democracy 1865–1876*. New York: International Publishers.

Allen, Ruth

1931 *The Labor of Women in the Production of Cotton*. Austin: University of Texas Press.

Amin, Samir

1978 *Accumulation on a World Scale*. New York: Monthly Review Press.

Anderson, Ellen, and F. P. Weaver

1939 *Prices and Pennsylvania Agriculture*. Pennsylvania State College Bulletin 384. University Park: Pennsylvania State College Press.

Armstrong, David L.

1969 Can Family Farms Compete?—An Economic Analysis. In *Corporation Farming: What Are the Issues?*, pp. 38–50. Report no. 53, prepared for the U.S.D.A. Washington, D.C.: G.P.O.

Bakker, Hans

1981 Bringing Weber Back In: Rural Values, Social Class and Rural Sociology. *Rural Sociologist* 1 (4): 221–30.

1987 Exorcising the Specters: Weber's Interpretive Sociology as Solution to Key Problems in Sociological Theory. *Comparative Rural and Regional Studies* 1 (Summer): 38–56.

Baran, Paul, and Paul Sweezy

1966 *Monopoly Capital: An Essay on the American Economic and Social Order*. New York: Monthly Review Press.

Bartley, Numan V.

1987 The Southern Enclosure Movement. *Georgia Historical Quarterly* 71 (3): 438–50.

Bell, Frederick W.

1978 *Food from the Sea: The Economics and Politics of Ocean Fisheries*. Boulder, Colo.: Westview Press.

Bendix, Reinhard

1960 Socialism and Bureaucracy. *Canadian Journal of Economics and Political Science* 9 (1): 501–14.

Benston, Margaret

1969 The Political Economy of Women's Liberation. *Monthly Review* 21 (September): 13–27.

Bernstein, Henry
1979 Concepts for the Analysis of Contemporary Peasantries. *Journal of Peasant Studies* 6 (4): 421–44.

Bethel, Elizabeth Rauh
1981 *Promiseland: A Century of Life in a Negro Community*. Philadelphia: Temple University Press.

Billings, Dwight B.
1979 *Planters and the Making of a New South*. Chapel Hill: University of North Carolina Press.

Blassingame, John W.
1972 *The Slave Community: Plantation Life in the Antebellum South*. New York: Oxford University Press.

Bloom, Jack M.
1981 The Political Economy of Southern Racism. Paper presented at the Annual Meeting of the American Sociological Association, Toronto, Ont.

Blumenfeld, Emily, and Susan Mann
1980 Domestic Labour and the Reproduction of Labour Power: Towards an Analysis of Women, the Family and Class. In *Hidden in the Household: Women's Domestic Labour under Capitalism*, edited by Bonnie Fox, pp. 267–307. Toronto: The Women's Press.

Bonnano, Alessandro
1987 *Small Farms: Persistence with Legitimation*. Boulder, Colo.: Westview Press.

Braverman, Harry
1974 *Labor and Monopoly Capital: The Degradation of Work in the Twentieth Century*. New York: Monthly Review Press.

Brenner, Robert
1977 The Origins of Capitalist Development: A Critique of Neo-Smithian Marxism. *New Left Review* 104:25–92.

Briggs, Harold E.
1932 Early Bonanza Farming in the Red River Valley of the North. *Agricultural History* 4 (1): 26–37.

Bringer, Gladys Stella
1927 Transition from Slave to Free Labor in Louisiana after the Civil War. M.A. thesis, Tulane University, New Orleans, La.

Burawoy, Michael
1970 The Functions and Reproduction of Migrant Labor: Comparative Material from South Africa and the United States. *American Journal of Sociology* 81 (5): 1051–87.

Busch, Lawrence, and William B. Lacy
1983 *Science, Agriculture, and the Politics of Research*. Boulder, Colo.: Westview Press.

Buttel, Frederick
1980 The Political Economy of Agriculture in the Advanced Industrial Societies: Some Observations from the United States. Paper pre-

sented at the Annual Meeting of the Canadian Sociology and Anthropology Association, Montreal.
1982a Farm Structure and Rural Development. In *Rural Policy Problems: Changing Dimensions*, edited by B. W. P. Browne and D. F. Hadwiger, pp. 213–35. Lexington, Mass.: Lexington Books.
1982b The Political Economy of Agriculture in Advanced Industrial Societies: Some Observations on Theory and Method. In *Current Perspectives on Social Theory*, edited by S. G. McNall, pp. 27–55. Greenwich, Conn.: JAI Press.
1982c The Political Economy of Part-Time Farming. *GeoJournal* 6 (4): 293–300.
1983 Beyond the Family Farm. In *Technology and Social Change in Rural Areas*, edited by G. F. Summers. Boulder, Colo.: Westview Press.
1985 Biotechnology and Genetic Information: Implications for Rural People and the Institutions That Serve Them. *Rural Sociologist* 5 (January): 68–78.
1986 Biotechnology and Agricultural Research Policy: Emergent Issues. In *New Directions in Agriculture and Agricultural Research*, edited by K. A. Dahlberg, pp. 312–40. Totowa, N.J.: Rowman and Allanheld.
1987 Biotechnology, Agriculture, and Rural America: Socioeconomic and Ethical Issues. Paper presented at the Iowa State University Agricultural Bioethics Symposium, Ames, Iowa.

Buttel, Frederick, Olaf Larson, and Gilbert Gillespie
1989 *The Sociology of Agriculture*. Westport, Conn.: Greenwood Press.

Buttel, Frederick, and H. Newby, eds.
1980 *The Rural Sociology of the Advanced Societies: Critical Perspectives*. Montclair, N.J.: Allanheld, Osmun.

Carlton, R. A.
1987 Durkheim, Human Ecology and Canadian Rural Studies. *Comparative Rural and Regional Studies* 1 (Summer): 1-7.

Carstensen, Vernon
1974 *Farmer Discontent 1865–1900*. New York: John Wiley and Sons.

Cash, W. J.
1969 *The Mind of the South*. New York: Vintage Books.

Chapman, Stephen
1979 Welfare Tractors. *The New Republic*, March 3, pp. 16–17.

Chayanov, A. V.
1966a On the Theory of Non-Capitalist Economic Systems. In *The Theory of Peasant Economy*, edited by Daniel Thorner, Basile Kerblay, and R. E. F. Smith, pp. 1-28. Homewood, Ill.: Richard Irwin.
1966b Peasant Farm Organization. In *The Theory of Peasant Economy*, edited by Daniel Thorner, Basile Kerblay, and R. E. F. Smith, pp. 31-299. Homewood, Ill.: Richard Irwin.

Chirot, Daniel, and Thomas Hall
1982 World-System Theory. *Annual Review of Sociology* 8:81–106.

Christidis, Basil G., and George J. Harrison
1955 *Cotton Growing Problems*. New York: McGraw-Hill.
Clark, Thomas, and Albert Kirwan
1967 *The South since Appomattox*. New York: Oxford University Press.
Cohen, R. L.
1940 *The Economics of Agriculture*. Cambridge: The University Press.
Collings, Gilbert H.
1926 *The Production of Cotton*. New York: John Wiley and Sons.
Conrad, David Eugene
1965 *The Forgotten Farmers: The Story of Sharecroppers in the New Deal*. Urbana: University of Illinois Press.
Contreras, Ariel José
1977 Límites de la producción capitalista en la agricultura. *Revista Mexicana de Sociologia* 39 (3): 885–99.
Cordtz, Dan
1972 A Tough Row to Hoe. *Fortune*, August, pp. 17–25.
Coulter, E. Merton
1947 *The South during Reconstruction*. Baton Rouge: Louisiana State University Press.
Courtenay, Philip P.
1965 *Plantation Agriculture*. New York: Praeger.
Coverman, Shelley W.
1989 Women's Work Is Never Done: The Division of Domestic Labor. In *Women: A Feminist Perspective*, edited by Jo Freeman. Mountain View, Calif.: Mayfield.
Daniel, Pete
1985 *Breaking the Land: The Transformation of Cotton, Tobacco, and Rice Cultures since 1880*. Chicago: University of Illinois Press.
Davis, John Emmeus
1980 Capitalist Agricultural Development and the Exploitation of the Propertied Laborer. In *The Rural Sociology of the Advanced Societies: Critical Perspectives*, edited by F. Buttel and H. Newby, pp. 133–53. Montclair, N.J.: Allanheld, Osmun.
Davis, Ronald L. F.
1982 *Good and Faithful Labor: From Slavery to Sharecropping in the Natchez District, 1860–1890*. Westport, Conn.: Greenwood Press.
Day, Richard H.
1967 The Economics of Technological Change and the Demise of the Sharecropper. *American Economic Review* 57 (3): 427–49.
De Beauvoir, Simone
1952 *The Second Sex*. New York: Bantam Books.
DeCanio, Stephen J.
1973 Cotton Overproduction in Late Nineteenth Century Southern Agriculture. *Journal of Economic History* 33 (3): 608–33.
1974 *Agriculture in the Postbellum South: The Economics of Production and Supply*. Cambridge, Mass.: MIT Press.

De Janvry, Alain
1980 Social Differentiation in Agriculture and the Ideology of Neopopulism. In *The Rural Sociology of the Advanced Societies: Critical Perspectives*, edited by F. Buttel and H. Newby, pp. 155–68. Montclair, N.J.: Allanheld, Osmun.

Dickinson, James, and Bob Russell, eds.
1986 *Family, Economy and State: The Social Reproduction Process under Capitalism*. London: Croom Helm.

Dobb, Maurice
1970 *Studies in the Development of Capitalism*. New York: International.

Dovring, Folke
1965 *Land and Labour in Europe in the Twentieth Century*. The Hague: Martinus Nijhoft.

Dowd, Douglas F.
1964 A Comparative Analysis of Economic Development in the American West and South. In *United States Economic History: Selected Readings*, edited by Harry Scheiber, pp. 271–88. New York: Alfred A. Knopf.

Du Bois, W. E. B.
1975 *Black Reconstruction in America, 1860–1880*. New York: Atheneum.

Durkheim, Emile
1964 *The Division of Labor in Society*. New York: Free Press.

Ellis, Dorothy Lois
1932 The Transition from Slave Labor to Free Labor, with Special Reference to Louisiana. M.A. thesis, Louisiana State University, Baton Rouge.

Elwood, R. B., L. E. Arnold, D. C. Schmutz, and E. G. McKibben
1939 *Changes in Technology and Labor Requirements in Crop Production: Wheat and Oats*. National Research Project, Report no. A-10, prepared for the Work Progress Administration. Philadelphia, Pa.

Emmanuel, Arghiri
1972 *Unequal Exchange: A Study of the Imperialism of Trade*. New York: Monthly Review Press.

Engels, Friedrich
n.d. *Engels on Capital*. London: Lawrence and Wishart.
1890 Engels to Vera Zasulich. In *Karl Marx and Friedrich Engels: Selected Correspondence*. Moscow: Progress.
1969 *Anti-Dühring*. Moscow: Progress.
1970 *The Peasant Question in France and Germany*. Moscow: Progress.
1974 *The Origin of the Family, Private Property, and the State*. New York: International.

Falk, William, and Jess Gilbert
1985 Bringing Rural Sociology Back In. *Rural Sociology* 47 (4): 561–77.

Federal Writers' Project
1975 *These Are Our Lives*. New York: W. W. Norton.

Fine, Ben

1979 On Marx's Theory of Agricultural Rent. *Economy and Society* 8 (3): 41–78.

1980 On Marx's Theory of Agricultural Rent. *Economy and Society* 9 (3): 327–31.

Finegold, Kenneth

1981 From Agrarianism to Adjustment: The Political Origins of New Deal Agricultural Policy. *Politics and Society* 11:1–27.

Fite, Gilbert C.

1984 *Cotton Fields No More: Southern Agriculture, 1865–1980*. Lexington: University Press of Kentucky.

Flora, Cornelia Butler

1981 Farm Women, Farming Systems and Agricultural Structure: Suggestions for Scholarship. *Rural Sociologist* 1 (6): 383–86.

1985 Women and Agriculture. *Agriculture and Human Values* 2 (1): 5–12.

Flora, Cornelia Butler, and Sue Johnson

1978 Discarding the Distaff: New Roles for Rural Women. In *Rural U.S.A.: Persistance and Change*, edited by Thomas Ford, pp. 168–81. Ames: Iowa State University Press.

Flora, Jan L., and John M. Stitz

1985 Ethnicity, Persistence, and Capitalization of Agriculture in the Great Plains during the Settlement Period. *Rural Sociology* 50 (Fall): 341–60.

Fogel, Robert William, and Stanley L. Engerman

1974 *Time on the Cross: The Economics of American Negro Slavery*. Boston: Little, Brown.

Foote, Richard J.

1970 *Concepts Involved in Defining and Identifying Farms*. Economic Research Service, Report no. 448, prepared for the U.S. Department of Agriculture. Washington, D.C.: G.P.O.

Fox, Bonnie, ed.

1980 *Hidden in the Household: Women's Domestic Labour under Capitalism*. Toronto: The Women's Press.

Frank, André Gunder

1970 The Development of Underdevelopment. In *Imperialism and Underdevelopment: A Reader*, edited by Robert Rhodes. New York: Monthly Review Press.

Franklin, John Hope

1967 *From Slavery to Freedom: A History of Negro Americans*. 3d ed. New York: Random House.

Freeman, Jo, ed.

1984 *Women: A Feminist Perspective*. 3d ed. Mountain View, Calif.: Mayfield.

Freund, J.

1968 *The Sociology of Max Weber*. New York: Pantheon.

Friedland, William H.

1980 Technology in Agriculture: Labor and the Rate of Accumulation.

In *The Rural Sociology of the Advanced Societies: Critical Perspectives*, edited by F. Buttel and H. Newby, pp. 201–14. Montclair, N.J.: Allanheld, Osmun.

1984a Commodity Systems Analysis: An Approach to the Sociology of Agriculture. *Research in Rural Sociology and Development* 1:221–35.

1984b The Labor Force in U.S. Agriculture. In *Food Security in the United States*, edited by L. Busch and W. B. Lacy, pp. 143–81. Boulder, Colo.: Westview Press.

1987 Women and Agriculture: A State of the Art Assessment. Paper presented at the Annual Meeting of the American Sociological Association, Chicago.

Friedland, William H., and Amy E. Barton

1975 *Destalking the Wily Tomato: A Case Study in Social Consequences in California Agricultural Research*. Department of Applied Behavioral Sciences, Research Monograph no. 15. Davis: University of California Press.

Friedland, William H., Amy E. Barton, and Robert J. Thomas

1981 *Manufacturing Green Gold: Capital, Labor, and Technology in the Lettuce Industry*. New York: Cambridge University Press.

Friedmann, Harriet

1976 The Transformation of Wheat Production in the Era of the World Market 1873–1935: A Global Analysis of Production and Exchange. Ph.D. dissertation, Harvard University, Cambridge, Mass.

1978a Simple Commodity Production and Wage Labour in the American Plains. *Journal of Peasant Studies* 6 (1): 71–100.

1978b World Market, State and Family Farm: Social Bases of Household Production in an Era of Wage Labour. *Comparative Studies in Society and History* 20 (4): 545–86.

1980a Economic Analysis of the Postbellum South: Regional Economies and World Markets, a Review Article. *Comparative Studies in Society and History* 22 (4): 639–52.

1980b Household Production and the National Economy: Concepts for the Analysis of Agrarian Formations. *Journal of Peasant Studies* 7 (1): 158–84.

1981 The Family Farm in Advanced Capitalism: Outline of a Theory of Simple Commodity Production in Agriculture. Paper Presented at the Annual Meeting of the American Sociological Association, Toronto.

1982 The Political Economy of Food: The Rise and Fall of the Postwar International Food Order. *American Journal of Sociology* 88 (Supplement): 248–86.

1986 Patriarchal Commodity Production. *Social Analysis* 20 (December): 47–55.

1988 Patriarchy and Property: A Reply to Goodman and Redclift. *Sociologia Ruralis* 26 (2): 186–93.

Frundt, H. J.
1975 *American Agribusiness and U.S. Foreign Agricultural Policy*. Ph.D. Dissertation, Rutgers University, New Brunswick, N.J.
Fulmer, John Leonard
1950 *Agricultural Progress in the Cotton Belt since 1920*. Chapel Hill: University of North Carolina Press.
Galeski, Boguslaw, and Eugene Wilkening, eds.
1987 *Family Farming in Europe and America*. Boulder, Colo.: Westview Press.
Gardiner, Jean
1975 Women's Domestic Labour. *New Left Review* 89 (January–February 1975): 47–59.
Garraty, John A., ed.
1968 *The Transformation of American Society, 1870–1890*. New York: Harper and Row.
Gartrell, John W., and C. David Gartrell
1980 Beyond Earth, Water, Weather and Wind. *Rural Sociology* 45 (Fall): 524–30.
Genovese, Eugene
1976 *Roll, Jordan, Roll: The World the Slaves Made*. New York: Vintage Books.
George, Henry
1901 *Our Land and Land Policy*. New York: Doubleday and McClure.
George, Susan
1977 *How the Other Half Dies: The Real Reasons for World Hunger*. Montclair, N.J.: Allanheld, Osmun.
Giddens, Anthony
1971 *Capitalism and Modern Social Theory*. Cambridge: Cambridge University Press.
Gilbert, Jess
1982 Rural Theory: The Grounding of Rural Sociology. *Rural Sociology* 47 (Winter): 609–33.
Gilbert, Jess, and Raymond Akor
1988 Increasing Structural Divergence in U.S. Dairying: California and Wisconsin since 1950. *Rural Sociology* 53 (Spring): 56–72.
Gilbert, Jess, and Carolyn Howe
1988 Beyond 'State *vs.* Society': Theories of the State and New Deal Agricultural Policy. Unpublished manuscript, Department of Rural Sociology, University of Wisconsin, Madison.
Glavanis, Kathy R. G.
1984 Aspects of Non-Capitalist Social Relations in Rural Egypt. In *Family and Work in Rural Societies: Perspectives on Non-Wage Labour*, edited by N. Long, pp. 30–60. New York: Tavistock.
Goldschmidt, Walter
1947 *As You Sow*. New York: Harcourt, Brace.

Goodman, David, and Michael Redclift
1982 *From Peasant to Proletarian: Capitalist Development and Agrarian Transitions*. New York: St. Martin's Press.
1985 Capitalism, Petty Commodity Production, and the Farm Enterprise. *Sociologia Ruralis* 13 (3/4): 231–47.
Goodman, David, Bernardo Sorj, and John Wilkinson
1987 *From Farming to Biotechnology*. London: Basil Blackwell.
Gordon, David M., ed.
1977 *Problems in Political Economy: An Urban Perspective*. 2d ed. Lexington, Mass.: D. C. Heath.
Goss, Kevin, Frederick Buttel, and Richard Rodefeld
1980 The Political Economy of Class Structure in U.S. Agriculture: A Theoretical Outline. In *The Rural Sociology of the Advanced Societies: Critical Perspectives*, edited by F. Buttel and H. Newby, pp. 83–132. Montclair, N.J.: Allanheld, Osmun.
Green, Gary P.
1984 Credit and Agriculture: Some Consequences of the Centralization of the Banking System. *Rural Sociology* 49 (Winter): 568–79.
1987 The Political Economy of Flue-Cured Tobacco Production. *Rural Sociology* 52 (2): 221–41.
Grubbs, Donald H.
1971 *Cry from the Cotton: The Southern Tenant Farmers' Union and the New Deal*. Chapel Hill: University of North Carolina Press.
Gutman, Herbert G.
1976 *The Black Family in Slavery and Freedom, 1750–1925*. New York: Pantheon Books.
Hacker, Louise M.
1970 *The Course of American Economic Growth and Development*. New York: John Wiley and Sons.
Hadinger, Don, and William Browne, eds.
1978 *The New Politics of Food*. Toronto: Lexington Books.
Hague, Douglas C.
1957 *The Economics of Man-Made Fibres*. London: Gerald Duckworth.
Harrison, Mark
1975 Chayanov and the Economics of the Russian Peasantry. *Journal of Peasant Studies* 2 (4): 122–42.
1977 The Peasant Mode of Production in the Work of A. V. Chayanov. *Journal of Peasant Studies* 4 (4): 323–36.
Hartmann, Heidi I.
1981 The Unhappy Marriage of Marxism and Feminism: Towards a More Progressive Union. In *Women and Revolution*, edited by Lydia Sargent, pp. 1–41. Boston: South End Press.
Havens, A. Eugene, ed., with Gregory Hooks, Patrick Mooney, and Max Pfeffer
1986 *Studies in the Transformation of U.S. Agriculture*. Boulder, Colo.: Westview Press.

Hawks, Joanne, and Sheila Skemp, eds.
1983 *Sex, Race, and the Role of Women in the South*. Jackson: University Press of Mississippi.
Haystead, Ladd, and Gilbert Fite
1956 *The Agricultural Regions of the United States*. Norman: University of Oklahoma Press.
Hedley, Max
1977 The Transformation of the Domestic Mode of Production. Paper presented at the Annual Meeting of the Canadian Sociology and Anthropology Association, Fredericton, New Brunswick.
1981 Relations of Production of the 'Family Farm.' *Journal of Peasant Studies* 9 (1): 71–85.
Hightower, Jim
1973 *Hard Tomatoes, Hard Times*. Cambridge, Mass.: Schenkman.
Hobhouse, Henry
1986 *Seeds of Change: Five Plants That Transformed Mankind*. New York: Harper and Row.
Holley, William C., and Lloyd E. Arnold
1938 *Changes in Technology and Labor Requirements in Crop Production: Cotton*. National Research Project, Report no. A-7, prepared for the Works Project Administration. Philadelphia, Pa.
Hooks, Gregory M.
1983 A New Deal for Farmers and Social Scientists: The Politics of Rural Sociology in the Depression Era. *Rural Sociology* 48 (3): 386–408.
1986 Critical Rural Sociology of Yesterday and Today. In *Studies in the Transformation of U.S. Agriculture*, edited by A. E. Havens, G. Hooks, P. Mooney, and M. Pfeffer, pp. 1-25. Boulder, Colo.: Westview Press.
Hopkins, John A.
1973 *Changing Technology and Employment in Agriculture*. New York: Da Capo Press.
Hoselitz, B. H.
1960 *Sociological Aspects of Economic Growth*. Glencoe, Ill.: Free Press.
Hufbauer, G. C.
1966 *Synthetic Materials and the Theory of International Trade*. Cambridge: Harvard University Press.
Hussain, Arthur, and Keith Tribe
1981a *Marxism and the Agrarian Question*. Vol. 1. *German Social Democracy and the Peasantry, 1890–1907*. London: Macmillan.
1981b *Marxism and the Agrarian Question*. Vol. 2. *Russian Marxism and the Peasantry, 1861–1930*. London: Macmillan.
Jaggar, Alison M., and Paula S. Rothenberg
1984 *Feminist Frameworks: Alternative Theoretical Accounts of the Relations between Women and Men*. 2d ed. New York: McGraw-Hill.
James, David R.
1981a The Local State and the Resistance to the Civil Rights Movement.

Paper presented at the Annual Meeting of the American Sociological Association, Toronto, Ontario, Canada.
1981b The State, Rural Class Structure and the Adoption of Innovation in Cotton Agriculture. Paper presented at the Annual Meeting of the Rural Sociological Society, Guelph, Ontario, Canada.
1981c *The Transformation of Local State and Class Structures and Resistance to the Civil Rights Movement in the South*. Ph.D. dissertation, University of Wisconsin, Madison.
1986 Local State Structure and the Transformation of Southern Agriculture. In *Studies in the Transformation of U.S. Agriculture*, edited by A. E. Havens, G. Hooks, P. Mooney, and M. Pfeffer, pp. 150–78. Boulder, Colo.: Westview Press.

Janiewski, Dolores
1983 Sisters under Their Skins: Southern Working Women, 1880–1950. In *Sex, Race and the Role of Women in the South*, edited by Joanne V. Hawks and Sheila L. Skemp, pp. 13–35. Jackson, Miss.: University Press of Mississippi.

Jaynes, Gerald David
1986 *Branches without Roots: Genesis of the Black Working Class in the American South, 1862–1882*. New York: Oxford University Press.

Jensen, Joan
1981 *With These Hands: Women Working the Land*. Old Westbury, N.Y.: Feminist Press.

Johnson, Leo A.
1978 Independent Commodity Production, Mode of Production or Capitalist Class Formation: A Critical Analysis. Unpublished manuscript, University of Waterloo, Waterloo, Canada.

Jones, Jacqueline
1985 *Labor of Love, Labor of Sorrow: Black Women, Work, and the Family from Slavery to the Present*. New York: Basic Books.

Kautsky, Karl
1899 *Die Agrarfrage*. Stuttgart: Dietz.
1976 Summary of Selected Parts of Kautsky's *The Agrarian Question*. Translated by J. Banaji. *Economy and Society* 5 (1): 2–49.

Kay, Geoffrey
1976 *Development and Underdevelopment: A Marxist Analysis*. London: Macmillan.

Kerblay, Basile
1966 A. V. Chayanov: Life, Career and Works. In *The Theory of Peasant Economy*, edited by D. Thorner, B. Kerblay, and R. E. F. Smith, pp. xxv–lxxv. Homewood, Ill.: Richard Irwin.
1971 Chayanov and the Theory of Peasantry as a Specific Type of Economy. In *Peasant and Peasant Societies*, edited by Teodore Shanin, pp. 150–60. Harmondsworth: Penguin.

Kester, Howard
1936 *Revolt among the Sharecroppers*. New York: Covici-Friede.

Kirby, Jack Temple
1983 The Transformation of the Southern Plantations, 1920–1960. *Agricultural History* 57 (3): 257–76.
1987 *Rural Worlds Lost: The American South, 1920–1960*. Baton Rouge: Louisiana State University Press.
Kirwan, Albert
1965 *Revolt of the Rednecks*. New York: Harper and Row.
Kloppenburg, Jack R., Jr.
1988 *First the Seed: The Political Economy of Plant Biotechnology, 1492–2000*. New York: Cambridge University Press.
Knox, John J.
1900 *A History of Banking in the United States*. New York: B. Rhodes.
Koc, Mustafa
1987 Uneven Development of Capitalism and the Persistence of Simple Commodity Production in Agriculture: The Case of Tobacco Producers in the Aegean Region, Turkey. Unpublished manuscript, Department of Sociology, University of Toronto, Ontario, Canada.
LaClau, Ernesto
1971 Perspectives on Imperialism: Feudalism and Capitalism in Latin America. *New Left Review* 67:19–38.
Langsford, E. L., and B. H. Thibodeaux
1939 *Plantation Organization and Operation in the Yazoo–Mississippi Delta Area*. Technical Bulletin no. 682, prepared for the U.S. Department of Agriculture. Washington, D.C.: G.P.O.
Laski, Harold
1948 *Communist Manifesto: Socialist Landmark*. London: G. Allen and Unwin.
Lehmann, David
1986 Two Paths of Agrarian Capitalism, or a Critique of Chayanovian Marxism. *Comparative Studies in Society and History* 28 (4): 601–27.
Lenin, V. I.
1939 *Imperialism, the Highest Stage of Capitalism*. New York: International.
1965 *Two Tactics of Social Democracy in the Democratic Revolution*. In *Collected Works*, Vol. 9, pp. 17–140. Moscow: Progress.
1967 *The Development of Capitalism in Russia*. Moscow: Progress.
1970 *The State and Revolution*. Peking: Foreign Languages Press.
1974 New Data on the Laws Governing the Development of Capitalism in Agriculture. In *Collected Works*, Vol. 22, pp. 17–102. Moscow: Progress.
Lerner, Gerda, ed.
1972 *Black Women in White America: A Documentary History*. New York: Pantheon Books.
Levine, Lawrence W.
1978 *Black Culture and Black Consciousness: Afro-American Folk Thought from Slavery to Freedom*. Oxford: Oxford University Press.

Lewin, M.
1968 *Russian Peasants and Soviet Power: A Study of Collectivization*. New York: W. W. Norton.
Lipton, M., with R. Longhurst
1985 *Modern Varieties, International Agricultural Research, and the Poor*. Washington, D.C.: World Bank.
Long, Norman, ed.
1984 *Family and Work in Rural Societies: Perspectives on Non-Wage Labour*. New York: Tavistock.
McMichael, Philip
1984 *Settlers and the Agrarian Question: Foundations of Capitalism in Colonial Australia*. Cambridge: Cambridge University Press.
1987a Bringing Circulation Back into Agricultural Political Economy: Analyzing the Antebellum Plantation in Its World Market Context. *Rural Sociology* 52 (2): 242–63.
1987b Reformulating Comparativism from a Non-Positivist World-Historical Perspective: A Fourth Research Strategy in Historical Sociology. Unpublished manuscript, Department of Sociology, University of Georgia, Athens, Georgia.
1987c What Can World System Theory Add to Comparative-Historical Inquiry? Unpublished Manuscript. Department of Sociology, Cornell University. Ithaca, New York.
Majka, Linda C., and Theo J. Majka
1982 *Farm Workers, Agribusiness, and the State*. Philadelphia: Temple University Press.
Mandel, Ernest
1970 *Marxist Economic Theory*. Vol. 1. New York: Monthly Review Press.
1975 *Late Capitalism*. London: New Left Books.
Mandle, Jay R.
1978 *The Roots of Black Poverty: The Southern Plantation Economy after the Civil War*. Durham, N.C.: Duke University Press.
Mann, Susan Archer
1982 Obstacles to the Capitalist Development of Agriculture: An Analysis of the Class Structure and Uneven Development of American Agriculture, 1870–1930. Ph.D. dissertation, University of Toronto, Canada.
1984a Marx and Weber on Bureaucracy and Rationality. In *Sociology in Action*, edited by Rawlein G. Soberano, pp. 207–35. New Orleans, La.: Alive Associates.
1984b Sharecropping in the Cotton South: A Case of Uneven Development in Agriculture. *Rural Sociology* 49 (3): 412–29.
1986 Family, Class and State in Women's Access to Abortion and Day Care: The Case of the United States. In *Family, Economy and State: The Social Reproduction Process under Capitalism*, edited by James Dickinson and Bob Russell, pp. 223–53. London: Croom Helm.
1987a Classical Sociological Theory and the Agrarian Question: The

Contributions of Marxism. *Comparative Rural and Regional Studies* 1 (Summer): 8–17.
1987b Review of *Farm Women: Work, Farm, and Family in the United States,* by Rachel Ann Rosenfeld. *American Journal of Sociology* 93 (1): 243–45.
1987c The Rise of Wage Labour in the Cotton South: A Global Analysis. *Journal of Peasant Studies* 14 (2): 226–42.
1988 Women in Agriculture: The Invisibility of Patriarchy. Paper presented at the Annual Meeting of the Southern Sociological Society, Nashville, Tenn.
1989 Slavery, Sharecropping, and Sexual Inequality. *Signs: Journal of Women in Culture and Society* 14 (4): 774–98.

Mann, Susan A., and James M. Dickinson
1978 Obstacles to the Development of a Capitalist Agriculture. *Journal of Peasant Studies* 5 (4): 466–81.
1980 State and Agriculture in Two Eras of American Capitalism. In *The Rural Sociology of the Advanced Societies: Critical Perspectives,* edited by F. Buttel and H. Newby, 283–325. Montclair, N.J.: Allanheld, Osmun.
1987a Collectivizing Our Thoughts: A Reply to Patrick Mooney. *Rural Sociology* 52 (2): 296–303.
1987b One Furrow Forward, Two Furrows Back: A Marx-Weber Synthesis for Rural Sociology? *Rural Sociology* 52 (2): 264–85.

Marcuse, Herbert
1971 Industrialization and Capitalism. In *Max Weber and Sociology Today,* edited by O. Stammer. New York: Harper Torchbooks.

Margavio, A. V., and Susan A. Mann
1989 Modernization and the Family: A Theoretical Analysis. *Sociological Perspectives* 32 (1): 109–27.

Martin, Elmer P., and Joanne Mitchell Martin
1986 The Black Woman: Perspectives on Her Role in the Family. In *Ethnicity and Women,* vol. 5, edited by Winston A. Van Horne, pp. 184–205. Ethnicity and Public Policy Series. Madison: University of Wisconsin Press.

Marx, Karl
1967a *Capital.* Vol. 1. Moscow: Progress.
1967b *Capital.* Vol. 2. Moscow: Progress.
1967c *Capital.* Vol. 3. Moscow: Progress.
1970 The Communist Manifesto. In *Selected Works in One Volume.* New York: International.
1972a The Eighteenth Brumaire of Louis Bonaparte. In *The Marx-Engels Reader,* edited by R. Tucker, pp. 436–525. New York: Norton.
1972b On Imperialism in India. In *The Marx-Engels Reader,* edited by R. Tucker, pp. 577–88. New York: Norton.
1973 *Grundrisse.* Harmondsworth: Penguin.

Meillassoux, Claude
1983 The Economic Bases of Demographic Reproduction: From the Do-

mestic Mode of Production to Wage Earning. *Journal of Peasant Studies* 11 (1): 50–61.

Melman, Seymour

1949 An Industrial Revolution in the Cotton South. *Economic History Review* 2 (1): 59–72.

Mies, Maria, Veronika Bennholdt-Thomsen, and Claudia von Werlhof

1988 *Women: The Last Colony*. London: Zed Books.

Miles, Robert

1987 *Capitalism and Unfree Labour: Anomaly or Necessity?* London: Tavistock.

Mitchell, Don

1975 *The Politics of Food*. Toronto: J. Lorimer.

Mitchell, H. L.

1979 *Mean Things Happening in This Land: The Life and Times of H. L. Mitchell, Co-Founder of the Southern Tenant Farmers Union*. Montclair, N.J.: Allanheld, Osmun.

Mitrany, David

1951 *Marx against the Peasant: A Study in Social Dogmatism*. Chapel Hill: University of North Carolina Press.

Mohr, James C.

1978 *Abortion in America: The Origins and Evolution of National Policy*. New York: Oxford University Press.

Moltmann, Jürgen

1984 The Alienation and Liberation of Nature. In *On Nature*, edited by Leroy S. Rouner, pp. 133–44. Notre Dame, Ind.: University of Notre Dame Press.

Mommsen, Wolfgang

1965 Max Weber's Political Sociology and His Philosophy of World History. *UNESCO International Social Science Journal* 17 (1): 23–45.

Moncrieff, R. W.

1954 *Artificial Fibres*. London: National Trade Press.

Mooney, Patrick H.

1982 Labor Time, Production Time and Capitalist Development in Agriculture: A Reconsideration of the Mann-Dickinson Thesis. *Sociologia Ruralis* 22 (3/4): 279–91.

1983 Toward a Class Analysis of Midwestern Agriculture. *Rural Sociology* 48 (4): 563–84.

1986 Class Relations and Class Structure in the Midwest. In *Studies in the Transformation of U.S. Agriculture*, edited by A. E. Havens, G. Hooks, P. Mooney, and M. Pfeffer, pp. 206–51. Boulder, Colo.: Westview Press.

1987 Desperately Seeking: One-dimensional Mann and Dickinson. *Rural Sociology* 52 (2): 286–95.

Moore, Barrington

1966 *The Social Origins of Dictatorship and Democracy: Landlord and Peasant in the Making of the Modern World*. Boston: Beacon Press.

Morgan, D. H. J.
1975 *Social Theory and the Family*. London: Routledge and Kegan Paul.
Mouzelis, N.
1977 Capitalism and the Development of Agriculture. *Journal of Peasant Studies* 4 (7): 483–92.
Murray, Robin
1977 Value and Theory of Rent: Part One. *Capital and Class* (3): 100–22.
1978 Value and Theory of Rent: Part Two. *Capital and Class* (4): 12–33.
Myrdal, Gunnar
1944 *An American Dilemma: The Negro Problem and Modern Democracy*. New York: Harper and Brothers.
Naisbitt, John
1982 *Megatrends: Ten New Directions Transforming Our Lives*. New York: Warner Books.
Nerlove, Marc
1958 *The Dynamics of Supply: Estimation of Farmers' Responses to Prices*. Baltimore: Johns Hopkins University Press.
Newby, Howard
1978 The Rural Sociology of Advanced Capitalist Societies. In *International Perspectives in Rural Sociology*, edited by H. Newby, pp. 3–30. Chichester, England: Wiley.
1983 The Sociology of Agriculture: Toward a New Rural Sociology. *Annual Review of Sociology* 9:67-81.
Nikolitch, Radoje
1962 Family and Larger than Family Farms—Their Relative Position in American Agriculture. Economic Research Service, Report no. 4, prepared for the U.S. Department of Agriculture. Washington, D.C.: G.P.O.
1965 The Adequate Family Farm—Mainstay of the Farm Economy. Economic Research Service, Report no. 247, prepared for the U.S. Department of Agriculture. Washington, D.C.: G.P.O.
1969 Family Operated Farms: Their Compatibility with Technological Advance. *American Journal of Agricultural Economics* 51 (3): 530–45.
Oakley, Ann
1974a *The Sociology of Housework*. New York: Pantheon Books.
1974b *Woman's Work: The Housewife, Past and Present*. New York: Pantheon Books.
O'Connor, A. M.
1966 *An Economic Geography of East Africa*. London: G. Bell and Sons.
O'Connor, James
1973 *The Fiscal Crisis of the State*. New York: St. Martin's Press.
Owens, Leslie H.
1976 *This Species of Property: Slave Life and Culture in the Old South*. New York: Oxford University Press.
Paarlberg, Don
1964 *American Farm Policy*. New York: Wiley.

Paige, Jeffery
1975 *Agrarian Revolution: Social Movements and Export Agriculture in the Underdeveloped World*. New York: Free Press.

Parsons, Talcott
1966 *Societies: Evolutionary and Comparative Perspectives*. Englewood Cliffs, N.J.: Prentice-Hall.

Perelman, Michael
1977 *Farming for Profit in a Hungry World*. Montclair, N.J.: Allanheld, Osmun.
1979 Obstacles to the Development of a Capitalist Agriculture: A Comment on Mann and Dickinson. *Journal of Peasant Studies* 7 (1): 119–21.

Petry, Ann
1975 Like a Winding Sheet. In *Women and Fiction: Short Stories By and About Women*, edited by Susan Cahill, pp. 133–42. New York: New American Library.

Pfeffer, Max J.
1982 The Labor Process and Capitalist Development of Agriculture. *Rural Sociologist* 2 (2): 72–80.
1983 Social Origins of Three Systems of Farm Production in the United States. *Rural Sociology* 48 (4): 540–62.

Potash, M.
1929 Marx and Engels on Narodnik Socialism. *Proletarskaya Revolyutsiya* 2:20–63.

Poulantzas, Nicos
1975 *Classes in Contemporary Capitalism*. London: New Left Books.

Prentice, A. N.
1972 *Cotton: With Special Reference to Africa*. London: William Clowes and Sons.

Ransom, Roger L., and Richard Sutch
1972 Debt Peonage in the Cotton South after the Civil War. *Journal of Economic History* 32 (3): 643–67.
1975 The 'Lock-In' Mechanism and Overproduction of Cotton in the Postbellum South. *Agricultural History* 49 (2): 405–25.
1977 *One Kind of Freedom: The Economic Consequences of Emancipation*. New York: Cambridge University Press.

Raper, Arthur
1946 The Role of Agricultural Technology in Southern Social Change. *Sociological Focus* 25:21–30.

Rasmussen, Wayne D.
1960 *Readings in the History of American Agriculture*. Urbana: University of Illinois Press.

Rasmussen, Wayne D., and Gladys Baker
1969 Programs for Agriculture 1933–1965. In *Agricultural Policy in an Affluent Society*, edited by Vernon W. Rattan. New York: W. W. Norton.

Raup, Phillip
1973 Corporate Farming in the United States. *Journal of Economic History* 33 (1): 274–90.
Ray, Victor K.
1968 *The Corporate Invasion of Agriculture*. Denver, Colo.: National Farmers Union.
Reid, Joseph D.
1973 Sharecropping as an Understandable Market Response: The Post-Bellum South. *Journal of Economic History* 33 (March): 106–30.
1975 Sharecropping in History and Theory. *Agricultural History* 49 (2): 426–39.
Riesebrodt, Martin
1986 From Patriarchalism to Capitalism: The Theoretical Context of Max Weber's Agrarian Studies, 1892–93. *Economy and Society* 15 (4): 476–502.
Ritzer, George
1983 *Sociological Theory*. New York: Alfred A. Knopf.
Robson, R.
1958 *The Man-Made Fibres Industry*. London: Macmillan.
Rochester, Anna
1940 *Why Farmers Are Poor: The Agricultural Crisis in the United States*. New York: International.
1942 *Lenin on the Agrarian Question*. New York: International.
Rodefeld, Richard D.
1975 Evidence, Issues and Conclusions on the Current Status and Trends in U.S. Farm Types. Paper presented at the Annual Meeting of the Rural Sociological Society, San Francisco, Calif.
1978 Trends in U.S. Farm Organizational Structure and Type. In *Change in Rural America*, edited by R. D. Rodefeld et al., pp. 158–77. St. Louis, Mo.: Mosby.
Rogin, Leo
1931 *The Introduction of Farm Machinery in its Relation to the Productivity of Labor in the Agriculture of the United States during the Nineteenth Century*. Berkeley and Los Angeles: University of California Press.
Roseberry, William
1983 From Peasant Studies to Proletarianization Studies. *Studies in Comparative International Development* 18 (1/2): 69–89.
Rosenfeld, Rachel
1985 *Farm Women: Work, Farm, and Family in the United States*. Chapel Hill: University of North Carolina Press.
Rosengarten, Theodore
1974 *All God's Dangers: The Life of Nate Shaw*. New York: Alfred A. Knopf.
Rostow, W. W.
1960 *The Stages of Economic Growth: A Non-Communist Manifesto*. Cambridge: Cambridge University Press.

Rowbotham, Sheila
1973 *Woman's Consciousness, Man's World*. Harmondsworth: Penguin.
Royce, Edward
1985 The Origins of Southern Sharecropping: Explaining Social Change. *Current Perspectives in Social Theory* 6:279–99.
Ryan, William
1986 Excerpts from *Blaming the Victim*. In *Taking Sides: Clashing Views on Controversial Social Issues*, 4th ed., edited by K. Finsterbusch and G. McKenna, pp. 45–52 and 158–65. Guilford, Conn.: Dushkin.
Sachs, Carolyn E.
1983 *The Invisible Farmers: Women in Agricultural Production*. Totowa, N.J.: Rowman and Allanheld.
Saloutos, Theodore
1960 *Farmer Movements in the South 1865–1933*. Lincoln: University of Nebraska Press.
1982 *The American Farmer and the New Deal*. Ames: Iowa State University Press.
Sargen, Nicholas P.
1979 *Tractorization in the United States and Its Relevance for the Developing Countries*. New York: Garland.
Schilletter, J. C., R. B. Elwood, and H. E. Knowlton
1939 *Changes in Technology and Labor Requirements in Crop Production: Vegetables*. National Research Project, Report no. A-12, prepared for the Work Progress Administration. Philadelphia, Pa.
Schlomowitz, Ralph
1979 The Origins of Southern Sharecropping. *Agricultural History* 53 (July): 557–75.
Schmidt, Alfred
1973 *The Concept of Nature in Marx*. London: New Left Books.
Schnittker, John A.
1970 Distribution of Benefits from Existing and Prospective Farm Programs. In *Benefits and Burdens of Rural Development*, pp. 89–104. Iowa State University Center for Agricultural and Economic Development. Ames: Iowa State University Press.
Schroeder, Emily, Frederick Fliegel, and J. C. van Es
1985 Measurement of the Lifestyle Dimensions of Farming for Small-Scale Farmers. *Rural Sociology* 50 (3): 302–22.
Schulman, Michael, Patricia Garrett, and Barbara Newman
1988 Differentiation and Survival among Smallholders: An Empirical Perspective on the Lenin/Chayanov Debate. Paper presented at the Annual Meeting of the Southern Sociological Society, Nashville, Tenn.
Schwartz, Michael
1976 *Radical Protest and Social Structure: The Southern Farmers' Alliance and Cotton Tenancy, 1880–1890*. New York: Academic Press.
Scofield, William H.
1969 Corporations in Agriculture. In *Corporation Farming: What Are the*

*Issues?*, pp. 1–12. Agricultural Economic Report no. 53, prepared for the U.S. Department of Agriculture. Washington, D.C.: G.P.O.

Seccombe, Wally

1973 The Housewife and Her Labour under Capitalism. *New Left Review* 83 (January–February 1973): 3–24.

1975 Domestic Labour—A Reply to Critics. *New Left Review* 94 (November–December 1975): 85–96.

1986 Marxism and Demography: Household Forms and Fertility Regimes in the Western European Transition. In *Family, Economy and State: The Social Reproduction Process under Capitalism*, edited by James Dickinson and Bob Russell, pp. 23–55. London: Croom Helm.

Shanin, Teodore

1971 *Peasants and Peasant Societies*. Harmondsworth: Penguin.

1972 *The Awkward Class: Political Sociology of Peasantry in a Developing Society, Russia 1910–1925*. Oxford: The Clarendon Press.

1973 The Nature and Logic of the Peasant Economy, Part I. *Journal of Peasant Studies* 1 (1).

1974 The Nature and Logic of the Peasant Economy, Part II. *Journal of Peasant Studies* 1 (2).

1986 Chayanov's Message: Illuminations, Miscomprehensions, and the Contemporary 'Development Theory.' Foreword to A. V. Chayanov, *The Theory of Peasant Economy*, edited by D. Thorner, B. Kerblay, and R. E. F. Smith. Madison: University of Wisconsin Press.

Shannon, Fred A.

1945 *The Farmer's Last Frontier: Agriculture, 1860–1897*. Vol. 5 of *The Economic History of the United States*. New York: Farrar and Rinehart.

Shaw, Eldon E., and John A. Hopkins

1938 *Trends in Employment in Agriculture, 1909–1936*. National Research Project, Report no. A-8, prepared for the Work Progress Administration. Philadelphia, Pa.

Shepherd, Geoffrey S.

1941 *Agricultural Price Analysis*. Ames: Iowa State College Press.

Silveira, Jeanette

1975 *The Housewife and Marxist Class Analysis*. Pittsburgh: Know Inc.

Singer, Edward G., Gary P. Green, and Jere L. Gilles

1983 The Mann-Dickinson Thesis: Reject or Revise? *Sociologia Ruralis* 23:276–87.

Sitterson, J. Carlyle

1943 The Transition from Slave to Free Economy on the William J. Minor Plantations. *Agricultural History* 17 (October): 216–24.

Sivakumar, S. S.

1976 Family Size, Consumption, Expenditure, Income, and Land Holding in an Agrarian Economy: A Critique of Some Populist Notions. *Economic and Political Weekly*, July 24, 1976, 1115–24.

Skocpol, Theda
1979 *States and Social Revolutions: A Comparative Analysis of France, Russia and China*. New York: Cambridge University Press.
1980 Political Response to Capitalist Crisis: Neo-Marxist Theories of the State and the Case of the New Deal. *Politics and Society* 10:155–201.
1982 Explaining Revolutions: In Quest of a Social-Structural Approach. In *Sociological Theory: A Book of Readings*, edited by L. Coser and B. Rosenberg, pp. 575–97. 5th ed. New York: Macmillan.

Skocpol, Theda, and Kenneth Finegold
1982 State Capacity and Economic Intervention in the Early New Deal. *Political Science Quarterly* 97 (2) (Summer): 255–78.

Soth, Laren
1957 *Farm Trouble*. Princeton, N.J.: Princeton University Press.

Stinchcombe, A. L.
1961 Agricultural Enterprise and Rural Class Relations. *American Journal of Sociology* 67 (2) (September): 165–76.

Street, James H.
1957 *The New Revolution in the Cotton Economy: Mechanization and Its Consequences*. Chapel Hill: University of North Carolina Press.

Summers, Gene F., ed.
1983 *Technology and Social Change in Rural Areas*. Boulder, Colo.: Westview Press.

Swanson, Louis E., and Lawrence Busch
1985 A Part-time Farming Model Reconsidered: A Comment on a POET Model, *Rural Sociology* 50 (Fall): 427–36.

Taylor, Henry, and Anne Taylor
1943 *World Trade in Agricultural Products*. New York: Macmillan.

Thomas, Robert J.
1981 The Social Organization of Industrial Agriculture. *Insurgent Sociologist* 10 (Winter): 5–20.
1985 *Citizenship, Gender, and Work: Social Organization of Industrial Agriculture*. Berkeley and Los Angeles: University of California Press.

Thomas-Lycklama a Niejholt, G.
1980 *On the Road for Work*. Boston: Martinus Nijhoff.

Thomsen, Frederick Lundy
1936 *Agricultural Prices*. New York: McGraw-Hill.

Thorner, Daniel
1966 Chayanov's Concept of Peasant Economy. In *The Theory of Peasant Economy*, edited by D. Thorner, B. Kerblay, and R. E. F. Smith, pp. xi–xxiii. Homewood, Ill.: Richard Irwin.
1971 Peasant Economy as a Category in Economic History. In *Peasant and Peasant Societies*, edited by Teodor Shanin, pp. 202–18. Harmondsworth: Penguin.

Tisdell, C. A., and P. M. McDonald
1979 *Economics of Fibre Markets: Interdependence between Man-Made Fibres, Wool and Cotton*. New York: Pergamon Press.

Todd, John A.
1915 *The World's Cotton Crops*. London: A. and C. Black.
Tribe, Keith
1981 *Genealogies of Capitalism*. Atlantic Highlands, N.J.: Humanities Press.
United States Bureau of Census
1900 *The Twelfth Census of the United States Taken in the Year 1900*. Vol. 5, part 1, Agriculture. Washington, D.C.: U.S. Bureau of Census.
1930a *The Fifteenth Census of the United States: 1930*. Vol. 2, part 2, Agriculture. Washington, D.C.: G.P.O.
1930b *The Fifteenth Census of the United States: 1930*. Vol. 3, part 1, Agriculture. Washington, D.C.: G.P.O.
1930c *The Fifteenth Census of the United States: 1930*. Vol. 4., Agriculture. Washington, D.C.: G.P.O.
1964 *Census of Agriculture*. Vol. 2. Washington, D.C.: G.P.O.
United States Bureau of Labor Statistics
1959 *Frequency of Change in Wholesale Prices: A Study of Price Flexibility*. Washington, D.C.: G.P.O.
United States Congress
1986 *Technology, Public Policy, and the Changing Structure of American Agriculture*. Washington D.C.: G.P.O.
United States Department of Agriculture
1901 *Yearbook of the Department of Agriculture*. Washington, D.C.: G.P.O.
1945 *Agriculture Situation, Jan. 1945–Dec. 1946*. Washington, D.C.: G.P.O.
Van Gigch, Francis
1972 Historical and Economic Summary of U.S. Agriculture. In *The Over-production Trap in United States Agriculture*, edited by Glenn L. Johnson and C. Leroy Quame, pp. 159–72. Baltimore, Md.: Johns Hopkins University Press.
Van Sickle, John
1943 *Planning for the South*. Nashville, Tenn.: Vanderbilt University Press.
Veblen, Thorstein
1962 The Independent Farmer. In *The Portable Veblen*, edited by Max Lerner, pp. 395–406. New York: The Viking Press.
Vergopoulos, Kostas
1978 Capitalism and Peasant Productivity. *Journal of Peasant Studies* 5 (4): 446–65.
Vollmar, Glen J.
1969 Factory Farms versus Family Farms . . . Some Concerns. In *Corporation Farming: What Are the Issues?*, pp. 28–34. Agricultural Economic Report no. 53, prepared for the U.S. Department of Agriculture. Washington, D.C.: G.P.O.
Von Werlhof, Claudia
1985 Why Peasants and Housewives Do Not Disappear in the Capital-

ist World-System. Paper presented at the Annual Meeting of the American Sociological Association, Washington, D.C.

1988a On the Concept of Nature and Society in Capitalism. In *Women: The Last Colony*, edited by Maria Mies, Veronika Bennholdt-Thomsen, and Claudia von Werlhof, pp. 96–112. London: Zed Books.

1988b The Proletarian Is Dead: Long Live the Housewife! In *Women: The Last Colony*, edited by Mariea Mies, Veronika Bennholdt-Thomsen, and Claudia von Werlhof, pp. 168–81. London: Zed Books.

1988c Women's Work: The Blind Spot in the Critique of Political Economy. In *Women: The Last Colony*, edited by Maria Mies, Veronika Bennholdt-Thomsen, and Claudia von Werlhof, pp. 13–26. London: Zed Books.

Wallerstein, Immanuel

1973 Dependence in an Interdependent World: The Limited Possibilities of Transformation within the Capitalist World Economy. Paper presented at the Conference on Dependence and Development in Africa, Carleton University, Ottawa.

1974a *The Modern World-System: Capitalist Agriculture and the Origins of the European World-Economy in the Sixteenth Century*. New York: Academic Press.

1974b The Rise and Future Demise of the World Capitalist System: Concepts for Comparative Analysis. *Comparative Studies in Society and History* 16 (4): 387-415.

1983 *The Capitalist World Economy*. New York: Cambridge University Press.

Warren, G. F.

1917 *Farm Management*. New York: Macmillan.

Warriner, Doreen

1969 *Land Reform in Principle and Practice*. Oxford: Clarendon Press.

Wayne, Jack

1981 Capitalism and Colonialism in Late Nineteenth Century Europe. *Studies in Political Economy* 5:79–103.

Wayne, Michael

1983 *The Reshaping of Plantation Society: The Natchez District, 1860–1880*. Baton Rouge: Louisiana State University Press.

Weber, Max

1949 *The Methodology of the Social Sciences*, edited by Edward Shils and Henry Finch. New York: Free Press.

1958 *The Protestant Ethic and the Spirit of Capitalism*. New York: Scribner's.

1968 *Economy and Society*. 3 vols. Vol. 1. Totowa, N.J.: Bedminster Press.

1972 Capitalism and Rural Society in Germany. In *From Max Weber: Essays in Sociology*, edited by H. Gerth and C. W. Mills, pp. 363–85. New York: Oxford University Press.

Wells, Miriam J.

1984 The Resurgence of Sharecropping: Historical Anomaly or Political Strategy? *American Journal of Sociology* 90 (1): 1–29.

Welty, Gordon

1983 Concrete versus Ideal Types. Paper presented to the Fifth Max Weber Colloquium on Comparative Historical Sociology, William Paterson College of New Jersey, Wayne, N.J.

1986 Concrete versus Ideal Types. *Bangladesh Sociological Review* 1 (1): 11–28.

1987 A Critique of A. V. Chayanov's Theory of the Family Labour Unit. *Comparative Rural and Regional Studies* 1 (Summer): 18–36.

White, Deborah Gray

1985 *Ar'n't I a Woman? Female Slaves in the Plantation South*. New York: W. W. Norton.

Wiener, Jonathan M.

1978 *Social Origins of the New South: Alabama 1860–1885*. Baton Rouge: Louisiana State University Press.

Wilcox, Walter, Willard Cochrane, and Robert Herdt

1974 *Economics of American Agriculture*. Englewood Cliffs, N.J.: Prentice-Hall.

Wiley, B. I.

1939 Salient Changes in Southern Agriculture since the Civil War. *Agricultural History* 13 (2): 65–76.

Williamson, Joel

1975 *After Slavery*. New York: W. W. Norton.

Wilson, John

1986 The Political Economy of Contract Farming. *Review of Radical Political Economics* 18 (4): 47–70.

Wimberley, Ronald C.

1983 The Emergence of Part-time Farming as a Social Form of Agriculture. *Research in the Sociology of Work* 2:325–56.

Wolf, Eric

1966 *Peasants*. Englewood Cliffs, N.J.: Prentice-Hall.

1973 *Peasant Wars of the Twentieth Century*. New York: Harper Torchbooks.

Woloch, Nancy

1984 *Women and the American Experience*. New York: Alfred A. Knopf.

Woodman, Harold D.

1977 Sequel to Slavery: The New History Views the Postbellum South. *Journal of Southern History* 53 (November): 524–54.

1979 Post–Civil War Southern Agriculture and the Law. *Agricultural History* 53 (January): 319–37.

Woodward, C. Vann

1951 *Origins of the New South, 1877–1913*. Baton Rouge: Louisiana State University Press.

1970 *The Burden of Southern History*. Baton Rouge: Louisiana State University Press.

Wright, Gavin

1974 Cotton Competition and the Post-Bellum Recovery of the American South. *Journal of Economic History* 34 (3): 610–35.

1978 *The Political Economy of the Cotton South*. New York: W. W. Norton.

1986 *Old South, New South: Revolutions in the Southern Economy since the Civil War*. New York: Basic Books.

Wright, Gavin, and Howard Kunreuther

1975 Cotton, Corn and Risk in the Nineteenth Century. *Journal of Economic History* 35 (3): 526–51.

Zaretsky, Eli

1973 *Capitalism, the Family and Personal Life*. Santa Cruz, Calif.: Loaded Press.

Zeichner, Oscar

1939 The Transition from Slave to Free Agricultural Labor in the Southern States. *Agricultural History* 13 (1): 22–32.

1940 The Legal Status of the Agricultural Laborer in the South. *Political Science Quarterly* 55 (3): 412–28.

Zeitlin, Irving

1973 *Rethinking Sociology: A Critique of Contemporary Theory*. Englewood Cliffs, N.J.: Prentice-Hall.

1981 *Ideology and the Development of Sociological Theory*. 2d ed. Englewood Cliffs, N.J.: Prentice-Hall.

# Index